The Margin Fades

The Margin Fades: Geographical Itineraries in a World of Islands

Eric Waddell
Patrick D. Nunn
Editors

Institute of Pacific Studies
1993

USP Library Cataloguing-in-publication data

The Margin fades : geographical itineraries in a world of islands /
Eric Waddell, Patrick D. Nunn, editors. - Suva [Fiji] :
Institute of Pacific Studies, The University of the South Pacific, 1994.

x, 297 p. : ill. ; 21 cm.

Bibliography:
ISBN 982-02-0092-X.

1. Human ecology - Oceania 2. Oceania - Environmental conditions 3. Oceania - Economic conditions I. Waddell, Eric II. Nunn, Patrick D. III. The University of the South Pacific. Institute of Pacific Studies. IV. Title.

GF851.M37 304.2'0995

Cover photo 'Ata island, Tonga; used by permission of the Government of Tonga
Cover design Graham Taylor
Word processing Akanisi Sakuwai
Typesetting Mark Garrett, Garrett's Consultants Limited
Production Linda Crowl
Printing Bluebird Printery Ltd.

" ... all experience is an arch wherethro'
Gleams that untravell'd world whose margin fades
For ever and for ever when I move."

Alfred Tennyson (*Ulysses*)

Acknowledgements

The editors would like to thank Sharon McGowan and Akanisi Sakuwai for help with typing the manuscript, Mark Garrett for typesetting, and Linda Crowl for her editorial assistance.

Contents

Prospective

Afterword

Illustrations

Figures

Plates

Chapter 1

Foreword: A View from the Islands

Geographers have made a significant contribution to research on the Pacific islands and that research has, in turn, made a substantial contribution to the development of certain sectors of the discipline. Names like Bonnemaison, Brookfield, Cumberland, Spate, Ward and Watters come immediately to mind, as do cultural ecology, environmental change, biogeography, subsistence agricultural systems, agroforestry and population migration. Those, such as Karl Butzer and Marvin Mikesell, concerned to chart the recent history of the discipline, even speak of of a "New Guinea syndrome" whose influence was felt in the halls of North American geography back in the 1970s.

Such Pacific geography emerged in the 1960s and was pioneered at Australian and New Zealand universities. It was a geography which focused on relationships between human populations and their environment, which accorded extreme importance to intensive fieldwork, which refused to be constrained by artificial disciplinary boundaries and which, with the notable exception of Isireli Lasaqa, was undertaken by scholars coming from beyond the Pacific islands.

Committed as they were to the development of a Pacific geography and to a view from within as distinct from beyond the islands, a number of these scholars chose to pursue their academic careers in the region's nascent tertiary institutions: the University of Papua New Guinea and the University of the South Pacific. In doing so they chose consciously to shift from an approach to the Pacific as an object of scholarly interest to one of the Pacific as home, as family and as workplace. Such a shift was much more than a concern to develop a new perspective. It was also a commitment to develop a new Pacific geography, one that is undoubtedly more applied in nature and, dare we say, more committed. It was also a concern to develop a geography that is more authentically 'of the islands', because it is done by Islanders, some of whom arrived thousands of years ago, some last century and others only 'yesterday'. The results of such a geographical shift in interest and in endeavour are now beginning to take form.

The University of the South Pacific was established in 1968 - some 25 years ago. Geography was one of its founding disciplines, in part no doubt because the Pacific *is geography* and in part because geographers are so important in the Pacific. It was inevitable that the Department of Geography be called upon to play a major role in the University, in terms of teaching, research, and scholarly and professional leadership. It has never faltered in this task. Pacific Island scholars have emerged from its ranks. Highly qualified and committed outsiders have come...and many of them have stayed. Prestigious visitors are frequent.

Owing to our fertile past, our energy and enthusiasm, it was perhaps inevitable that one of us, Rajesh Chandra, then Pro-Vice Chancellor, suggest that we produce a volume to mark the passage of 25 years of the discipline at the University, review the past and chart some pathways to the future. The idea was accepted enthusiastically by all colleagues and it was decided, in late 1992, to invite all present staff plus those who had spent a minimum of one year in the Department to contribute to a collective 'Festschrift'. Potential contributors were invited to write either scientific or more reflective personal statements and the result of their efforts has been, we feel, a creative balance between scholarship and experience, some of the papers welding the two together as a striking expression of the Pacific as a geographer's home and a place from which to read the larger world. Hopefully it will provide the reader with some measure of a distinctive Pacific geographical scholarship, one which bears the imprint of the scholarship of institutions in Canberra, Auckland, Wellington, Berkeley and other metropolitan centres, but one which has taken their messages and their skills and transformed them through contact with the native land and native scholars, thereby producing a new vision, new preoccupations from the fertile interaction of the two geographical and cultural realms.

Perspectives on the Pacific islands do differ, depending on one's origins. One only need consider the distinction currently made between "islands in a far sea" and "a sea of islands", or concerns about the "terrestrial fixation" of expatriate geographers, or the increasing irritation in the Pacific upon being confronted with naive distinctions between Polynesia, Melanesia and Micronesia, and the straitjacketing of island peoples into narrow, national identities.

Geographical research in the Pacific has suffered, sometimes cruelly, from these divergent perspectives. In the following pages, the various contributors set out to highlight these dichotomies, to focus on misunderstandings, and to identify new priorities and new strategies for the future.

For Nunn, there are even radical divergences in our reading of prehistory. For Bryant, Chandra, Thaman and Veitayaki, there are new priorities, new agendas. For Gibson and Overton, dominant development philosophies and strategies need urgent reconsideration. For David and McShane, divergent resource management strategies are the foci of grave misunderstanding and conflict. For Manner and Walsh, it is the progressive unfolding of the Pacific world through their personal itineraries which results in new visions, new perspectives.

Running through most of the contributions, implicitly or explicitly, is the delicate issue of detachment in scientific research. Should one be, indeed can one be, objective? What transpires clearly from *The Margin Fades: Geographical Itineraries in a World of Islands* is, we believe, the conviction that detachment is impossible. The appreciation of this fact made us Pacific geographers in the first place, by birth or by adoption. It kept us here, if not physically then most certainly in spirit. An excellent illustration of this is provided Clarke's account of the manner in which he was, and continues to be, influenced by Ngirapo. In a similar vein, Waddell's analysis of the thoughts of Jean-Marie Tjibaou concerning the future of his people and his country, illustrates the need for a distinctive island vision, not only for the region's future but perhaps for the entire world.

The broad grouping of the papers into three sections, Contemporary Issues, Retrospective and Prospective, followed by an Afterword, highlights our particular quest and experience. We see a common thread running through them all: a Pacific thread of time and space, of people and the great forces of nature. Through the continuing dialogue between scholar and villager or urban dweller, between humanity and the natural world that forms our setting we seek to journey on in this great ocean.

Eric Waddell

Patrick D. Nunn

Suva

November 1993

Chapter 2

Beyond the Naive Lands: Human History and Environmental Change in the Pacific Basin

Patrick D. Nunn

Introduction

In 1992 a book entitled *The Naive Lands* (prehistory and environmental change in Australia and the South-west Pacific) was published (Dodson, 1992). It explains the stage to which archaeological and related research in the region has reached. It examines the likely interactions between people and their environments since the time the region was first inhabited. In doing so, it gives credence to a number of propositions which can be as equally well denied on the basis of the available evidence.

Several alternative interpretations of selected issues are given below. In doing so, they are not intended in any way to disparage the work which has been done and the people who have done it, but only to provoke a wider debate on issues which are critically important to any understanding of past, present and future environmental change and human behaviour in the region.

Naive Lands?

The title of *The Naive Lands,* while never properly explained therein, is believed to refer to the premise that, before people arrived in Australia and the islands of the south-west Pacific, their environments were naive; that is, they were simple and lacked the manifold complexities which the modern environments of these areas exhibit. To my mind, this premise is derived from some astonishingly naive assumptions deriving, not from a reasoned appraisal of what is known, but from shallow assumptions about what is not known.

The principal assumption is that humans are the major reason why environments change: in other words, without humans, environmental change is negligible. Even on a human timescale, this assumption fails to acknowledge the effects of non-human agencies, such as climate change, tectonic and sea-level change and even the impacts of exotic fauna and flora on environments worldwide.[1] In the south-west Pacific, I recently assembled the available evidence for the effects of non-human agencies on island environments (Nunn, 1992) from which I argued that such changes had not miraculously ceased once humans arrived in these environments but had continued. Much of what had once been naively regarded as the consequence of human impact appears more probably to have been the result of non-human impacts.

The debatable premise implicit in the title of *The Naive Lands* might put off many potential readers, and this would be a shame because the book contains much of interest. Many chapters concentrate wisely on descriptions of what is known: those on environmental change in New Guinea (Swadling & Hope, 1992) and parts of Australia I found compelling. Facts abound throughout the rest of the book, but the authors often find it difficult to detach facts from interpretation. Some specific examples are given in the following sections.

A Moa Sighted

When many people think of changes that took place in New Zealand before Europeans arrived, it is the moa that first springs to mind. Moas or dinornithiformes were giant flightless birds, the bones of which commonly litter Maori archaeological sites leading to the idea that the first inhabitants of New Zealand hunted the birds to extinction. Moas are believed to have disappeared several hundred years ago yet early in 1993, in an incident which made headlines around the world, one was claimed to have been seen and photographed by three hikers in bushland 80 kilometres (km) west of Christchurch. Once the initial excitement had subsided, it was generally agreed that the 'moa' had probably been a red deer.

The incident poses interesting questions for the understanding of the region's prehistory. There is immense interest in the past, and many people do not share the caution that most professionals demonstrate when interpreting the meagre evidence. They want answers. They want to know not just that the moa existed, but how it lived, the colour of its eyes, the sounds it made and a hundred other things about it. Questions about our islands' earliest human inhabitants are equally numerous and the temptation to sacrifice academic self-discipline to satisfy public interest is great. Some people have succumbed and their 'science' is more a creative art. Elsewhere, and this comes across in parts of *The Naive Lands,* even the scientific establishment appears to have partly yielded to public interest by abandoning the cool, rational evaluation of evidence in favour of the relentless development of one interpretation over all others. Such an approach is not dangerous where it is made explicit; however, where this is not so, it may lead to all kinds of unwarranted developments and impinge unhelpfully on the contemporary human-environment debate.

These points can be illustrated with reference to the moas. Remains of moas in New Zealand were first described on paper in 1839, at which time "there was no evidence that they had survived into the era of human colonisation" (Anderson & McGlone, 1992: 212). The subsequent discovery of moa bones at Maori archaeological sites demonstrated that they had indeed survived into the era of human colonization. How does one get from this to the idea that "extinctions [of moas] began only after the arrival of humans about AD 1000" (White & Flannery, 1992: 6)? Could the number of moas not have been declining before humans arrived as the result perhaps of contemporaneous climate and vegetation change (Figure 2.1a)? After all, the numbers of moa bones found is only a small percentage of the total population (White & Flannery, 1992). Why close our minds to the alternative interpretation? The answer is, first, because the view that moas became extinct only because of being hunted by Maori is simplest and neatest and, second, because it was a view first expressed by Julius Haast, who spent much of his professional career as Director of the Canterbury Museum looking at Maori archaeological sites full of moa bones. He did not have a palaeontologist's interest in the moas, seeing only their relationship with the early human inhabitants of New Zealand.

While writing of New Zealand, it is opportune to address the question of the decline in area of its forest cover over the last 2,000 years. Most writers want to make the point that it was humans who were responsible for clearing many of the forests which once existed. To support this view, they typically show maps of New Zealand's forests about 1500 BP[2] (just before human arrival) and about AD 1850 (e.g. Cumberland, 1962). These leave the reader in no doubt that the forest acreage declined during that time, but the coincidence of forest decline and human settlement of New Zealand does not prove that the two were connected. It is quite possible that forests were already declining during the late Holocene in New Zealand and that people either merely witnessed a process over which they had no control or, more realistically, accelerated a process already in operation.

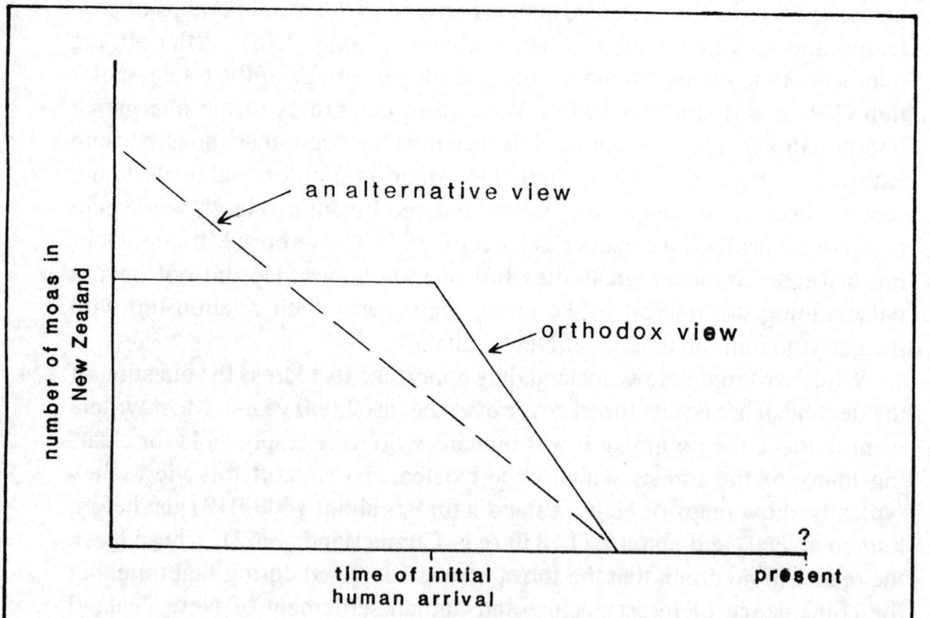

Figure 2.1a. Graphic illustration of the orthodox view of the decline and extinction of the moa contrasted with one of a number of alternative views.

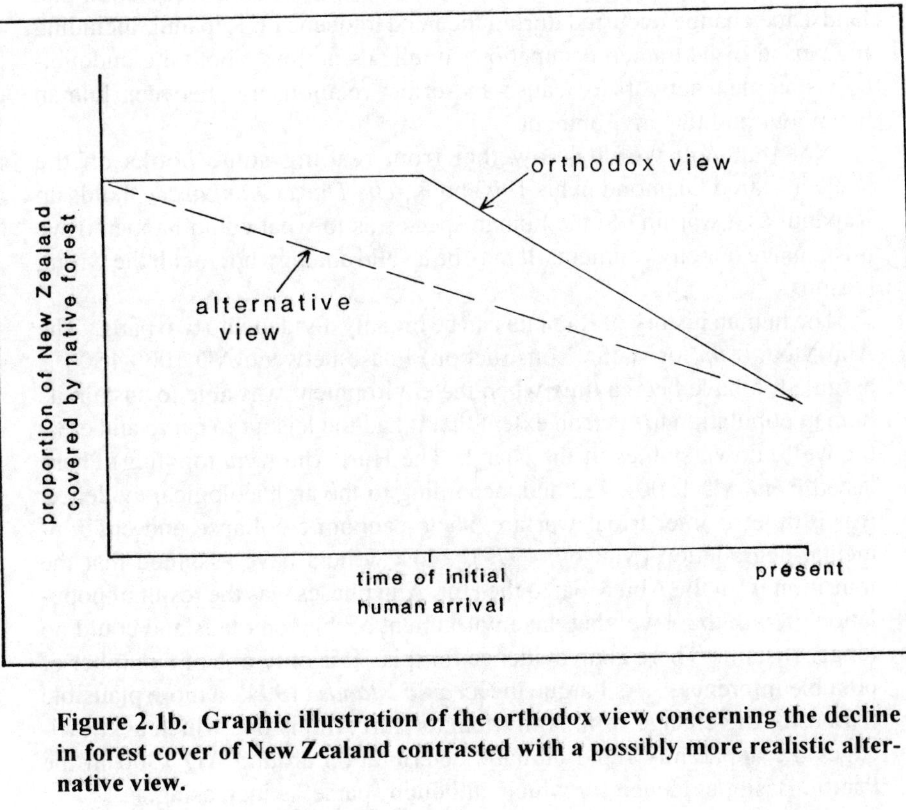

Figure 2.1b. Graphic illustration of the orthodox view concerning the decline in forest cover of New Zealand contrasted with a possibly more realistic alternative view.

Yet, because people are seen to clear forests today, whereas climate change is not observed to do so, it is perhaps understandable (though naive) for the cause of ancient forest decline to have been blamed on humans rather than non-human agencies. All such inferences are a bit like moa sightings: more the products of wishful thinking than of a cool appraisal of all possible explanations for a particular observation.

The cause of vegetation change on Pacific Islands during the period of human occupation has long appeared clear to most writers. A good example is that of Rapanui (Easter Island),

> which pollen records show was at least partly covered with forest when people arrived. The treeless grassy landscapes reported by European explorer-sailors in the eighteenth century *show how effectively humans can alter the vegetation of entire islands* (White & Flannery, 1992: 7, my emphasis).

It shows no such thing. What it shows is that substantial vegetation and landscape change occurred during the late Holocene on Rapanui, including the period of its human occupation. It tells us nothing about the undoubtedly complex network of cause-and-effect relationships between human behaviour and the environment.

Not that you would know that from reading some books on the subject. Jared Diamond in his 1992 book, *The Third Chimpanzee,* holds up Rapanui as a warning to the human species as to what could happen if we mismanage our environment. It may be a valid analogy but for all the wrong reasons.

The human history of Rapanui can be broadly divided into two parts. The Ahu Moai (*ahu,* or statue, construction) Phase between AD 1000-1500 is assumed to have been a time when the environment was able to sustain its human population to such an extent that it had the leisure to carve and erect the well-known statues of the island. The Huri Ahu (*ahu* toppling) Phase lasted from AD 1500-1722 and, according to the archaeological evidence, was a time of inter-tribal warfare, socio-economic collapse and environmental degradation (McCoy, 1979). Most writers have assumed that the transition from the Ahu Moai to the Huri Ahu phases was the result of population growth to a level that the environment of this remote island could no longer sustain. There is no evidence for this. It is only one of a number of possible inferences. As I argue in *Oceanic Islands* (1994), a more plausible reason for the change from Ahu Moai to Huri Ahu is one which acknowledges the apparently rapid climatic deterioration around AD 1300 in the Pacific Basin, evidence for which, although sparse, is increasing.

A Catastrophe Around AD 1300?

Many of the fallacious propositions underlying some of the conclusions in *The Naive Lands* derive from a lack of information about the environmental history of the areas in question. Some of the contributing authors are open about this,[3] others not so. Much of the information available is found only in obscure journals or 'grey literature'. Little of it has been systematically analysed; yet, it occasionally reveals surprises. The example is given here of the period about AD 1300 (650 BP) which is believed to approximate in the Pacific Islands to the wet transition between the warmer, drier Little Climatic Optimum and the cooler, initially quite wet but overall also dry compared to the present, Little Ice Age.

Rainfall records from such places as China and California around the Pacific rim suggest that this transition was a period of about 100 years marked by rainfall averaging 4-5 times as much as during the periods either before or after (Nunn, 1992). Some data for the Galapagos, Marquesas and Society Islands support the interpolation of this wet period, presumably associated with an abnormally high frequency of tropical cyclones, across the Pacific Basin, perhaps slightly later than it occurred around the periphery.[4]

There is also a mass of data which could be interpreted in several ways, including one involving the effects of a prolonged period of catastrophic rainfall. The societal changes on Rapanui, discussed at the end of the preceding section, are a good example. Similar human behavioural changes about the same time in Fiji and Hawaii could also be plausibly linked to unprecedented rainfall levels having caused wholesale destruction of artificial terracing and other strategies for enhancing agricultural production which the generations living through the much drier Little Climatic Optimum had developed. Catastrophic forest destruction in New Zealand and Japan could also have been linked to this event (Nunn, 1992).

Several sites in the Hawaii group also illustrate the situation. At Kawai Nui Marsh on Oahu, increased sedimentation around AD 1300 hastened infilling of an offshore lagoon, a process attributed by most investigators to the commencement of swidden agriculture on the upland slopes. This view has since been cogently challenged by Athens (see following section). In the Halawa valley on Molokai, an erosional cycle which produced a large colluvial fan began no later than AD 1100-1320 (Kirch & Kelly, 1975). Surrogate measures of population growth in times before records were kept peak in Hawaii about AD 1500-1650. This peak has been interpreted as meaning that "the capacity of the indigenous technological productive sys-

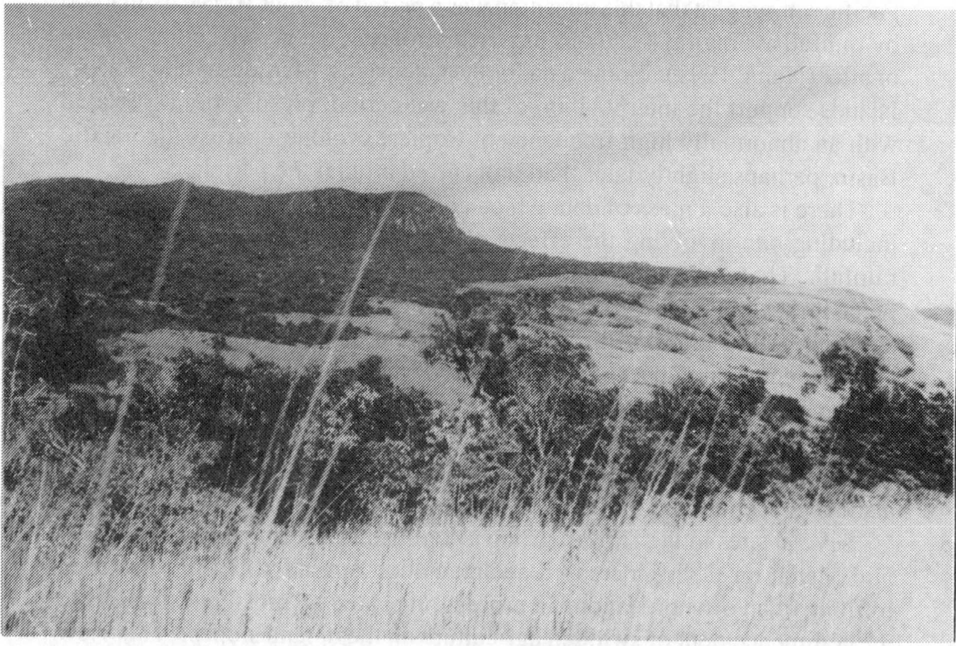

Plate 2.1. Looking from the grassland landscape of western Viti Levu towards its rainforest cloaked windward side in the vicinity of Navunidakua in the upper Sigatoka valley. The orthodox view of the origin of such grasslands is that they are anthropogenic, but it appears increasingly that they existed in the Pacific Islands before people arrived and are therefore properly regarded as climatogenic.

Plate 2.2. Rainforest behind Naceva on the island of Beqa grows here because the site is windward and faces the south-east tradewinds. When forest is cleared and the ground left alone, forest will eventually return not grassland.

tem to support increased population had reached its limits" (Kirch, 1982b: 4), but it could equally well mean that the agriculturally productive area had been devastated to such an extent by the effect of an abrupt climate change that it could no longer support the number of people it had previously.

Most such events, particularly the societal changes, have been interpreted in terms of the relationship between a growing population and an island's carrying capacity reaching a critical point beyond which the island's population would have to have been reduced if anyone was to survive. Clearly, a climatic catastrophe which abruptly reduced an island's carrying capacity might bring its relationship with island population (growing or otherwise) to the critical point with similar results (Figure 2.2).

Human and Non-human Causation

Consider this statement: "We can see human effects on the islands of the eastern Pacific both because they happened only quite recently and because human impacts on the landscape often caused site burial" (White & Flannery, 1992: 7). This is an alternative form of the idea mentioned earlier that, because we (and earlier observers) can see changes in contemporary landscapes which humans are occupying, we assume that the first humans caused similar changes to the islands which they inhabited. This idea, seemingly quite innocuous to most people interested in environmental change, actually contains some highly challengeable assumptions.

First, it assumes that modern environmental change is caused wholly by modern humans. The corollary of this idea is that contemporary climate change (rising temperatures and increasing tropical-cyclone frequency in particular) have had no effect on the landscape, an idea which many subsistence agriculturalists in the Pacific Islands regard as highly implausible. Furthermore, there have been no quantitative studies of the comparative roles of human and non-human causes of modern environmental change in the Pacific Islands. Most outside 'experts' brought in to advise Pacific Island governments on environmental problems routinely blame human activities and make no mention of potential non-human causes of environmental change.

Second, it transfers this somewhat dubious assumption to the 'quite recent' past, thus explaining away contemporary environmental changes without even acknowledging the possibility of either the contemporary climate or the contemporary sea level having been changing, which they undoubtedly were. This view is one which is based, as illustrated by the example of Rapanui above, on prejudiced interpretations of the few known

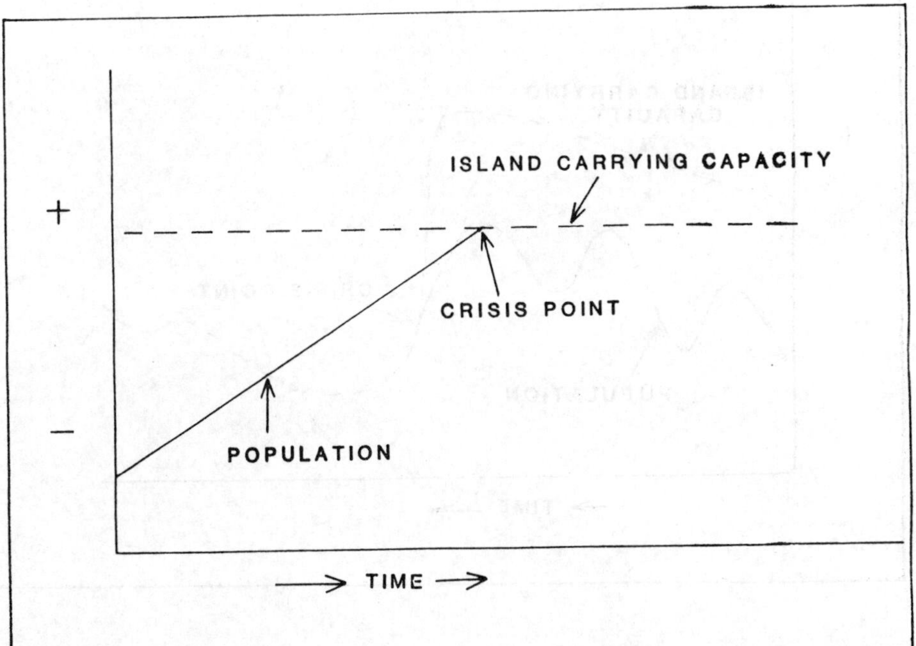

Figure 2.2a. Graphic illustration of the orthodox view of the relationship between island carrying capacity and population growth. A crisis will occur when the two lines intersect which may see a reduction in population allowing only a smaller number of people to survive.

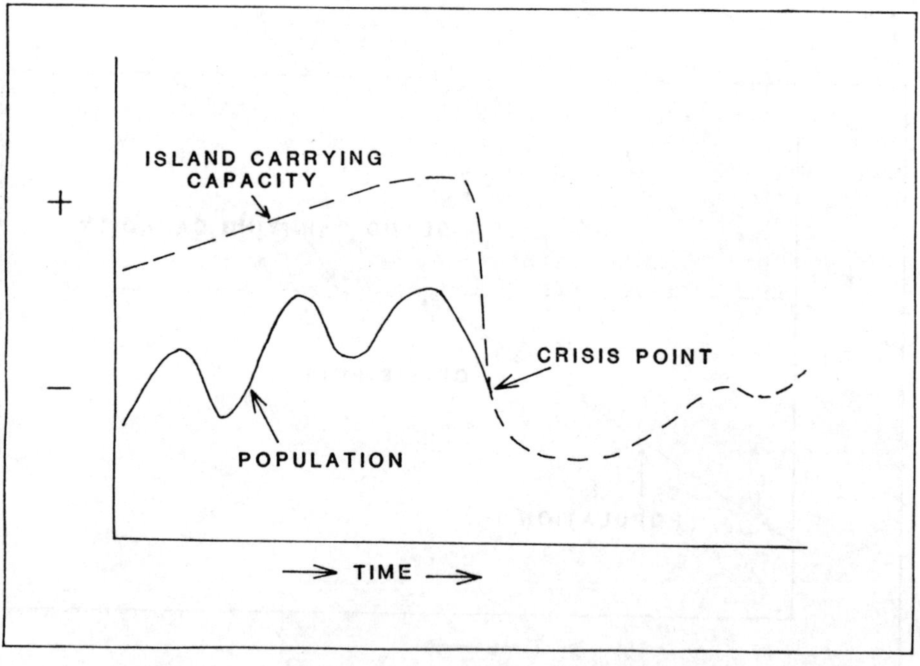

Figure 2.2b. Graphic illustration of an alternative view of the relationship between island carrying capacity and population growth. In this the carrying capacity is more variable and highly changeable in response to climatic changes. A catastrophic climatic change might see an abrupt decrease in carrying capacity which might cause it to intersect rapidly with population, itself a changeable variable rather than one rising uniformly.

Plate 2.3. Emerged coral reef at Poloa in north-west Tutuila, American Samoa, was living 500-700 years ago when sea level was slightly higher. The high sea level was associated with slightly higher temperatures, the climax of the Little Climatic Optimum, which lasted from about AD 750-1300.

facts about these islands. If a person has a fixed idea that only humans cause environmental change then, upon finding evidence of environmental change, it is no surprise to find that this person regards humans as its cause. No surprise, perhaps, to find also that it is regarded as 'proven' by many such persons and by those who subsequently read their work without seeing the original data.

It is encouraging to see that some archaeologists and others working on environmental change in the early Pacific do not have such preconceived ideas. The results of investigations by such people are proving illuminating although they are still very much in a minority. The origins of Pacific Island grasslands are one such example and are discussed in a later section. Other examples are given below.

Throughout Pacific Islands, marshes and lakes have proved favourite sites for coring in order to work out rates of sediment accumulation (surrogates for upland soil erosion) during the last few thousand years. At Kawai Nui Marsh on Oahu in Hawaii, recent investigators have found, contrary to the conclusions of previous researchers, that the sediment accumulation rate *decreased* during the period of early human occupation, thereby implying that the island's first inhabitants had no significant effect on the island's landscape. This was a situation which did not change throughout the course of prehistory, even with the radical alteration of inland natural vegetation communities and the intensification of agriculture (pers comm, J. Stephen Athens, 1993).

An analogous situation was found in New Caledonia where slope erosion leading to a major phase of inorganic sedimentation in two lowland basins began around 25,000 years ago yet ceased around 10,000 years ago (pers comm, Geoff Hope, 1992), more than 6,000 years before humans are believed to have arrived in the area.

There are a few other examples of situations where the role of non-human factors in environmental change during the early settlement history of Pacific Islands has been realistically appraised. Among the earliest was the work of Kirch and Yen (1982) who recognized that emergence over the last few thousand years of the island of Tikopia in Solomon Islands was the product of *both* increased terrigenous sediment being eroded off the island's uplands (perhaps largely a human impact) *and* contemporary sea-level fall (a non-human impact). Similarly, in the Channel Islands off California, the work of Cushing et al. (1986) on 'fire areas' demonstrated that these were the result of low-temperature, non-heating processes in groundwater rather than having been created by humans, as earlier investigators had assumed. The decline in large shellfish in the lagoons of Tongatapu island in Tonga during its early human occupation was attributed partly by Spennemann (1989) to increased predation (by humans) but largely to changing environment.

A Lesson from Lou

It seems generally agreed by prehistorians, archaeologists and others interested in the early settlement history of the south-west Pacific Islands that the first wave of human migration into western Melanesia (the Bismarck Archipelago and the main group of Solomon Islands) stopped at Makira in Solomon Islands. It did not extend into the eastern outer Solomon Islands (Santa Cruz group) nor into Vanuatu, New Caledonia or points east. The main reason claimed for this is that the earliest inhabitants of this region did not apparently possess the maritime technology (neither boat building nor navigational skills perhaps) to cross successfully the sea gaps separating Makira at the eastern end of the Solomons chain from islands to the south and east (Wickler & Spriggs, 1988; Enright & Gosden, 1992).

Superficially, this explanation seems to explain adequately the observation that there is evidence of human settlement along the Solomons chain as far east as Makira[5] around 30,000 BP yet none to the south and east before about 3500 BP. Other explanations are possible. John Gibbons, formerly of the Biology Department at the University of the South Pacific, was fond of speculating about the probability of much earlier settlement in Fiji, Vanuatu and island groups to the east than has been discovered to date. He pointed out that, had people arrived in Fiji, for example, 10,000 years ago, the sea level would have been lower and that any coastal settlement they established would now be buried beneath at least 10-20 metres (m) of sediment and water.[6] Gibbons argued that prehistorians were wrong to shut their minds to such alternative explanations.

It is much better if such alternative explanations are not only considered for negative reasons. In the question of crossing sea gaps, there is a strong positive reason for thinking that people may have colonized areas south and east of Makira before about 3500 BP. Consider what is known about early settlement in the Bismarck Archipelago (Figure 2.3a).

The first people in the Bismarcks arrived there a little over 30,000 years ago, probably a few millennia after human settlement had become established on the Papua New Guinea mainland. Most of the early settlements in the Bismarcks were on New Ireland, but there was one on the island of Lou in the Admiralty Islands.

Lou was an important place for the earliest settlers of Papua New Guinea (including the Bismarck Archipelago) and Solomon Islands for it was the site of several obsidian quarries. Obsidian is a rock which was prized by the earliest inhabitants of the Pacific Islands on account of its hardness and consequent suitability for tools and weapons. To judge from the widespread occurrence of Lou obsidian in ancient settlement sites from the Papua New Guinea mainland throughout Solomon Islands to Vanuatu (Ambrose, 1978), Lou must have figured large in the earliest trading network of western Melanesia.

Lou is very isolated. It is 293km from the Papua New Guinea mainland yet flakes of Lou obsidian have been found at Wom and on the Moem Peninsula, both near Wewak. The direct distance from source to site is about 400km (Ambrose, 1978). Can we assume that the earliest settlers of the region crossed such a distance? We have little choice, although there is a more circuitous route through New Ireland and New Britain which involves crossing marginally shorter sea gaps. The direct distance from Lou to New Ireland is about 349km. It is possible that obsidian was transported at the time via Mussau (St Matthias Group) which is only 250km from Lou, but there is no trace of early (pre-Lapita) settlement on Mussau and it was probably unknown to these traders. There seems no way out of acknowledging that the earliest settlers of the Bismarck Archipelago did indeed have the boat-building and navigational skills to cross ocean gaps of 350-400km.

So why should anyone be so reluctant to admit that the earliest people in the region did not cross from Makira to islands south and east? The shortest ocean gap is from Makira to Nendö and is about 399km (Figure 2.3b). At the height of the last ice age, some 17,000 BP, this distance would have been a few kilometres shorter owing to the lower sea level. There may have been islands between Makira and Nendö then which are now underwater. Are we really to suppose that people settled in Makira without utilizing the skills of their kinsfolk trading with and from Lou for 23,000 years? That is what the evidence we have to date suggests if one interprets it uncritically. Yet, because the evidence is so sparse, perhaps we should not be so reluctant to admit that this interpretation is improbable.

In practical terms this means that the search for early (pre-Lapita) settlement sites in the islands east and south of Makira should be renewed. If such a search eventually proves worthless because older sites than those we presently know about are not found, then that will tell us something about

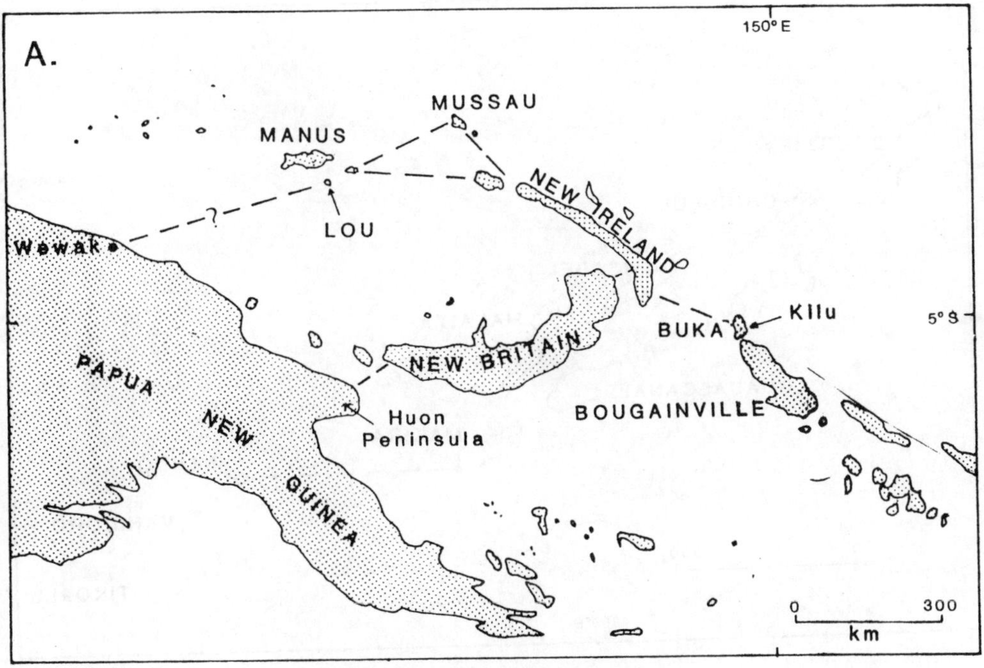

Figure 2.3a. Early human settlement in western Melanesia extended from the Papua New Guinea mainland at least to Kilu on Buka Island at the north-west end of the Solomons chain (from Nunn, submitted). The connection between Wewak and Lou is of particular interest. Broken lines represent possible journeys made, perhaps regularly, by pre-Lapita inhabitants of the region.

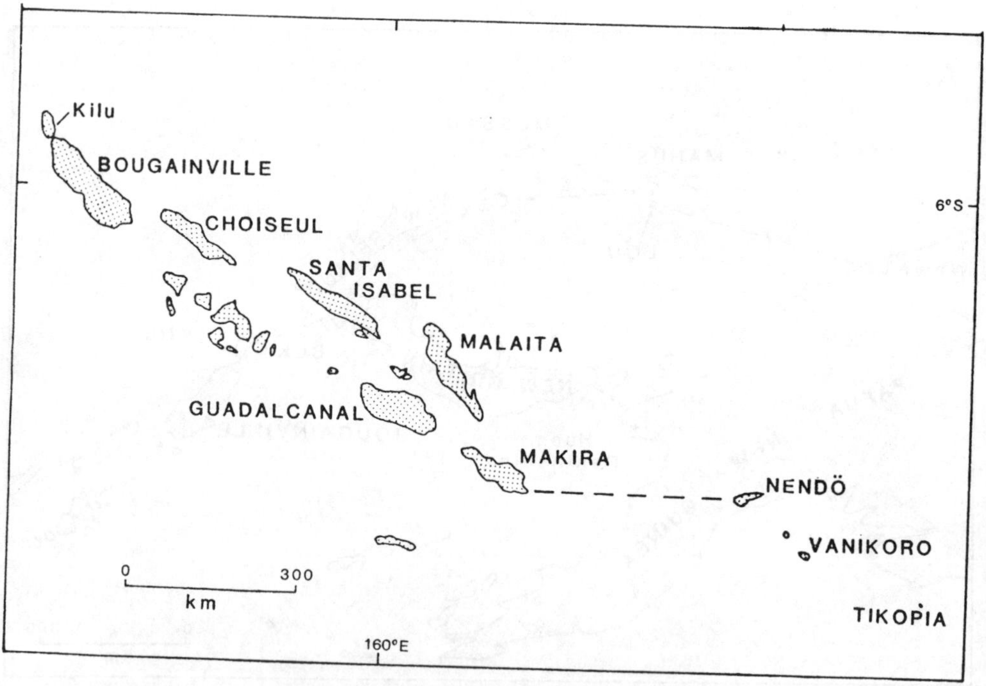

Figure 2.3b. The Solomons chain, most of which west of and including Makira, was probably colonized by people before about 30,000 BP (from Nunn, submitted). The eastern outer islands were apparently not colonized until about 3200 BP. Was the Makira-Nendö sea gap really such an effective barrier to earlier eastward migration or will future discoveries demonstrate, as they have in western Melanesia, that people crossed this gap much earlier?

the behaviour of the earliest settlers of western Melanesia. If, however, earlier settlements are found one day, and we shall probably have to look underwater to find them, only then will an accurate picture of the peopling of the Pacific Islands begin to emerge.

Wisdom from the Amazon

The question of the cause of forest decline in New Zealand was discussed above. The issue is part of a much larger question about vegetation changes and their cause(s) during the period of early human settlement in the Pacific Islands.

The orthodox view is well represented in *The Naive Lands* where we are informed, for example, that deforestation associated with *anthropogenic* burning began on the Nadrau Plateau on Viti Levu island in Fiji about 2000 BP (p 190). On the same page, we are told that abundant charcoal particles and grass pollen in post-2900 BP sediments on Aneityum island in Vanuatu "suggests *anthropogenic* burning as the major agent of forest clearance here also" (Enright & Gosden, 1992: 190, my emphases).

Not only is the cause of deforestation clearly identified in *The Naive Lands* but also its antiquity: we are told (p 108) that, because Australian Aborigines have been seen to use burning as a form of vegetation control during the "ethnographic present", such a practice "must" also have existed in the past. It is explained to us in great detail (p 69) how humans modified the Australian environment through the systematic use of fire from the time they first arrived in it.

Two attributes common to these examples are that they are all unsupported and empirically unsupportable inferences liable to be mistaken for unassailable truths. For example, it is only assumed that burning 2000 BP in Fiji was caused by people because people were living there at the time. Charcoal found in sediments in Australia and Vanuatu is proof that fires occurred, not that humans lit them.

There is something to learn about all this from a study in the northern Amazon Basin by Saldarriaga and West (1986). They dated charcoal from forest fires here from 6260 BP until the present day. Hitherto these fires had been regarded as anthropogenic but evidence for a human presence, in the form of ceramic sherds, was dated only from 3750 BP. The inescapable conclusion is that, for at least the first 2510 years during which there were forest fires in the northern Amazon Basin, there were no people there, so we can hardly regard the fires as anthropogenic. They must have been caused naturally, perhaps by lightning, particularly during periods of prolonged aridity. Then what about the last 3,750 years in the northern Amazon Basin? Just because humans were there, are we to believe that the same processes which had once caused fires in the absence of humans abruptly and miraculously ceased once humans arrived? It seems unlikely.[7]

Given the above study of Amazonian fires, one is forced to question the continued attribution of forest burning on Pacific Islands to human rather than non-human causes (or a combination of both) during the last few thousand years.

Complementary to the orthodox view that people destroyed the forests on Pacific Islands by burning is the view that all Pacific Island grasslands developed as the result of anthropogenic burning. Besides the few native grasslands in the Pacific (Nunn, 1990), it has long been assumed that the grasslands covering large parts of Melanesia and Polynesia (including New Zealand) formed only as the result of indiscriminate burning of forests by humans when they first settled these islands. It is not hard to trace the antecedents of this idea. Burning is part of the way of life of many people living in these grassland areas today; it is tempting to accede to the romantic notion that this is an age-old tradition dating from a time when there were forests there. Furthermore, many early European visitors to the Pacific saw people burning forests and assumed that this was not just a response by former subsistence agriculturalists to external demands for a change in land use but part of an long-established tradition.

We now know differently. Pacific grasslands, once assumed to be wholly anthropogenic, are now known to have considerably pre-dated human arrival on many islands. Southern (1986) thought that grassland on the dry side of Viti Levu island in Fiji may have persisted since the last ice age (when grasslands were widespread owing to the drier climate), so its presence there today cannot be entirely attributed to human impact.[8] In the islands of Micronesia, it has long been entrenched wisdom that the grassland-savannas existing there were solely the result of the forests having been burned by humans when they first arrived. Careful work by Zan and Hunter-Anderson (1987) showed that Micronesian savannas are composed of endemic plant species and that traditional agricultural practices were highly unlikely to have led to the formation of savanna in areas which were once forested. Similar conclusions about New Zealand's grasslands were reached by Holloway (1954) whose views, widely condemned at the time for flying in the face of the prevailing orthodoxy, are due, I feel, to be rehabilitated (Nunn, 1992).

Despite the above, it is not denied that burning by humans will cause grasslands to extend into areas occupied by other types of vegetation. Nor is it deniable that many grassland areas are today kept in that state by regular burning. Such statements do not invalidate the earlier comments about the origins of such grasslands and savannas.

One final point of interest refers to the supposed cause(s) of anthropogenic burning during the early settlement history of Pacific Islands. Reasons for modern burning of grasslands vary greatly[9] and much has been inferred *a posteriori* about early human behaviour in the Pacific Islands by assuming that once forest-clad islands were devastated by their earliest human settlers. If it can be demonstrated that the islands on which the first humans landed in the South Pacific were not forest-clad but largely covered with grassland and savanna, that would significantly alter our premises about contemporary human behaviour and subsequent socio-cultural development.

In my view, a reassessment is needed now. We can no longer justify these slick assumptions about human behaviour three millennia or more ago. We need to approach the subject in a more rational and less prejudiced frame of mind if we are going to uncover the truth.

Conclusion

I fear that through the elaborate system of inferences about the Pacific past, such as is aired in *The Naive Lands,* we are creating a world which never existed; a world which we consider wholly understandable and less complex (more naive) to an improbable degree than the world we inhabit; a world in which people were rational and predictable, albeit in retrospect; not a world where people were temperamental, where behaviour was far from uniform, where prejudices did not run rife and produce irrational acts.

There is much more to discover about early human history and contemporary environmental change in the Pacific Islands and Australasia. Most of this involves simply looking and recording. In *The Naive Lands,* some writers emphasize the lack of information we have. Yet, from the accounts of others, the unwary reader might be deceived into thinking that just about everything we need to know is known and that only agreeing on the correct interpretation matters now. This is manifestly untrue.

The interpretation matters too. Nevertheless, all of us with an interest in this field must be continually reminded that in dealing with the distant past we can know little with certainty and that much of what we might pretend we know is actually only inferred, thereby liable to change as new information emerges. If this means that prehistorians and all they associate with are the pariahs of the academic world, ridiculed as adherents of a science without facts, then so be it.

Notes

1. Thom, in contributing a short background chapter to *The Naive Lands,* mentions that people who investigate long-term environmental change "are often faced with very patchy records, and with inadequate opportunities to fully convey their knowledge of these records to others" (1992: 11-12). It might have been expected that some of the more extreme statements in the book would have been tempered with this in mind.
2. BP is an abbreviation for Before Present and refers to a radiocarbon age determination in which present is the year 1950 AD.
3. For the island of New Guinea, Swadling and Hope write that "much of this vast island is still scientifically unexplored" (1993: 13).
4. For example, the lower 2m of a 5-m core from the bed of Lake Vaihiria in Tahiti indicate greater evidence of erosion between about AD 1500-1700. Flenley et al. (1991) interpret this as meaning either that tropical cyclones were more frequent during this period and/or that the contemporary population of the interior of Tahiti (thus clearance of forest on the slopes surrounding the lake) was higher.
5. Actually, there is no known evidence of early settlement on Makira: I know of no investigations thereon. This inference is based on the date of 28,740 BP for a settlement on Buka island at the western end of the Solomon chain and the assumption that negligible sea gaps separating islands between Buka and Makira within that chain would have been crossed easily (White & Flannery, 1992).
6. The essence of the argument is in Gibbons and Clunie (1986). I attempted an extension of John Gibbons' thinking on this subject following his untimely death (Nunn, 1988).
7. The debate is slightly more complex. Although other writers (e.g. Sanford et al., 1985) broadly agree, still others find a strong correlation between forest burning and a human presence in parts of the Amazon Basin (e.g. Piperno, 1990).
8. People are believed to have arrived on Viti Levu within the last 3,500 years; the last ice age ended 10,000 years ago.

9. In the Sigatoka valley (on Viti Levu, in Fiji), where I have had students asking local people this question over the years, the most common answers are ground clearance for planting, insect control and to encourage rain to fall. The latter is explained by the smoke providing hygroscopic nuclei in the air.

Chapter 3

Contemporary Industrialization in Fiji

Rajesh Chandra

Introduction

Deane (1965: 4) has argued that "it is now almost an axiom of the theory of economic development that the route to affluence lies by the way of an industrial revolution". Although there are now growing concerns regarding the consequences of industrialization, particularly of the type of industrialization undergone by the currently industrialized countries, it nonetheless remains true that most developing countries still see industrialization as the proven path to high standards of living (Chandra, 1992; World Bank, 1987; Thirlwall, 1991).

The development literature in the past was of the view that industrialization was out of reach of small countries; writers felt that certain economies of scale were needed in manufacturing, and that these were to be found only in large countries (for reviews of smallness and development, see Jalan, 1982; Selwyn, 1985; Shand, 1980). Yet the development of technology that does not need large production runs and the enviable, almost dramatic industrial progress of small countries, such as Hong Kong, Singapore, and Taiwan, have made industrialization a realizable goal for other such countries. In any case, almost every country needs a degree of industrialization to maximize value from its agricultural sector and to assist other sectors.

Fiji began to encourage industrialization when it gained political independence in 1970, both to complement the agricultural sector and to provide employment. Yet the government did not see manufacturing as a driving force in the economy, which was seen as based very much on agriculture and tourism.[1] Only after the military coups of 1987 did the government begin to view manufacturing as a leading sector and begin articulating a view of Fiji society as an industrial one.

This chapter provides a description and analysis of contemporary industrialization in Fiji. Beginning with a discussion of the level of industrialization, it analyses the structure of manufacturing – what kind of manufacturing activities are to be found in Fiji? It then examines the orientation of the manufacturing sector – is it geared to the supply of domestic demand, or does it produce for exports? Economic activities, and most of all activities that involve large capital investment and entail significant risks, are influenced greatly by government policies. The chapter, therefore, also analyses public policies as they have related to the manufacturing sector, and assesses their impact. Finally, it attempts to present a view of the future prospects of manufacturing in Fiji.

How Industrialized Is Fiji?

The starting point of any discussion of industrialization in any country is its level. The level of industrialization is most commonly measured in terms of the manufacturing sector's share of the Gross Domestic Product (GDP), although sometimes its share of total employment is also used.

In 1991, the latest year for which data are available, the manufacturing sector contributed 12% to the GDP (in 1977 constant prices at factor cost, calculated from Fiji Bureau of Statistics, 1993). This is a high level compared with other Pacific Island countries where, with the exception of Papua New Guinea, levels of industrialization are extremely low, but it is much lower than many other developing countries, and is close to the level of industrialization of the least developed countries. What is even more significant than the low level of industrialization is the fact that the manufacturing sector's contribution to the GDP has not changed very much in the last 30 years. This is in spite of the fact that the economy of Fiji has changed considerably (agriculture becoming less important, and tourism and services becoming more important).

This is not to imply that important changes did not take place within the manufacturing sector during the last few decades. There were very important changes: the sector became diversified, and the importance of food manufacturing declined as new forms of manufacturing developed.

The Structure of Manufacturing

The make-up of the manufacturing sector is usually discussed with reference to International Standard Industrial Classification of All Economic Activities (ISIC), which has categories to describe any economic activity. The structure of the manufacturing sector in Fiji is depicted in Figure 3.1. The largest component is still food; in 1990, it accounted for

48% of the value added[2] of the sector. Garment and wood product manufacturing follow closely behind, with a wide range of activities making up the rest.

Two main points should be made regarding the structure of manufacturing in Fiji. First, the sector is still at an early stage of development. Figure 3.2 presents data on the composition of manufacturing in developing countries as a whole.[3] The importance of the food sector has declined markedly in the latter, from 26% of manufacturing value added in 1963 to 16% in 1984, declining even further to 15% in 1990 (UNIDO, 1982; UNCTAD, 1988; United Nations, 1990). Thus Fiji's figure of 48% for foodstuffs indicates its early stage of industrial development. Second, garment manufacturing has become very important, particularly in the last five years (Chandra, 1990, 1992). A dramatic increase occurred in garment manufacturing in response to the decision by Australia and New Zealand to open up their domestic markets, and the consequent pressure on their producers to seek cheaper production sites, and in response to the South Pacific Regional Trade and Economic Co-operation Agreement (SPARTECA), which allows non-reciprocal trade benefits to the South Pacific Forum states in Australian and New Zealand markets.[4] In addition, the government's tax free system, which offers (among other things) 13-year tax holidays, assisted the expansion of garment production.

What is not so obvious from the data is that Fiji has developed a very extensive range of manufacturing, from food to shipbuilding, from matches to the production of video and audio tapes.

The market structure of the manufacturing sector has been largely monopolistic and oligopolistic, although less pronounced today than previously (Chandra, 1988). This has resulted from the small domestic market and the previously import-substituting industrialization strategy pursued by the government. Yet in recent years, the government has changed the orientation of its economic policies towards export production in a competitive environment, thus enabling additional firms to set up operations. In addition, the presence of fewer firms no longer means that they divide the market among themselves because the government has reduced the level of protection. Domestic producers now have to compete with imports. Imports of items that are also produced in Fiji have grown significantly in some cases. For instance, import of flour increased 320 fold (or by 31,900%) between 1988 and 1992, while import of beer increased by 789% over the same period (calculated from data in Fiji Bureau of Statistics, 1993).

Most manufacturing firms in Fiji are family concerns. Many of these

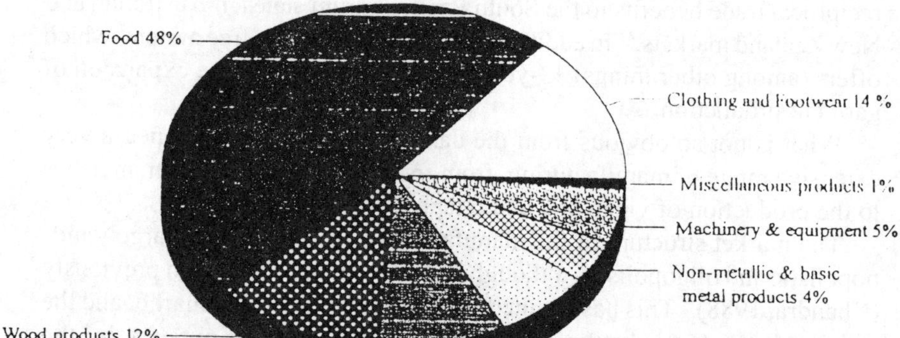

Source: Fiji Bureau of Statistics, 1993:26.

Figure 3.1. The structure of manufacturing in Fiji, 1990

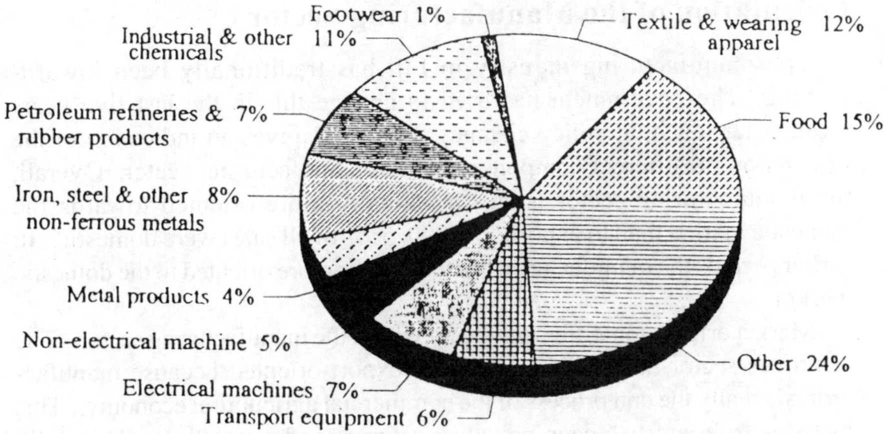

Source: United Nations, 1990:69.

Figure 3.2. The structure of manufacturing in the developing countries

firms, such as the Motibhai, Punja and Lees Trading groups of companies, originated from retailing and wholesaling. The government's incentives to firms to enter manufacturing were critical in their involvement and success. Foreign manufacturing companies are subsidiaries of multinationals, although some individual foreign entrepreneurs are also setting up operations in Fiji. Fiji does not have a tradition of public companies, although a Stock Exchange has been set up and the government is encouraging firms to trade their shares publicly.

One question that has interested researchers for a long time is whether the family holding company becomes a handicap in the future development of enterprises. In the case of the leading companies in Fiji, there is no evidence that this is so. One family firm, Maganlal Jiwa and Sons Limited, a very successful producer and exporter of confectionery, has sold its shares to the giant Nestlé corporation, although the previous owners continue to provide management support. There is some pressure on family owned firms to become public, partly to enable ethnic Fijians to purchase shares and play a larger role in the manufacturing sector.[5]

Orientation of the Manufacturing Sector

The manufacturing industry in Fiji has traditionally been inward-looking. The government has tried to change this in the last five years through far-reaching policy changes. Table 3.1 gives an indication of the orientation of different components of the manufacturing sector. Overall, the manufacturing sector is still marginally more oriented towards the domestic market than to export: in 1990, 55% of all sales were domestic. In earlier periods the manufacturing sector was far more oriented to the domestic market.

Market orientation differs markedly within the manufacturing sector. The resources sector has traditionally been export-oriented because manufacturing is really the end process of the commercial agricultural economy. This includes fruit and fish canning, sugar refining and sawmilling. The really strong export-orientation among new industries is focused on garment and footwear manufacturing. Yet there is a growing tendency among traditionally import-substituting activities to export. For instance, 17% of confectionery production is exported, 16% of paper products are exported, 11% of paint sales are foreign, and 14% of cement, concrete products, and basic metal sales are foreign (Table 3.1).

We can conclude that the manufacturing sector has a mixed foreign and

Table 3.1. The orientation of manufacturing in Fiji, 1990

FSIC*	Industry	Local Sales (F$000) Amount	%	Export ($F000) Amount	%	Total sales ($F000)
3111	Butchering & meat packing	1,624	100	0	0	1,624
3112	Dairy products	27,514	99	146	1	27,660
3113/4	Fruit, fish	17,604	25	51,437	75	69,041
3115	Edible & coconut oil	31,714	100	0	0	31,714
3116	Rice & flour milling	34,847	100	0	0	34,847
3117	Bakery products	19,843	82	4,414	18	24,257
3118	Sugar milling	22,892	9	237,784	91	260,676
3119	Confectionery	11,574	83	2,333	17	13,907
3121	Miscellaneous food	4,940	97	149	3	5,089
3122	Animal feed	11,390	100	50	0	11,440
3131/2 /3140	Beer, spirits, cigarettes & tobacco	78,558	100	371	0	78,929
3133	Non-alcoholic drinks	10,364	100	0	0	10,364
3210	Textiles & clothes	18,152	21	67,528	79	85,680
3220	Footwear	1,237	27	3,430	73	4,667
3311	Sawmilling	20,287	39	31,367	61	51,654
3312 & 3319	Curios & artifacts	1,161	93	89	7	1,250
3320	Furniture & upholstery	14,571	95	700	5	15,271
3410	Paper products	19,092	84	3,535	16	22,627
3420	Printing & publishing	25,910	100	33	0	25,943
3511	Paint	10,791	89	1,323	11	12,114
3512	Soap, toiletries, & chemical products	20,049	99	162	1	20,211
3519	Misc. chemicals	4,876	97	158	3	5,034
3520	Retreading	5,706	100	0	0	5,706
3530	Plastics	14,201	99	153	1	14,354
3600& 3700	Cement, concrete & basic metals	20,468	86	3,216	14	23,684
3811	Metal furniture & fixtures	1,337	100	0	0	1,337
3812	Structural metal products	17,079	87	2,485	13	19,564
3819	Fabricated metal products except machinery & equip	16,271	92	1,390	8	17,661

Continued overleaf

Table 3.1 continued

FSIC*	Industry	Local sales (F$000) Amount	%	Export (F$000) Amount	%	Total sales (F$000)
3821	Agricultural machinery & equipment	3,183	100	0	0	3,183
3829/30	Repair & maintenance of industrial machinery & electrical equipment	2,774	94	172	6	2,946
3841	Shipbuilding & repair	5,645	100	0	0	5,645
3849	Bus manufacture	2,260	100	0	0	2,260
3901	Jewellery and related items	6,761	100	0	0	6,761
3909	Misc. products	3,254	57	2,419	43	5,673
Total		507,937	55	414,844	45	922,781

* FSIC refers to Fiji Standard Industrial Classification, a slight modification of ISIC to suit Fiji's circumstances.

Source: Calculated from data in Fiji Bureau of Statistics, 1993: 27.

domestic market orientation and that, while an export orientation exists primarily among resource industries and garment and footwear industries, exporting is developing in sectors that have traditionally catered solely to the domestic market.

Public Policies

As was noted in the introduction, government policies play a critical role in determining most facets of a country's industrialization process. It has been argued:

> Perhaps the strongest lesson of the development experience of the last 30 years is that no matter how well or ill countries are endowed naturally (in terms of minerals, climate, location, etc.), their economic performance depends primarily on their commitment to growth and the appropriateness of the policy framework they evolve to implement their growth strategy (Black-Metzner & Hughes, 1982: 85).

The view is perhaps an extreme one, but there is no doubt of its pertinence.

The colonial government in Fiji, as elsewhere, did not favour industrialization. During World War II, however, it did encourage certain initiatives to overcome shipping difficulties. After the war, the government continued its limited encouragement of industrialization, although without much determination or enthusiasm.

The colonial government began the process of import substitution industrialization (ISI). In 1947 it introduced the Protected Industries Ordinance, which empowered the governor to provide protection to industries he considered to be in the national interest. Although only three industries were given assistance under this scheme prior to 1960 – and all of them failed – it set the pattern for subsequent industrial development in Fiji. It was natural that newly independent Fiji should follow this path.

The government followed an incremental policy for the manufacturing sector in the 1970s and 1980s. Manufacturing was not seen as a leading sector of the economy; this role was accorded to agriculture and tourism. Yet the importance of manufacturing was realized and policies were formulated to encourage it.

The Income Tax Act in 1974 consolidated the government's industrial policies. Under the new act, where enterprises were deemed to assist the economic development of Fiji, exemptions from tax were granted. Exemptions were to be for five years initially, with provision for extension (Fiji Government, 1975).

In addition, the government continued to levy high rates of tariffs on imports, particularly where these items were being produced in Fiji. Until the late 1980s the government looked upon tariffs as essential revenue generators. In 1983, for instance, customs and port dues accounted for 35% of its current revenue (calculated from Fiji Bureau of Statistics, 1989a). Additionally, licences and quotas were imposed on a wide range of products, often in response to direct pressure from manufacturers. By the early 1980s the Fiji Employment and Development Mission (FEDM) pointed out that protection had reached "dangerously high levels" (FEDM, 1984: 510). The World Bank (1986) also pointed to very high levels of effective protection, even leading to negative value added in some instances (Narsey, 1989).

Although the government had wished as early as Development Plan Six (1971-1976), the first plan for independent Fiji, to see increasing export orientation in manufacturing, its policies, nonetheless, continued its domestic market bias. The government did attempt a reform of its incentives, but it could not overcome the very strong domestic market orientation lobby. In any event, it had begun to view tariff on imports as a major source of revenue. As a result of government policies, as well as international recession, the manufacturing sector stagnated in the 1980s.

On 14 May 1987 Sitiveni Rabuka staged a coup that brought the country to the brink of economic collapse as capital and people fled and domestic demand for non-essential goods all but disappeared. The government devalued the Fiji dollar by 17.75% on 29 June 1987 and by a further 15.25% on 7 October to reduce the flight of capital and to dampen import demand. It also introduced a tax-free system to attract foreign capital in export-oriented industries. These actions set the tone of future economic policies, which were more clearly enunciated in the mini-budget of 1989, following the National Economic Summit.

Post-Coup Economic Policies

Post-coup economic policies centred around the following (Kamikamica, 1991), each of which is elaborated and critically evaluated in the following sections.

1. Export promotion as the main development strategy.
2. Deregulation of the economy, particularly in terms of reduction of protection, elimination of licensing, and labour market reforms.
3. Reform of the taxation system to encourage savings and investment.
4. Mobilization of all sectors of the economy in support of the new policies, particularly increased participation of ethnic Fijians in commerce and industry.
5. Restraint in government expenditure and a reduction in the government's role in the economy.

Export Promotion and Deregulation

The government has pursued export promotion by increased competition in the manufacturing sector through a sharp reduction in the level of protection and through labour market reforms designed to introduce greater flexibility in the labour market and to ensure international competitiveness.[6] Tariffs were reduced in the 1991 budget to a standard maximum fiscal duty of 40% (from 50%). The 1992 budget reduced this to 30%, and it was reduced to 25% for 1993. In addition, licences have been all but eliminated: import licences were lifted on 34 non-agricultural products in 1989; 7 products were freed in the 1991 budget (Fiji Ministry of Finance and

Economic Planning, 1991), and 4 in the 1992 budget. The only products remaining under licence control now are seed potatoes, butter in bulk packs, canned fish, rice, skimmed milk, full cream powdered milk, coffee, lubricants, and mineral fuels (Kamikamica, 1991). Price control has been lifted from most commodities. The role of the Prices and Incomes Board, previously the controller of prices, has been changed to that of price monitoring. The government has also attempted to remove other distortions in the economy by removing and reducing subsidies.

Tax-free system

After vacillating on the issue for almost 15 years, the tax-free system was introduced in late 1987. For manufacturers and export service providers, the government offered an attractive package, provided they exported at least 95% of their output (Chandra, 1990).

The investment and incentive package involves a total waiver of licensing for import of capital goods and other production materials, duty-free import of capital goods and equipment, duty exemption on importation of raw materials, components, spares and packaging materials. Building materials, furniture, and office equipment used to establish tax-free factories are also exempt from import duty. Products manufactured within the zone do not attract Value Added Tax (VAT). All materials supplied to the zone from outside it are treated as exports, and are therefore eligible for export benefits (Fiji Trade and Investment Board, 1988).

Companies are offered a tax holiday of 13 years. There is no withholding tax on interest, dividends and royalty paid abroad. Final dividend is taxed at the rate of 5% when paid to resident shareholders. There are no restrictions on the repatriation of capital and profits.

The tax-free system also streamlined bureaucratic procedures, with the Fiji Trade and Investment Board (FTIB) handling most of the paperwork on behalf of the investor. The FTIB has promised a turnaround time of six weeks from application to notification, though in practice a turnaround time of about ten weeks now prevails. Recent changes have made the FTIB a "one-stop shop" for investors.

In addition, the tax-free status entitles firms to import specialist personnel for enterprises subject to requirements under the Immigration Act. The immigration rules have been considerably relaxed to encourage foreign investment.

Tax Reform

The government has also undertaken a major review of the taxation system. It reduced the highest level of marginal personal tax rate by 20% in the 1990 budget. On 1 July 1992 the government introduced these additional changes:

1. reduction of the highest personal marginal rate to 35% and the standardization of company and personal tax rates;
2. simplification of the personal tax structure to 3 bands (from 10);
3. abolition of most allowances;
4. raising of the tax threshold to $F4,500; and
5. introduction of a Value Added Tax of 10%.

Summary

Industrial policies in Fiji have changed radically from import-substitution to export-oriented production. The government has sought to deregulate the economy, provide incentives for export production, and generally to work towards a competitive economic environment in Fiji. How successful have these changes been?

An Evaluation of the Success of the Policy Changes

One can discuss the performance of the new policies in terms of the importance of the manufacturing sector in the economy, inflow of foreign capital, growth in employment in manufacturing, the extent to which manufacturing goods are now being exported, and the establishment of a sound basis for long-term growth.

Yet, changes can only be confidently observed over a reasonably long period of time. In the case of Fiji, most of the policy changes have been since 1988 and, given this short time and the time lag in the availability of data, any assessment of their effectiveness has to be tentative.

Industrialization in the Economy

Table 3.2 presents data on the share of the manufacturing sector in the Fiji economy. Unfortunately, this information is not current to 1992. The data do not indicate a major change. In fact, the share of GDP contributed by manufacturing in 1989 was less than it was in 1980. If another series is used, however, based on constant 1977 prices (Table 3.3), for which 1991 data are available (but not earlier data), it can be seen that there has been a positive trend since 1989, but even here the level of industrialization in 1991, of 12%, is lower than what had already been achieved in 1986, prior to the coups of 1987.

Table 3.2. Share of the manufacturing sector of the GDP at current prices at factor cost, 1980-1989

Year	Share of the GDP
1980	11.9
1981	10.5
1982	10.7
1983	9.2
1984	9.8
1985	9.5
1986	10.3
1987	11.8
1988	9.6
1989	10.5

Sources: Calculated from Fiji Bureau of Statistics (1989) and Fiji Bureau of Statistics (1993).

Table 3.3. Share of the manufacturing sector of the GDP in constant prices of 1977 at factor cost, 1985-1992

Year	Share of the GDP
1985	11.3
1986	12.4
1987	11.8
1988	11.4
1989	11.4
1990	11.6
1991	12.0

Source: Calculated from Fiji Bureau of Statistics, 1993.

There may have been a positive movement in the level of industrialization, but firm evidence will only come from statistics derived from a longer period.

Growth of Investment

One of the main aims of the new economic policies was to restart the flow of foreign investment into Fiji, which had largely dried up in the 1980s (Gunasekera, 1985). Table 3.4 indicates that foreign direct investment into Fiji has increased substantially. Foreign direct investment jumped significantly in 1990. This was to be expected as foreign investment takes time to react to changes in country policies.

Table 3.4. Foreign direct investment inward flows into Fiji, 1986-1990

Year	Amount (US$ million)
1986	8
1987	-11
1988	24
1989	13
1990	66

Source: United Nations, 1992.

In addition to increasing foreign investment, the new policies have played their part in the growing local investment in manufacturing. In the tax-free sector, for instance, large amounts of local capital have been forthcoming since the introduction of the tax-free system. Table 3.5 indicates that at the end of June 1991, tax-free factories had a total investment of F$60.1 million, of which F$27.5 million or 43% was local. Furthermore, local entrepreneurs contributed a portion of the F$14.8 million investment in joint ventures (Table 3.5).

Table 3.5. Investment in tax free factories in Fiji, June 1991

Ownership	Investment	
	Amount (F$ million)	Per cent
Local	25.7	42.8
Foreign	19.6	32.6
Joint venture	14.8	24.6

Source: Unpublished data supplied by the Fiji Trade and Investment Board.

Employment

There has been major growth in employment. In the 1980s manufacturing jobs had begun to contract. From a peak in 1980 of 15,413 in the manufacturing sector, manufacturing employment decreased to 13,973 in 1986, prior to the coups, and to 13,680 in 1987 (Table 3.6). Largely as a result of the new policies, particularly the tax-free system, manufacturing employment then increased rapidly, reaching an all-time record of 23,400 people in 1991, comprising just over one quarter of all employees in the country. Yet manufacturing employment fell by almost 10% in 1992, raising questions as to whether the growth of the last few years will be sustained in the future.

Table 3.6. Manufacturing sector employment in Fiji, 1970-1992

Year	Employment	Share of Total Employment
1970	na	17.7
1971	na	17.9
1972	na	16.8
1973	na	16.5
1974	11,840	17.7
1975	12,760	18.2
1976	11,444	16.3
1977	11,253	15.6
1978	13,484	17.6
1979	13,948	17.8
1980	15,413	19.2
1981	14,223	17.5
1982	13,522	17.5
1983	14,702	18.4
1984	14,184	18.0
1985	14,057	17.3
1986	13,973	17.5
1987	13,680	17.5
1988	14,040	18.1
1989	19,666	22.3
1990	21,051	23.6
1991	23,400	25.6
1992	21,181	22.9

Sources: Fiji Bureau of Statistics, 1989, 1993.

Growth of Manufacturing Value Added

Table 3.7 presents data on the growth of manufacturing value added from 1973 to 1990. During most of the 1980s, manufacturing value added was stagnant and erratic. Since the introduction of new policies, it has grown. The most positive trend is that value added grew by 14% between 1989 and 1990, although, given the decline in employment, one should await the 1991 and 1992 figures before drawing firm conclusions.

Table 3.7. Growth of manufacturing sector value added, 1973-1990

Year	Value Added ($F Million)	Change (%)
1973	29.7	—
1974	45.7	53.9
1975	51.1	11.8
1976	65.1	27.4
1977	73.1	12.3
1978	65.9	-9.8
1979	93.0	41.1
1980	97.7	5.1
1981	91.3	-6.1
1982	101.0	10.6
1983	85.0	-15.8
1984	105.4	24.0
1985	106.7	1.2
1986	136.1	27.6
1987	161.9	19.0
1988	112.7	-30.4
1989	191.7	70.1
1990	218.9	14.2

Sources: Narsey (1989) and Fiji Bureau of Statistics, 1991, 1993. Data for 1988 are from World Bank, 1991. Percentages calculated by the author.

Growth of Exports

Perhaps the most significant achievement of the new policies has been to increase exports of manufactured goods from Fiji. This can be seen at two levels. First, they have helped the development of export industries, most notably the garment industry. Table 3.8 shows just how dramatically exports of garments have grown in Fiji. From less than F$5 million in 1986, garment exports reached F$131 million in 1991, a major achievement from any perspective.

Table 3.8. Fiji's garments exports, 1982-1992

Year	Value of Exports ($F)	Per Cent Change
1975	58,464	---
1976	62,296	7
1977	70,889	14
1978	87,297	23
1979	119,557	37
1980	115,043	-4
1981	108,751	-5
1982	170,793	57
1983	516,675	203
1984	848,513	64
1985	2,058,809	143
1986	4,862,771	136
1987[a]	8,803,744	81
1988[b]	30,118,000	242
1989	99,261,000	230
1990	115,774,000	17
1991	131,123,000	13
1992	105,543,000	-20

[a]The Fiji dollar was devalued by 33% in 1987.

[b]The government has revised garment export figures due to irregularities in customs entries. The new figures are more accurate, although even these have been changing in different issues of Current Economic Statistics.

Source: Fiji Bureau of Statistics, 1986 and unpublished trade data from Fiji Bureau of Statistics,and Fiji Bureau of Statistics, 1993.

As I have argued elsewhere (Chandra, 1990), not all the credit for this huge surge in garment exports can be given to Fiji government policies. Some credit must go to the changing trade policies in Australia and New Zealand and to the generous provisions of SPARTECA. Nonetheless, the government created an environment in which local entrepreneurs and overseas investors were able to combine to take the garment industry to new heights.

The second level at which the export performance of the new policies can be evaluated is that of existing industries. To what extent did industries originally set up as import-substituting turn to exporting? Table 3.9 presents data on the exports of these industries. Just after the devaluation of the Fiji dollar and the collapse of domestic demand, there was an increase in exports from this group of industries. However, except for a few items, such as bakery products, the exports of other items appear to be petering out. This raises important question as to whether Fiji manufacturers are able to hold on to markets.

Table 3.9. The export performance of import-substituting manufacturing in Fiji, 1970-1992

Year	Cement ('000 tonnes)	Bakery Products ('000 kg)	Cigarettes ('000 kg)	Paints ('000 litres)
1970	11	716	67	164
1971	24	913	67	168
1972	14	893	54	186
1973	12	786	28	241
1974	15	1,074	11	177
1975	12	724	5	123
1976	10	752	8	116
1977	8	671	17	151
1978	10	744	9	154
1979	3	940	6	137
1980	2	827	6	124
1981	1	848	5	109
1982	0	787	3	193
1983	2	1,003	9	229
1984	4	1,013	3	162
1985	8	857	5	217
1986	3	901	6	208
1987	3	676	4	212
1988	4	880	10	219
1989	21	1,165	12	145
1990	30	1,111	10	217
1991	17	949	3	258
1992	4	1,145	0	190

Sources: Fiji Bureau of Statistics publications.

Conclusions

This paper has presented an overview of contemporary industrialization in Fiji, with an emphasis on its level, structure, orientation, and public policies. It has been established that the level of industrialization is not very high by international standards and that it has not increased consistently over the last decade. The manufacturing sector is dominated by food manufacturing, an indication that industrialization is at an early stage of development. In the last decade, the manufacturing sector has diversified away from resource processing to other areas. Starting from a predominantly domestic market orientation, the manufacturing sector now has a mixed orientation, although the new push is towards export production. The export orientation is expected to increase in the future.

Industrialization policies underwent a dramatic re-orientation in the aftermath of the two coups of 1987. The government introduced new incentives for export production, chiefly through the introduction of the tax-free system. It also deregulated the economy through the near elimination of licensing, and the lowering of tariffs on all except luxury goods. It has tried to introduce a competitive economic environment in Fiji.

There is little doubt that government policies have had a major impact. In the areas of employment generation, exports, and attraction of investment, there has been considerable success. Yet the share of the manufacturing sector of the GDP has not changed very much.

The data for 1992 raise serious concerns. The decrease in exports of garments leads one to question the earlier optimism that Fiji was going to be the South Korea of the future in clothing exports. Manufacturing employment also fell by almost 10% in 1992, raising for the first time fears that deregulation policies may have a negative impact on the manufacturing sector. These findings indicate that the government and entrepreneurs must keep the situation under close scrutiny and, where necessary, take appropriate action. Yet they do not cast doubt on the basic thrust of the new policy because, given the stagnation of the 1980s and the economic consequences of the coups, the present policies are the only logical ones.

Where to now? There is little doubt that Fiji has considerable scope for further industrialization, particularly in resource-related areas where it has a comparative advantage and where links with the local economy are strong. It also has scope for the continued production of garments, provided Fiji realizes that many of its market-access advantages are short term, and that the government prepares the industry for competitive production. There is a particular need to focus on improving the quality of labour and on productivity in general. It is also important to take a detailed look at the impact of deregulation, not because of any doubts about the appropriateness of the basic thrust of the policies, but to assess the speed of reforms and identify areas where adjustment assistance may be required.

Notes

1. For a comprehensive survey of public policies on industrialization in Fiji, see Chandra (1985, 1992) and the various national development plans.
2. Manufacturing value added refers to the difference between gross output (sales, stock changes and self-consumption) and intermediate consumption, which comprises all costs of production except labour and capital depreciation. Value added comprises, therefore, labour costs and gross profits.
3. Developing countries are defined as all countries not included in the category of developed countries. It excludes countries of the former Soviet Union, some of which will no doubt be included in this category in the future.
4. The members of the Forum are Australia and New Zealand and independent Pacific Island countries.
5. One development objective of the government is to encourage ethnic Fijians to play a larger role in Fiji's commercial life. The government has provided large amounts of money to bring this about. One indication of the success of the initiative is that the approval of loans to ethnic Fijians by the Fiji Development Bank under the commercial loans to ethnic Fijians scheme increased from F$2,656,000 in 1988 to F$18,037,000 in 1992, an increase of 579% (calculated from Fiji Bureau of Statistics, 1993).
6. The future of labour market reforms, however, is uncertain as the government develops a new relationship with the Fiji Labour Party.

Chapter 4

Pacific Island Biodiversity: A Basis for Ecological, Cultural and Economic Survival

Randolph R. Thaman

Introduction

Since my first visit to Fiji almost 30 years ago, one aspect of life in the Pacific Islands which has permeated my consciousness has been the paramount role that plants and animals play in rural life. Even urban Pacific peoples, when asked which aspects of their cultural heritage they value most, include myths, songs, dances, traditional feasts, seafood, leis and garlands, kava, betel-nut, whales' teeth, shell money, fine mats, tapa cloth, yam or taro gardens or their own home island or village to which they ultimately intend to return. Most of these have one thing in common: they depend on, are derived from, or focus on the island environment and its constituent plants and animals. The latter are being referred to increasingly as 'biodiversity', the conservation of which has become a *cause célèbre* of the international community.

The biodiversity of the region constitutes both the bounty which was largely responsible for the mutiny on the *Bounty* and, more importantly, the bounty upon which rests the sustainability of the relatively benign and peaceful ways of life of the small-island states of the Pacific Ocean. Pacific biodiversity also includes the intimate knowledge that Pacific peoples have of this bounty and their time-tested 'biodiversity-use' systems which provided for its relatively sustainable use for thousands of years. If these resource-use traditions are not maintained, there will be a mutiny of the biodiversity bounty which will undermine the push for environmentally sustainable social and economic development in the Pacific Islands.

One of the most important roles that geographers and non-geographers alike can play at the University of the South Pacific (USP) is to foster among our students and the emerging Pacific Islands managerial elite, a better understanding and appreciation of this biodiversity and its role as a foundation for environmentally sustainable development in a rapidly expanding, but economically and politically unstable world. For this to be successful, biodiversity, ethnobiology (the study of the cultural uses and husbandry of plants and animals) and biodiversity conservation must increasingly serve as a focus of our teaching, research and community out-reach.

It is also suggested that island biodiversity and the biodiversity-use traditions have been among the reasons that the Pacific Islands have been so widely romanticized. Why did Fletcher Christian and his crew mutiny on the *Bounty* over two centuries ago, thus aborting Captain William Bligh's mission to load breadfruit and carry part of the Pacific's biodiversity to the West Indies as a staple diet for slaves on British plantations? Why did Paul Gauguin and Robert Louis Stevenson, to mention only two, leave behind the material affluence and *haute culture* of their European homelands for the South Pacific? Why do Bikini Islanders insist on returning to their ancestral island, despite the fact that it will probably never be safe for human habitation owing to radioactive contamination? Why do Nauruans choose to remain on their devastated phosphate-mined island despite their monetary wealth and easy access to Australia? Why do most Pacific Island emigrants dream of eventually returning home? Why has "subsistence affluence" become etched so indelibly in the publications of academics?

It is argued here that it is, to a large extent, because of the biodiversity of the islands and the intimate relationship that Pacific peoples have with it. The Pacific Islands remain among the most serene and benign places on the earth's surface in terms of the bounty and beauty that nature has to offer. Its pelagic fisheries resource, its reefs and lagoons, its forests, grasslands and croplands and household gardens still constitute one of the world's most diverse and untapped bases for sustainable development.

This paper makes three points:

1) That the biodiversity of the Pacific Islands and the intimate relationship with it that Pacific peoples developed have made the Pacific Islands one of the most romanticized and peaceful areas on earth;
2) That the erosion of both this biodiversity and the people's knowledge of its use and management herald the end of subsistence affluence and the relatively benign social and political systems which have made the islands of the Pacific Ocean pacific;
3) That, as geographers, one of the most important roles that we can play is to foster a geography which synthesizes the most appropriate aspects of traditional and modern geography (regional, global, quantitative, Geographical Information Systems) with a truly 'human biogeography'

(human ecology) which places humans clearly at centre stage in all Pacific ecosystems. Only through such a shift from a Eurocentric and increasingly technocratic geography can we maximize the contribution that we can make as the only discipline which focuses on the link between human societies and their dependence and impact on their ecosystems.

Why Biodiversity as a Focus: My Biodiversification

By virtue of the USP's location, it is almost impossible to avoid seeing the importance of biodiversity to rich and poor alike. Whereas the Australian National University, the centres for Pacific studies that have sprung up in Christchurch and Auckland and at the University of Hawai'i are located in highly urbanized and monetized areas from which academics must venture out from their libraries and word processors to study their 'subjects' in their diverse island environments, the USP is situated squarely in the middle of the tropical plants, animals and ecosystems. It is surrounded and peopled by the men and women who know and depend on them. We border the mangrove swamp and intertidal zone of Laucala Bay; we know the squatters and low-income families that depend on them every day. We are surrounded by cassava, taro, *bele* (*Hibiscus manihot*), sugar-cane gardens and groves of coconuts, breadfruit, pandanus and bananas and plantains, the trees of life of the Pacific. We are within ten minutes by bus of the Suva Municipal Market, Nabukalou Creek and the Handicraft Market where the fruits of the land, sea and the Pacific handicraft tradition constitutes a living testimonial to the importance of biodiversity in the context of the life of a small-island Pacific's modern city. Finally, our students from 12 Pacific countries, eager to share and teach us about their familiar traditions while we often try to jam ours down their throats, constitute our most important window to the importance of their biodiversity inheritance...if we are willing to listen.

My first encounters with Pacific families and their marine and terrestrial resources had a lasting and irreversible impression on me. Spear-fishing and snorkelling for the first time in the lagoons and reefs of Viti Levu, Tahiti, Moorea and Borabora; foraging with Tahitians for shellfish at low tide on the reefs of Raiatea by torchlight; being dumbfounded by, and attempting to sample, the tropical diversity of the Suva and Papeete markets; serving as a porter to help Pita, our Tahitian guide, collect and carry orchid specimens from Lake Vaihiria and the mountains of Tahiti Nui for the future director of the Bishop Museum; taking part in a traditional presentation of *isevusevu* (first fruits) and *yaqona* (kava) ceremony in Nadroga, Fiji;

sharing 'real' curries and their culture with an Indian family in Suva; and living three days and eating fish with a Tahitian extended family on Moorea. All had such a profound impact upon me (culturally and scientifically) that I henceforth resolved to spend the rest of my life with Pacific peoples in their island ecosystems.

Upon completion of my Master's thesis, I applied to join a recently advertised U.S. Peace Corps programme in Western Samoa. On being told that I had been selected for Tonga, I immediately accepted.

By teaching science, biology and physical education to Tongan children at Tonga High School; playing rugby for my town team of Fasi; tending my own food garden and chickens (part of the Peace Corps philosophy at the time); and spear-fishing for food, I began to gain greater insight into the Pacific's biodiversity and cultural traditions. To cut a long story short, I did my PhD at the University of California at Los Angeles on 'Tongan Agriculture: With Particular Emphasis on Plant Assemblages' (1976), for which I mapped and recorded all plants and land uses on 100 8-acre Tongan bush allotments and administered over 200 questionaires on Tongan use of plants and animals and the nature of plants on town allotments. After a brief time at the University of California at Santa Barbara, where my Tongan wife and I worked for a Geography Remote Sensing making inventorying crops and ecosystems using high altitude and satellite images, we were hired by the University of the South Pacific.

My teaching, research and consultancy interests over my 20 years at the USP have ranged from Pacific ethnobotany, vegetation, food systems and urban gardening to sustainable development and the impact of nuclear technology on Pacific ecosystems.

Most recently, I was fortunate enough to get a sizeable grant from the MacArthur Foundation in Chicago to mount a major Community-Based Biodiversity Conservation Project which involves University staff and students and the South Pacific Action Committee on Human Ecology and the Environment (SPACHEE) in rapid rural assessments of the biodiversity and biodiversity-use traditions of inland and coastal communities in Fiji, Vanuatu, Solomon Islands and New Caledonia. The final objective is to use the findings to devise and implement formal and non-formal education programmes to encourage landowners to protect their biodiversity – for their benefit.

Fate and fortune have guided me in an continuing process of 'biodiversification' and increasing appreciation of the critical role that biodiversity and its conservation and management has played, and should continue to play, as the foundation of Pacific Island human development. Pacific peoples were, by tradition, extremely biodiversified: economically, socially, ecologically and nutritionally. Pacific peoples were not highly specialized and individualistic. They shared and managed their resources and their knowledge for the benefit of the community and future generations. They were communal societies based on the sustainable management and sharing of their biodiversity traditions. These traditions were, and are, their strengths and insurance against unforeseen natural and economic disasters and life crises.

Every day it becomes increasingly clear to me that a sustainable future scenario for the Pacific Islands must be based on community-based biodiversity conservation (CBBC). Owing to geographic, demographic, economic and management constraints, large-scale, national-level, top-down biodiversity conservation is probably doomed to failure.

Biodiversity and its Conservation in the Changing Pacific

For most Pacific Island societies, biodiversity is not just a matter of scientific, economic (in monetary terms), recreational or ecological value. It is a capital inheritance, which has been passed on by past generations to current and future generations of Pacific Islanders. Biodiversity is not income that should be spent or destroyed. It is the 'capital' needed for development and maintenance of Pacific societies and from which "subsistence affluence" and almost all 'income' (both cash and non-cash) are derived. Whereas the predominant focus for most rich-country motivated biodiversity preservation includes uniqueness or endemism, scientific importance, importance as potential gene pools for plant breeding, medicinal discoveries or other technical breakthroughs, for most Pacific Island societies, the focus of biodiversity preservation should be its central role as the basis for ecological, cultural and economic survival of local communities. Particular stress is placed on the fact that for semi-subsistence societies, 25-90% of the real income of rural peoples is in the form of non-cash income derived from local terrestrial and marine plant and animal resources. Moreover, this income is relatively unaffected by inflation and deterioration in terms of trade which make imported goods increase in cost more rapidly than wages or what is received in return for exports overseas.

If we are indeed worried about cultural survival and sustainability in some of the biologically poor areas on earth, the focus of biodiversity preservation programmes must include not only endemic (unique) terrestrial and marine taxa, and larger "charismatic megafauna", such as the dugong, sea turtles, whales, birds-of-paradise, the bird-wing butterflies of Papua New Guinea and the *cagou* (*Rhynochaetos jubatus*) of New Caledonia, but also ecologically and culturally important ubiquitous species or varieties which are also endangered. This is particularly critical in the context of smaller islands which have limited ecosystem diversity and few endemic plants or animals of global scientific interest.

Pacific Island Biodiversity

Biodiversity can be assessed in terms of both the diversity of different types of ecosystems or in terms of the overall diversity of the different plant and animal species or varieties found in a given place. Although there is a wealth of biodiversity in the Pacific Islands, there is both great diversity and great disparity in the biota of different countries at the island and ecosystem levels. The larger islands of western Melanesia have the greatest ecosystem diversity and among the richest flora and fauna in the world, whereas the smaller low-lying atolls of the eastern Pacific have the lowest ecosystem diversity and among the most impoverished terrestrial flora and fauna in the world. In terms of marine biota, the disparity is not so great, although there is still an attenuation of species from west to east (Stoddart, 1992).

A survey by Dahl (1980) identified over 70 ecosystem or biome types found in the Pacific Islands. These included:

1) terrestrial or freshwater ecosystems, such as tropical lowland and upland forests, swamp and riverine forests, mangrove and coastal beach forest, woodlands and savannas, meadows, scrublands, deserts, marshes, rivers, streams and lakes;
2) marine ecosystems, such as algal and seagrass beds, beaches, a range of reef and lagoon types, estuaries, offshore slopes, terraces, shelves, canyons, seamounts and abyssal plains;
3) what seem to be subsets of these, such as seabird rookeries, sea turtle nesting areas, and upwelling systems in the ocean. These are further broken down into approximately 600 individual ecosystems based on different island types, substrates, slope exposures, climate and other factors.

The South Pacific Regional Environment Programme (SPREP), with support from The Nature Conservancy, the U.S. Agency for International Development, the U.S. Fish and Wildlife Service, the East-West Center and the Worldwide Fund for Nature has been refining the Dahl system which can be used to produce an inventory of ecosystems on a regional, national and island scale. This will then be used as a basis to prioritize biodiversity conservation action.

Although both the Dahl and SPREP systems provide excellent bases for systematic regional and national inventories of ecosystems and biodiversity and their endangerment status, the predominant emphasis is still on identifying systems that can be set aside for nature conservation rather than on the preservation of biodiversity. There is a need for a simpler, more functional ecosystem classification system, which could be used at the community or landowner level, and in schools in the region, to promote community-based biodiversity conservation. I have proposed such a system in a more-detailed paper (Thaman, 1993). Ecosystems classified included indigenous, inland, coastal and mangrove forests, grasslands and scrublands, shifting and permanent agricultural lands, monocultural plantations and plantation forests, pasturelands, urban/built areas, beaches and bare rock, rivers, lakes, wetlands, estuaries, lagoons, reefs, island shelves, seamounts, the open ocean and aquacultural/maricultural areas.

The utility or advantage of such a classification system is that it:

1) includes most of the major resource-use zones, in both the traditional and modern contexts;
2) roughly corresponds to local classification systems, which would have distinct vernacular terms for each resource-use zone;
3) identifies ecosystem types or resource-use zones which have relatively distinct biological communities in terms of habitat, ecological niches, species diversity, and the degree of human modification and endangerment status;
4) identifies ecosystems which can be managed by local communities to protect, conserve or enhance the constituent biological resources on a sustainable basis as part of a multi-ecosystem CBBC strategy.

To further appreciate what biodiversity means to Pacific societies, it is useful to identify the main classes or categories of taxa that constitute the biodiversity of each of these ecosystems, and which could be protected a part of CBBC initiatives (Table 4.1). The system presented is a first attempt at providing a system that could be used at the community, school and policy-making levels to bring people's attention to both the diverse biological resources found in 'their' ecosystems, and their ecological and functional utility as a basis for sustainable development at the household, community, national and regional levels.

Table 4.1. Classification and utility of community-level ecosystems in the Pacific islands

Class	Sub-classes	Specific types	Utility
Lower life-forms		Bacteria	E,s,c
		Viruses	E,s,c
Plants	Indigenous	Phytoplankton	E,s,c
	Aboriginal introductions	Algae	E,S,C
	Recent introductions	Fungi	E,S,c
	Wild plants	Mosses	E,s
	Domesticated plants	Other lower plants	E,s,c
	Food plants	Ferns	E,S,C
	Non-food plants	Herbs/forbs	E,S,C
	Terrestrial	Grasses/sedges	E,S,C
	Freshwater	Vines	E,S,C
	Marine	Shrubs	E,S,C
		Trees	E,S,C
Animals	Indigenous	Protozoa	E,s,c
	Aboriginal introductions	Zooplankton	E,s,c
	Recent introductions	Sponges	E,s,c
	Wild animals	Corals	E,S,c
	Domesticated animals	Jellyfish	E,S,c
	Food species	Worms	E,S,C
	Non-food species	Molluscs	E,S,C
	Terrestrial	Insects	E,C,C
	Freshwater	Crustaceans	E,S,c
	Marine	Echinoderms	E,S,C
		Holothurians	E,s,c
		Other Invertebrates	E,S,C
		Fish	E,s,c
		Amphibians	E,S,C
		Reptiles	E,S,C
		Birds	E,S,C
		Non-human mammals	E,S,C
		Humans	E,S,C

E, S and C = direct major Ecological, Subsistence or Commercial or Export utility to people at the community *and* national level in Melanesia, Polynesia or Micronesia; e,s and c = minor or indirect ecological, subsistence or commercial/export importance

From such a perspective, it can be seen that the biodiversity of almost all island ecosystems would be almost incomprehensible to a reductionist economist or 'pure scientist' but not to Pacific peoples and hopefully not to human biogeographers and their students.

Functional Utility of Biodiversity to Pacific Societies

If one were to list all the species, subspecies, forms, varieties, cultivars, races, breeds and provenances of wild and domesticated plants and animals present in each class, subclass or type of biota in each ecosystem represented in a given community, island or Pacific Island country, the magnitude of biodiversity, even for a small atoll community, becomes all too apparent.

The true cultural importance and diversity of 'biodiversity' becomes even more astounding when we add an ethnobiological dimension to the equation and attempt to catalogue all uses (the 'bio-utility') of all taxa to a given community. For example, preliminary analyses of the results of a survey of Ucunivanua Village in Fiji indicate that for shellfish alone there are over 70 different edible species, many of which are the main sources of cash income to the village. In north Ambrym, Vanuatu, there are over 300 plant species considered useful.

An attempt to categorize the cultural utility of Pacific trees (Thaman & Clarke, 1987) shows that trees serve at least 12 distinct ecological functions, have over 70 cultural uses, and provide from 10-90% of the real income and production of rural Pacific peoples. To replace these products with imported substitutes would either be impossible or too expensive. To eliminate these trees would, thus, constitute a major ecological, cultural and economic disaster which would seriously undermine self-reliance and sustainability in the Pacific Islands.

Similarly, an analysis of the ecological and cultural importance of 140 ubiquitous or locally important coastal and mangrove plants found from the continental islands of New Guinea and New Caledonia in the west to the smallest atolls, Rapanui (Easter Island) and the Hawaiian Islands in the east showed their 'bio-utility' to be high wherever they are found (Thaman, 1992).

In terms of the ecological utility of coastal plant resources, the most important functions include the provision of shade, animal and plant habitats, protection from wind, erosion, flood and salt-water incursion, land stabilization, protection from the desiccating effects of salt spray, soil improvement and mulching, and as animal food or links in important terrestrial and marine food chains.

Of particular importance are mangrove ecosystems which contribute either directly or indirectly, through primary and secondary productivity, to the nutritional requirements of a high proportion of marine food species (Watling, 1985). Research in Fiji has shown that over 60% of commercially important animal species live in mangroves or depend on mangrove food webs at some stage in their life cycle (Lal *et al.*, 1983). More rigorous research gives figures of 67% and 80% for eastern Australia and Florida respectively (Watling, 1985). Destruction and reclamation of mangroves have deleterious effects on fisheries, with studies in the Malacca Straits indicating that mangrove reclamation for industrial expansion led to a substantial drop in catches per effort (Khoo, 1976). Baines (1979) argued that mangrove removal can lead to offshore fisheries yield declines of 50-80%.

Similarly, *Pisonia grandis* is the most important seabird rookery species throughout the atoll Pacific. It is a species under which phosphate-rich, guano-derived soil and rock are found. It is an important pig feed in many parts of the Pacific. Where *Pisonia* has been removed, seabird populations decline and the location of schools of tuna based on the presence of seabird flocks becomes problematic for fishermen.

One of the most important ecological roles played by coastal plants is the protection of inland agricultural areas, non-coastal vegetation and fauna, settlements, and water supplies from salt-water spray and storm surges. Of particular value because of their remarkable tolerance to high levels of salinity are plants with high tolerance to salt spray and saline soils. Farmers throughout the Pacific purposely leave strand or mangrove forests intact seaside of their gardens, knowing that to remove these trees would adversely affect farming.

To provide greater detail on Pacific coastal plants is beyond the scope of this paper but can be found elsewhere (Thaman, 1992b). Examples are given here of only the medicinal, ceremonial or spiritual and body ornamentation or perfumery use of coastal plants.

Medicinal use is most widespread. Almost a quarter of Pacific coastal plants are used medicinally throughout the Pacific, as well as in South-east Asia (Perry and Metzger, 1980).

The ceremonial and spiritual importance of plants cannot be overstated. Those of more ceremonial importance include species used in rituals associated with death, war and peace, human sacrifice and cannibalism, circumcision or coming of age, house or temple building, canoe making and launching, fishing, planting cycles, love-making, wave-making or control of the sea, prayer sessions, as well as serving as symbols or totems and mediums for communicating with spirits or gods or those planted in sacred groves or burial grounds. Other species are associated with times of revelry or are used in the production of baskets, mats, and other articles reserved for ceremonial exchange or dress. As noted by Setchell (1924) for Samoa, plant names were given to gods. Songs and legends have developed around them and the heroes, families, or villages they represent. One particular Samoan text of the battle of trees and stones mentions 70-80 tree names.

The importance of body ornamentation and perfumery is attested to by the considerable time and expense devoted by most societies to clothing, jewellery, perfumes, and other items of personal adornment. Pacific Island societies place great importance on the importance of plant products for body ornamentation and perfumery, with 44% of all coastal species being used in body ornamentation and 15% used to scent coconut oil or for perfumery.

Many places, such as Hawaii or Tahiti, are commonly associated with flower leis or sweet smelling flowers, such as the *tiare Tahiti.* The *salusalu, kahoa* and *sisi, ula,* and *te bau,* the Fijian, Tongan, Samoan, and Kiribati equivalents of the Hawaiian *lei,* are all of great social, ceremonial, magical or spiritual importance. Powell (1976), Bonnemaison (1985), Neal (1965) and McDonald (1978) all stress the ceremonial or magical importance of body ornamentation in Papua New Guinea, Vanuatu, Tuvalu and Hawaii respectively, with Koch (1983) noting that ornaments used for special occasions in Tuvalu are now almost exclusively made of plants because the longer-lasting ornaments succumbed to the puritanical zeal of the Samoan missionaries.

These few examples from the analysis of the utility of the plants of Pacific Island coastal ecosystems shows the cultural sophistication and storehouse of empirical knowledge possessed by Pacific Island societies in relation to their biodiversity. It is sad that the economic, cultural and ecological value of biodiversity is rarely acknowledged in development plans, project documents, or aid proposals, despite the fact that the products and benefits provided by it would be extremely expensive or impossible to replace with imported substitutes.

The Need and Potential for Community-Based Biodiversity Conservation Strategies

Centuries of exploitation and, more recently, urban-industrial development have led to endangerment and extinction of biodiversity throughout the Pacific. Forests, both primary and secondary, continue to be transformed into degraded savannas and fern-grasslands, mangroves and lagoons into housing and industrial estates, airports and other lifeless landscapes; polycultural traditional gardens into monocultural plantations; mineral deposits and their associated biota totally destroyed; and villages and urban areas divested of their remaining plants and animals to make way for industrial, commercial, and residential areas. Although some countries and territories have conservation legislation and systems of conservation areas, forest and marine products continue to be shipped off for a fraction of their world market price to Hawaii, Japan, South Korea and Australia. The trends of biodiversity endangerment and extinction are the same from the high continental islands of Melanesia to the smallest atoll islets of Polynesia and Micronesia (Thaman & Clarke, 1987).

Deforestation in the Pacific is proceeding at a frightening rate and has undoubtedly been the main cause of the extensive anthropogenic grasslands of highland New Guinea, the xerophytic *niaouli* (*Melaleuca leucadendron*) savanna lands of New Caledonia, the highly degraded 'sunburnt lands' or *talasiga* found throughout Fiji, and the rapidly expanding *saafa* (*Panicum maximum*) grasslands of Tongatapu in Tonga. Deforestation has led to severe erosion in Wallis and Futuna, the Cook Islands, French Polynesia and Hawaii where most of the indigenous forest has been removed, leaving degraded fernlands and grasslands no longer suitable for agriculture (Kirch, 1982a). Flenley and King (1984) go as far as to suggest that deforestation was responsible for the collapse of the pre-European megalithic culture on Rapanui.

In perhaps the most extreme case, by the turn of the century, the entire indigenous forest and most of the coastal strand forest of the 24 square kilometre(km^2) island of Nauru will have been transformed into a virtually unusable moonscape by open-cast phosphate mining and associated urbanization (Manner et al., 1984).

The same holds true for marine resources. Sea turtles, whales, sharks, giant clams and black coral are endangered or extinct in some areas of the Pacific because of overexploitation. Two species of giant clams (*Hippopus*

hippopus and *Tridacna gigas*) are now extinct in Fiji, the former having been brought to extinction in both Fiji and Tonga within recent times and the latter having become extinct in Fiji in the last two decades, owing mainly to illegal poaching by Asian fishing vessels (Lewis et al., 1988).

An issue of particular concern is the endangerment of 'human biodiversity' (Pacific peoples) by the shift from the state referred to by Fisk (1972) as "subsistence affluence", where food supplies were diverse and abundant and people were reportedly well-nourished, to a situation where Pacific peoples, especially in urban areas, now have some of the highest or most rapidly increasing rates of malnutrition and nutrition-related metabolic and degenerative diseases in the world. This alarming development seems to be related for the most part to a dietary shift, primarily in urban areas, from fresh traditional plant and animal foodstuffs and breastfeeding to nutritionally inferior, highly processed imported foods, such as breast-milk substitutes, white rice and flour, sugar, alcohol and tinned foods (Coyne, 1984; Thaman, 1988c). This nutrition and health crisis is clearly related to the declining diversity and consumption of both wild and domesticated foodstuffs from wildlands and marine and agricultural ecosystems: in other words, a loss of nutritional biodiversity.

Associated with all these aspects of biodiversity erosion, and with modern institutionalized education and development planning, has been a loss of traditional biological knowledge and an appreciation of the subsistence and developmental importance of biodiversity.

As stressed above, the loss or impoverishment of biodiversity and the loss of ethnobiological knowledge represent an ecological, cultural and economic disaster which will lock Pacific societies more tightly into the vicious circle of economic and cultural dependency. There is a critical need for biodiversity conservation and education before it is too late.

A positive sign, and a recognition of the need for biodiversity conservation regionally, is the recent approval of the South Pacific Biodiversity Conservation Programme (SPBCP), a US$10.5 million programme designed to promote biodiversity conservation in the Pacific Islands. The SPBCP will focus on the promotion of biodiversity conservation and sustainable development through the establishment of a number of Conservation Area Projects (CAPs) in the SPREP member countries. Particular emphasis will be placed on the establishment of Conservation Areas (CAs) at the community or landowner level. In the establishment of CAs, emphasis will be placed on achieving a balance between the management and utilization of CAs and their biological resources to provide for both the cash and subsistence needs of resident communities, at the same time maximizing the conservation of biodiversity, particularly plant and animal species which are rare, endangered or of major economic, cultural and ecological importance. Where biodiversity conservation could result in landowners forgoing opportunities for economic development, alternative economic activities may be facilitated.

Other members of the international aid and development community, such as the United Nations Development Programme, the Asian Development Bank, the World Bank, the Australian International Development Assistance Bureau and non-government organizations, such as Greenpeace, the World Wildlife Fund, The Nature Conservancy, the Foundation for the Peoples of the South Pacific and SPACHEE, to mention only a few, are also boarding the biodiversity bandwagon. Unfortunately, most have focused their efforts on expensive conservation area projects instead of on the systematic nationwide promotion of biodiversity conservation at the community level. Most money earmarked for biodiversity conservation is spent on administration and on the salaries, travel, per diem and consultancy fees of grossly overpaid and overpriced staff and consultants (usually from 'privatized' overseas consultancy firms which tap into tied aid funds), and not on community-based self-help programmes and environmental education that could empower people at the community level to conserve biodiversity.

In terms of cost- and biodiversity-conservation effectiveness (measured in terms of the number of endangered and ecologically and culturally important ecosystems and taxa that are protected or increase in numbers), the major effort should be placed on conservation of biodiversity at the local community or landowner level through the implementation of multi-ecosystem CBBC. In other words, local communities and landowners (including reef, lagoon and ocean owners) must be given the tools and incentives to protect all important ecosystems and plants and animals so that they will be available for use by future generations of landowners. This is not to suggest that national initiatives for the establishment of conservation areas is not also a priority.

For such broad-based community or national biodiversity conservation programmmes to be successful, a major component, in terms of both funding and personnel, must be devoted to formal and non-formal public education to create awareness of the importance of biodiversity and biodiversity conservation to sustainable development.

Recommendations

To promote multi-ecosystem CBBC, individuals, local bodies, governments and non-governmental international organizations and academic institutions must create an environment which will foster the protection and enhancement of important ecosystems and biodiversity at the community level. Extensive, primarily self-help programmes must be mounted to encourage biodiversity preservation, not only in rural areas and wildlands, but also in and around towns and cities. Although there are countless recommendations that could be made with respect to the systematic promotion of multi-ecosystem CBBC in the Pacific Islands, the following are some general recommendations that could serve as an initial blueprint for optimal biodiversity preservation:

1. that multimedia programs be developed in the vernacular to stress the nature and long-term economic, social, and ecological importance of existing biodiversity and the problems associated with the loss of biodiversity;
2. that units be written for use in school science or social science/geography curricula, at appropriate levels, on the nature and importance of biodiversity to Pacific societies (such units should be examinable and include field activities for both rural and urban areas);
3. that intersectoral working groups or committees be established in all countries to compile published lists (with both vernacular and Latin names) of the biological diversity in representative ecosystems at the the community and national levels;
4. that in-depth research be funded and conducted to study important ecosystems, their component plants and animals, cultural ecology and husbandry, and their economic importance in the context of national and community development;
5. that all landholders/owners be encouraged to preserve representative areas of all ecologically important and culturally utilitarian components of the land and marine use and tenure systems;
6. that national park and conservation area development include the promotion and establishment of village-level or landowner reserves or micro-parks in an effort to spread the benefits of park and biodiversity conservation initiatives;
7. that the nutritional and economic importance of wild foods and other

wild-land and marine resources be widely stressed and included as capital items in development plans and be made a component of environmental impact assessment procedures;

8. that important wild or cultivated medicinal plants, perfume and ornamental plants and other culturally important plants and animals be identified and consciously planted or protected;
9. that the magico-religious, spiritual and cultural importance of biological resources be popularized in an attempt to get landowners to protect representative species and ecosystems;
10. that, where possible, the protection or enhancement of useful plants, animals and components of terrestrial and marine ecosystems be required or encouraged in all agricultural, forestry, fisheries, livestock, tourism, and urban-industrial development projects;
11. that deliberate planting, transplanting, translocation or protection of endangered indigenous plant and animals species from endangered ecosystems to other appropriate areas or islands be actively encouraged, with appropriate quarantine procedures;
12. that severe pruning, pollarding, and coppicing be encouraged as alternatives to complete plant removal, when clearing new garden areas for both commercial and subsistence crops or livestock production.

There are obviously other means of promoting multi-ecosystem CBBC by individuals, communities, local bodies, governments and non-governmental and international organizations. The main point is that biodiversity conservation in the Pacific Islands should benefit local communities rather than preserving endemic plants and animals for science or in the hope of finding in our forests or lagoons a cure for AIDS. Biodiversity will probably remain the basis for cultural, economic and ecological development and maintenance for most Pacific Island communities, although undoubtedly new technologies and some new plant and animal species could enhance cash incomes and the quality of life in all areas of the Pacific.

Although biodiversity conservation has been one of the strengths of both the Geography Department and the University of the South Pacific over the past 25 years, there is considerable scope for an expansion of such activities. It is an exciting prospect. Owing to our location and the composition and knowledge of our students, staff and member countries, no other institution on earth can compete. By working closely with Pacific peoples at the community level to promote CBBC, our work could become much more enjoyable, stimulating and relevant to the developmental and conservation needs of our region. If we fail to imbue our future leaders with the need and tools to treasure and protect their Pacific biodiversity inheritance, for the benefit of people at the community level, what has made us love the Pacific will be lost.

Plate 5.1 Jean-Marie Tjibaou (ADCK/AVENIR).

Chapter 5

Jean-Marie Tjibaou: Kanak Witness to the World

Eric Waddell

Preamble

Are not words, and words alone, the raw material, the grist of any geographical dream?[1] Let me quote Jean-Marie Tjibaou for you:

> Me? I'm only momentarily here. But I must do everything in my power to ensure that the country I will leave to my sons is the most beautiful possible. For it to be rich in thought, in wisdom, in flowers and in food (Bellow, 1989a: 39).

What a remarkable reflection on the part of a man deemed by some to have been a 'mere' politician.

On the Relative Merits of Surfing and Diving

My friend and colleague, Epeli Hau'ofa, made the observation some time ago that those who study and reflect on the Pacific can be broadly divided into two categories, surfers and divers. Surfing is a spectacular sport, entertaining but essentially ephemeral in nature. Its practitioners capture powerful waves and speed across the surface of the ocean. Diving is, by contrast, a much less public pastime. It requires the development of considerable skills to plunge beneath the waves and slowly explore the silence and not only the intimacy, but also the enormity, of the ocean depths. The rewards are immense, and not easily shared.

I have been captured by the metaphor, turning it over in my mind for weeks now, reflecting on it, exploring its many dimensions. Surfers, in Epeli's view are, I believe, concerned with brief moments in time, with the present as some two-dimensional reality, largely detached from the past and future worlds. Their preoccupations are fashionable, intense perhaps, but essentially superficial in nature. They are concerned with knowledge. They collect vast amounts of information. And they speed on.... Divers, on the other hand, are slower moving, less concerned with sensations and show, more attracted by reflection and meditation, and with that which lies concealed beyond the surface of a momentary world. They are concerned with roots, the past, with understanding and with pathways to the future. Theirs is a three-dimensional universe.

I thought at first the analogy was trivial, designed more to entertain young, leisure-oriented people than nourish reflective scholars. It seemed to have a *Palagi* (Caucasian), tourist-oriented, South Sea island air about it. It was distractive and essentially alien. Then it suddenly hit me: both are profoundly Pacific Island activities. Surfing, the sport of Polynesian kings; diving, practised by all coastal populations in their quest for marine resources on and within the fringing reefs and lagoons. Both figure in the great myths of these islands. The metaphor *is* relevant. More important, perhaps, it can be used in speaking of administrators, politicians, planners and statesmen as much as of scholars. It has a much wider relevance.

The vast majority of politicians and statesmen are concerned only with tomorrow, next week, next year, their present mandate, their personal credibility, their quest for power...and for personal wealth and renown. All these aspirations are expressed in the programmes of political parties, the lives of governments, the implementation of development projects, management and investment strategies, the preparation of triennal submissions and 5-year plans. The horizons of such people are inevitably narrow, their expertise and spheres of action of limited dimensions.

I suppose I was once a surfer myself; a body surfer; a scientific surfer. I collected vast amounts of data, wrote scholarly articles for academic journals, such as *Human Ecology, Mountain Research and Development* and *Pacific Viewpoint.* Then a violent wave threw me up on the beach at Taharaa (near Mahina), Tahiti, my neck broken, my writing arm largely paralysed. The Pacific Ocean had rudely halted my progress. I was stopped for six months and obliged by circumstances to reflect. It was, ironically, a euphoric period, listening forcibly to the voices of others. I believe the nurses in the Clinique Cardella in Papeete thought I was crazy, glued to the words of Joe Dassin, anthropologist-turned-singer, recounting his tropical sentiments, reading constantly, then slowly negotiating the city's streets in my bodycast – to build up strength for the long voyage home to Canada and the necessary operation to put my body back in working order. I ceased thereafter to surf, but whenever I had the chance I went to gaze at the magnificent boards lined up in the Bishop Museum in Hawaii, and I delved into Ben Finney and James Houston's book on the subject (Finney & Houston, 1966). This fascination later developed into a casual interest in outrigger canoe racing, another Pacific-wide sport whose roots run deep and whose presence is largely invisible to experts and to organizers of the South Pacific and Oceania Games. And my interests shifted progressively to words rather than figures, to listening rather than observing, to emotions rather than to graphical representations of reality.

I never became a diver, of course. I don't have the training, the experience, or the guts perhaps. Rather, I practise snorkelling. Gliding just beneath the surface, appreciating the silence and the magic of a new-found world and peering into the depths into which only the more courageous and perceptive among us may venture.

Jean-Marie Tjibaou was one such person. A politician perhaps, but also, above all, one who ventured deeply into the past and future worlds. He was committed, deeply committed, to the independence of his country, but he was concerned much more with what he called "the after-independence", the country his people would inherit, the kind of future they would build for themselves and for those around them, the way his Melanesian people would insert themselves into, and contribute to, the great family of peoples and nations that have inherited the earth. He sought to transcend the experience of our daily lives, our immediate needs, to find the message which gives a philosophical dimension to that which we experience in life itself, and in life on earth. It was a singular quest which he paid for with his life, on 5 May 1989:

> He is dead. Struck down by one of his own.
> This death, he had seen it coming and he had accepted in advance
> the risk, he who often spoke of the "great black hole".
> Today, let us simply say that it is not in the power of the
> "great black hole" to swallow everything up.
> Jean-Marie Tjibaou, in essence, remains with us.
> He will have invented a new way: the Kanak way of
> decolonisation. (Césaire in Musée, 1990:15)

It was the great poet *martiniquais*, Aimé Césaire, author of *Cahier d'un retour au pays natal* and architect of the concept of "négritude", who penned those words....

The Holes That are Made in our Soul

Hence, my wish to explore the world of Jean-Marie Tjibaou and, through him, to reflect on culture and identity in the contemporary Pacific. It is a vaguely impertinent task for a geographer to set himself. After all, we are supposed to focus our interests on the environment, on ecology and, perhaps, adaptation. That's what I used to do, before that wave left me on the beach at Mahina, my body riddled with pain and my mind in a trance. Since then I've become terribly sceptical about the environment, biodiversity, resource management, beach clean-ups and all the rest. I have a strange feeling, when I listen to such discourses, that I am not at the helm, that there are other interests setting the agenda and, because of them, there is something fundamental missing from the all invasive ecological debate.

It was Norman Mailer, enfant terrible of contemporary American literature, who remarked recently in an interview published in the *Magazine littéraire*:

> Ecology, if you wish, is not my principal preoccupation, but I agree with them. However, if it is true that we destroy nature, what do we do with men's souls? We are victims of plastics, of publicity, of television. No one has considered the horrors of capitalism. For 70 years the Communists did their best to brainwash the Russians, but they were not entirely successful because the Russians were conscious of it. It was too obvious: when you see on the roadside enormous hoardings with quotations from Lenin, you are aware of what is happening; but when you watch a television programme, are enjoying yourself, and the programme is interrupted by a commercial, it is brainwashing which we are oblivious of. Over the past 40 years the average American television viewer, according to one researcher, has been subject to one million publicity flashes. That, that's brainwashing. It is damage which belongs to the realm of spiritual ecology. The ravages are, without a doubt, more serious than the famous holes in the ozone layer: these are holes that are made in our soul (1993: 102).

The holes that are made in our soul: such was the principal preoccupation of Jean-Marie Tjibaou. Untiring worker for the independence of Kanaky, yes. Without a doubt, one of the great political leaders of the Pacific. But also a man imbued with an incredible sense of responsibility, and with a message for us all, wherever we may live, wherever we may dream:

> The great word is let loose.
> Responsible for the future. Responsible for the present and for that

which is to be. Responsible for maintaining, strengthening and transmitting life... (Césaire in Musée, 1990:15).

Such is the reason why I believe it so urgent to reflect on him: to sound his values, identify his conception of an independent Kanaky, explore his vision of the world.

A Man I Never Knew

My tools are limited. I never had the honour of meeting Jean-Marie Tjibaou. My contacts with those who knew and worked with him are minimal to say the least. I have only set foot in New Caledonia three times. Yet, I do have a comprehensive collection of documentary material on and by Jean-Marie, very generously offered to me by Mme Lêdji Bellow of the Agence de Développement de la Culture Kanak. Such, and such alone, are the raw materials on which my reflection is based.[2] However, I do sincerely believe it is sufficient because it filters out the ephemeral, the noise of action and events which are mere passing phenomena.

Consequently, I'm scarcely going to write about politics or explore in detail the recent history of New Caledonia, the suffering and carnage that *Territoire* has experienced. I will simply limit myself to a few dates and events that will allow me to set the scene, provide some essential references which will, in turn, permit me to appreciate the tribulations of a people, then explore the visions, reflections and acts of a singular man who was placed by history on centre stage for little more than a decade in the long trajectory of a civilization; who brought that civilization back from near oblivion, offered it direction, hope and meaning, all with remarkable tact and generosity – and, I repeat, paid for it with his life.

Jean-Marie Tjibaou arrived, for me, on centre stage on 3 September 1975, with Mélanésia 2000, the festival over which he presided and into which he infused a vision, notably through the drama *Kanaké*. He left it, brutally, struck down by one of his own, on 5 May 1989. He is still with us, as he was with us long before 1975, because he is merely the thread in the weave of a civilization, a moment in its history – and a man who was called upon to speak for all, and for all time.

Jean-Marie Tjibaou's Itinerary

I can fix for you a succession of dates in the life of Jean-Marie as any competent journalist or biographer could do. He was born in 1936 at

Tiendanite, tucked away in the hills behind Hienghène on the north-east coast of La Grande Terre. One of nine children.

He left home for school with the Marist Brothers at the age of nine, first in Canala, then on the Ile des Pins. There followed three years as a primary school teacher, at Lifou and at Thio, prior to entering the Seminary at Païta in 1959. Six years later, in 1965, he was ordained at Hienghène. His first year was spent as a parish priest at Bourail and a military chaplain at Nandaï. This was followed by two years as the second vicar at the cathedral in Nouméa. There he decided he wanted to pursue his studies, and he obtained a year's leave to prepare for university entrance in France.

In 1968 Jean-Marie left for France, spending his first year at Lyon, divided between the Institut Politique, the Université d'État, and the Institut Social and the Institut de Sociologie of the Faculté Catholique. Armed with a diploma, he went on to the Sorbonne, to study ethnology at the École des Hautes Études en Sciences Sociales. Two years were spent in research in Paris, broken only by a brief return visit to New Caledonia in 1970, as a result of the death of his father. On this occasion he chose, along with a number of other Kanak priests, to leave the Church and devote his life to the service of his people.

Jean-Marie returned to Paris for the 1970-1971 academic year, coming back to New Caledonia at the end with the intention of conducting research on Kanak culture and identity. Not having a scholarship, he was obliged to work, and he chose the field of popular education and grass-roots action. First he worked on a project to re-establish tribal councils on the East Coast of La Grande Terre, and it was there he met his future wife, Marie-Claude. There followed a crucial period with a women's group dedicated to improving the appearance and the quality of the village environment: Souriant Village Mélanésien. A concern with the physical environment evolved rapidly into an involvement in cultural rejuvenation and, inevitably, political action.

Events and experiences followed in increasingly rapid succession: publications, marriage (in 1973), political action in the context of his tribe at Hienghène, involvement in the Union des Indigènes Calédoniens Amis de la Liberté dans l'Ordre (UICALO), the organization of the Festival Mélanésia 2000 in 1975, mayor of Hienghène in 1977, entry into the Union Calédonienne (UC), the party's initial declaration in favour of the independence of New Caledonia and the election of Jean-Marie as vice-president and as deputy in the Territorial Assembly – all in 1977. Another UC congress in 1978 resulted in a much more vigorous declaration in favour of independence for New Caledonia. This led directly to the creation of a Front Indépendantiste in 1979 and to its obtaining a majority in the Territorial Assembly in 1982. Jean-Marie was appointed vice-president of the Conseil du Gouvernement. He was one of the architects of the creation, in 1984, of the Front de Libération National Kanak Socialiste (FLNKS) and was appointed its first leader, a role he was to maintain until his death.

The Front immediately boycotted the territorial elections, planned for November of the same year. The boycott provoked a succession of bloody confrontations between Melanesians and the Territorial Administration, Kanaks and Caldoches,[3] which brought New Caledonia to the verge of civil war. In one confrontation, the massacre of ten FLNKS militants at Hienghène on 5 December 1984, two of Jean-Marie's brothers died. In an explosive atmosphere, subsequently marked by the killing of Elio Machoro by gendarmes, Jean-Marie pleaded for dialogue and negotiation rather than vengeance.

In the few short years that followed, he sought to calm the tensions and bitterness that characterized the independence movement, give it dignity, hence the power to negotiate from a position of strength, without ever losing sight of its fundamental generosity. In other words, he was concerned to move from discourse to the construction of an independent Kanaky, to evolve from road-blocks to the creation of political, economic and social institutions and to "take root in the land". However, history and a right-wing government in France were against him. A regime concerned to thwart Kanak aspirations banned and violently broke up a series of peaceful demonstrations in 1987 – the 10-day March for Kanaky and the pro-independence gathering on the Place des Cocotiers (Nouméa). Those accused of the 1984 Hienghène massacre were acquitted in the same year. By virtue of these events, the fragile consensus that Tjibaou had constructed within the FLNKS was shattered. Confrontation and insurrection were the rule for 1988, culminating in April and May in the attack on the Gendarmerie of Fayaoué (Ouvéa) and the massacre of Gossanah: 19 deaths by violence on one side and 6 on the other.

Again, Jean-Marie chose dialogue, aided by the return of the Socialists to power in France and the recognition by Jacques Lafleur, leader of the Rassemblement pour la Calédonie dans la République (RPCR) and by extension of the Caldoche and metropolitan French communities, that New Caledonia had returned to the brink of civil war. In June of that year – only two months after the attack on the Gendarmerie in Ouvéa – the Accords de

Matignon were signed. New Caledonia was divided into three provinces, two dominated by the Kanak nationalists. A development strategy directed to the two Kanak provinces was elaborated, and a referendum on the political future of New Caledonia approved, with participation restricted to those identified on the 1988 electoral lists and their descendants.

Another fragile consensus had been achieved. It was, however, a consensus for which Jean-Marie Tjibaou paid the ultimate price. The violence to which the Kanak community had been victim, first in 1984 and again in 1988, had left indelible scars.

Post-war New Caledonia

The itinerary is an extraordinarily long and complex one for so short a life, but it was dictated in no uncertain way by the post-war history of New Caledonia. A settler colony, born of the violent confrontation between 19th century imperial design and a 3,000-year-old Melanesian civilization condemned to systematic marginalization, if not pure annihilation, it had been aroused by the shock of the coming of a million American troops during the Second World War. They brought with them immense material wealth and displayed the evident permeability of racial barriers. Theirs was a dynamic order, seemingly devoid of prejudice and injustice.

In their wake, France accorded citizenship to the Melanesians and, until the early 1960s, set out to democratize the territory's institutions and provide equal opportunities, justice and dignity for all. However the sense of euphoria – that a century of systematic dispossession of property, of racism and of intolerance had come to an end – was short-lived. By 1963, an alignment between the local, Caldoche bourgeoisie and the political right wing in Paris, sought to suppress the integration of the Melanesians into Caledonian society and reinforce the hegemony of metropolitan France. The nickel boom of 1969-1972, with its attendant wealth and labour requirements, served only to strengthen the initiative. A policy of massive immigration from metropolitan France and its Overseas Departments and Territories to New Caledonia, was designed to swamp the Melanesians.

A response was not long in coming: the creation of new political parties and, henceforth, an unequivocal association of justice and independence. Polarization, leading to violent confrontation, was inevitable. The arrival of the Socialists to power in France in 1981 offered an intermission. Nevertheless, when it became evident that Mitterand was incapable of offering independence for New Caledonia and that democratic institutions provided little hope for a Melanesian community that had become a minority in its own land, hostilities recommenced. The Statut Lemoine (1984) made it clear that the Socialists were committed to the rule of the majority, with no consideration to be given to what the Melanesians considered to be overriding ethnic interests. The return of the Right to power in France in 1986 served only to inflame the situation.

In perspective, these events of the post-war years took the form of an ascending curve, that was bringing New Caledonia closer and closer to the brink of civil war. Extended periods of tension and violence were from time to time punctuated by dialogue between Kanaks and Caldoches and glimmers of comprehension by Paris, hence brief hopes of compromise. First the Loi-Cadre (Loi Defferre) in 1956, then the Plan Dijoud in 1978, Pisani's proposal for "independence-association" in 1985 and, finally, the Accords de Matignon in June 1988. As a man of consensus, Tjibaou played a crucial role in the last two initiatives to build a common future for all the peoples of New Caledonia. That he devoted his life to his people and to his country and that he chose to work for consensus rather than confrontation and the creation of a truly multi-ethnic nation, all the while recognizing the primacy of his own people's interests, was the fruit of certain formative experiences in his own life and of his particular cultural consciousness.

The Essential and the Accessory

Strangely, in all the articles I have read, none identify Jean-Marie's date of birth or mention his age. There is uncertainty over whether he died on 4 or 5 May (probably because of the International Date Line which divides New Caledonia from a remote metropolitan France – thereby adding another ironic twist to the drama of his people). He himself hesitated over the exact number of his brothers and sisters, in part because two were torn from him in violence and two others succumbed to premature deaths. It is as if such points of detail were not important. Rather, it was the sentiments, the long silences, the meditation, the progressive unravelling of the world around him, and the momentous decisions which ensued that counted for him.

Jean-Marie was a product of the circumstances that surrounded him – of place, of people and of history. If he had not assumed the role he did in two decades of the life of a country, someone else would have. He was projected on to centre stage, obscuring only marginally the presence of those that stood at his side, slightly behind, before or after him: Yeiwéné Yeiwéné, Eloi Machoro, Pierre Declercq and so many others. Consider that, within a year of Jean-Marie's death, the FLNKS had elected a new president, Paul Néaoutyine who shares exactly the same philosophy and goals as his predecessor: building an independent Kanaky that is generous and viable. Consider also the observation of the journalist Jean-Paul Besset:

> Even before he was born, Jean-Marie Tjibaou had a rendezvous with the destiny of the Kanak people. One day in 1917 a detachment of the French army, in pursuing a Kanak, shot down his grandmother, whose silhouette stood out high on a ridge top. As she slumped to the ground she let fall the child she was carrying. The child rolled down to the bottom of the ravine, unscathed. It was Wencelas Tjibaou, the father of Jean-Marie (1989: 21).

Jean-Marie's formative years were marked by a range of crucial experiences, many of them described in the remarkable interview conducted by Jacques Violette in 1987 (Violette, 1989). Childhood memories of the despising looks of Caldoche settlers when they entered tribal lands in search of stray cattle. Segregation and censorship in the Catholic Church in New Caledonia: the different material comforts accorded to Kanak and Caldoche children at the school in Canala, the European priest eating apart, and differently, from the Melanesian teachers at Lifou, the systematic separation of seminarists at Païta, the frequent interrogations by the European priests as to the content of the sermons given by the two Melanesians at the Cathedral in Nouméa. The underside of spiritual life in Nouméa: gathering up drunken 'weekend warriors' from the streets of the city. The explosion of ideas in the France of 1968. The meeting with students and lecturers from Africa, South America and other Third World regions in the universities of Lyon and Paris: universities where Jean-Marie learned of the profound economic inequities that have persisted beyond political independence and where he acquired the tools of political analysis necessary to escape from underdevelopment. The frequenting of Jean Guiart and Roger Bastide in Paris, and the discovery of ethnology, particularly, the nature and importance of myths for a people condemned to self-hatred, alienation and defeat. The return to New Caledonia in the early 1970s, to witness the invasion of the tribes by alcohol – and the recognition that it was not that, or the new-found wealth that accompanied it, which was the root of his people's problems, but rather their lack of self-respect.

These, and other such events, led Jean-Marie Tjibaou to the conviction in the early 1970s that, if, as a people, the Kanaks were no longer condemned to extinction, as a civilization they were riddled by despair and self-depreciation. They had become paupers in their own land, and they were confronted by a terrible choice: to live and flourish as a civilization or to be subjected to slow, but inevitable, spiritual death. He had no choice but to take up the challenge, to act. That action required that he leave the ministry and place himself at the service of his people. But first, he had to articulate the philosophy that had been slowly taking form in his mind.

The Heart of the Matter

The crucial years in Jean-Marie's life began with his year at the cathedral in "Nouméa-la-Blanche" and terminated with his return from his studies in France and his commitment to work in the Melanesian community. Five short years between 1966 and 1971 which took him from a bourgeois Catholic milieu in town to grass-roots action in the peri-urban area and the bush with, as a crucial intermission, three years in France which brought him into contact with the rest of the world.

On the desperate evening streets of Nouméa, he had been witness to the tears and the anger of the Melanesian community: of broken men who sought solace in drink, who momentarily rediscovered their manhood and their pride in themselves, and who tearfully shared their profound distress: "... references to the ancestors, to deaths of kin, the allusions to abandoned cemeteries, the suicidal instincts created by the rupture with their place of birth" (Rollat, 1989: 107-108). Here he became fully conscious of the resignation of the Kanak people, the sense of alienation and submission that was a direct result of their colonial experience.

Here, too, the thesis of the recently deceased Father Apollinaire Ataba was brought to his attention, *Histoire et psychologie des Mélanésiens,* presented for the Bachelor's degree in Theology at the Institut catholique in Paris in 1965 and thereafter carefully dissimulated by the Catholic hierarchy, its publication forbidden. He was dumbfounded by the first Kanak analysis of the history of his country to come to his attention, by its overt criticism of the struggles between the Catholic and Protestant churches to which his people were victim, by his reflections on the implications of a Christian culture which gives excessive attention to the individual compared with a Melanesian one which gives primacy to the group, and by its recognition of the inevitability of political independence for his people.

As a result of his being, on one hand, witness to the terrible cul-de-sac in which his people had found themselves and, on the other, seized by the enormity of the intellectual and moral challenge confronting him, Jean-Marie decided to leave for France: "I didn't leave in order to study, I left above all in order to acquire the analytical tools which would allow me to understand more clearly the reality right here" (Violette, 1989: 17).

This concern found tangible expression in a research paper he wrote while at Lyon and in a proposal he subsequently developed in Paris. Here he outlined the desperate resignation of the Kanaks as a people. He saw this as a permanent state of powerlessness, intimately bound with the colonial experience. He concluded that the only possible solution to this tragedy lay in actions which would allow both the individual and the people as a whole to recreate a positive image of themselves: to recognize their right to exist as Kanaks.

It had by now become inevitable that he abandon the priesthood and, by virtue of it, the Catholic Church, a church dominated by European clergy and metropolitan values which had progressively reneged on its social responsibilities with respect to the Kanak people. He had no wish to remain trapped "...in a mystical-religious ghetto without any commitment to society" (Rollat, 1989: 175). In its place he chose solidarity and action, committing himself to the Souriant Village Mélanésien programme in the suburbs of Nouméa.

The issue was again alcoholism among the men, but the solution this time focused not on the symptom but on the root of the problem. Energy was invested in improving the quality of the habitat: houses, their surroundings, the neighbourhoods. The objective? To allow wives to "reconquer" their husbands, to develop a sentiment of self-respect and the consciousness of belonging to a group. Culture, and specifically identity, had by now emerged as the linchpin of Jean-Marie Tjibaou's preoccupations. It was to dominate his thoughts and actions in the years to follow, as it was to dominate those of the FLNKS that he was instrumental in creating.

It had become transparent in his eyes that the colonial experience and European domination had "prevented the Kanaks from being". Emptiness, despair and self-destruction prevailed. In order to achieve the political and economic goals set by their leaders, the Kanaks first would have to liberate themselves intellectually, sociologically and psychologically. That would have to be achieved while all the time remaining faithful to their past. Hence, the question which came to be at the centre of all of Jean-Marie's concerns: "How can one be Kanak in the modern world?" It was a preoccupation which figured constantly in his speeches and in his long silences, in his travels through the world and in his 'rootedness' in his tribal home. The nature of culture. The weight and importance of tradition. The place of the past in the modern world. The need to construct a bridge between the past and the present. The conviction that the Kanak people must be able to take possession of the modern world without losing their soul. Hence, the realization, on one hand, that it was necessary to mobilize the traditional resources of his people, transforming them into a source of strength rather than weakness and, on the other, that "the return to the traditional world is a myth". The challenge was to create a people "profoundly impregnated by a past that was rich in traditions and values but who were resolutely oriented to the future". As he would repeatedly insist: "Notre identité est devant nous" – "Our identity is before us."

The quest was long and arduous. The Kanaks were not simply a colonized people. They had been marginalized territorially and demographically and systematically excluded from the destiny of their land. They had no choice but to construct a future which would be based on mutual respect and dialogue with those whom history had placed at their sides, notably the Caldoches. Their culture dictated that they be generous and welcoming.

Jean-Marie's philosophy and strategy was elaborated piecemeal through experiences and actions. It found its first significant expression in an unprecedented cultural event: Mélanésia 2000.

Mélanésia 2000

The event was a festival of Melanesian arts which was held in Nouméa in September 1975. Jean-Marie was the driving force behind this great public manifestation in which 2,000 Melanesians 'invaded' Nouméa and revealed to the assembled 50,000 spectators their rich cultural heritage, voiced their refusal of subordination and the white man's 'mask', and openly demanded the recognition of their distinctive identity.

For Jean-Marie, the Souriant Village Mélanésien project had addressed the material conditions of people's existence. This time he was concerned to go much further, to what he believed to be the essence of the drama of his people, their identity crisis. He was concerned to give his people the moral and cultural dignity they desperately lacked. He was intent on tackling their minds, by projecting an image of Melanesian society in which they would recognize themselves and which would also be recognized by others. In achieving it, they would acquire pride in themselves, which would in turn strengthen and legitimize Melanesian society as a whole.

Mélanésia 2000 was at once an extremely ambitious, courageous and generous project. Ambitious because it was concerned to give hope and direction to Melanesian society in a context where all hope had been lost and an entire people was succumbing to self-hatred and drowning its tragedy in alcohol. Courageous because, for it to happen, it required convincing a local administration and petty bourgeoisie which were at best ambivalent and at worst openly opposed to the initiative. Generous because it was articulated around the notion of dialogue between Kanak and European cultures, of each recognizing the other as distinct, free and equal such that they might both be reborn together and a new country constructed.

Essentially a 'cultural inventory', the festival was designed to confront the Kanaks with their world, inviting them thereby to rediscover and redefine their contemporary identity, making them appreciate that they too constituted a 'civilization' which, like all others, was invited freely to participate in the family of civilizations. To be recognized, one must first recognize oneself, and to recognize oneself one must know oneself. Without culture, there can be no political project. Without the mutual recognition of European and Melanesian cultures and co-operation between them, there could be no political project for New Caledonia.

Perhaps the most important element of the festival was the stage play *Kanaké,* written by Georges Dobbelaere and Jean-Marie Tjibaou. Presented in three acts, the play summarizes the history of Melanesian civilization: a ceremonial yam exchange, which is interrupted by the coming of Europeans, leading to the systematic destruction of traditional Kanak spirituality, and terminating with a long march in the night, over the ruins of their past, in which the Kanaks confront European civilization and their necessary relation to it. For the first time

> ...Melanesians had the opportunity to say – and they said it magnificently – what they thought of the colonial experience and what it had been intended to do to them: economic slavery, land alienation, conscious utilisation of alcohol to destroy them, an attempt at cultural alienation that was developed to the highest degree (Rollat, 1989: 143).

For the first time the other citizens of New Caledonia were confronted by the strength and orginality of Kanak culture, of the Kanaks' refusal to be dominated and of their quest for self-determination. Significantly, the play ends with, once again, the sharing of yams, where Europeans and Melanesians offer gifts in friendship and as a manifestation of their desire to construct a common future.

The two key figures in the play are Kanaké and l'Homme blanc (the White Man). In his Introduction to the book produced for the festival, Jean-Marie states:

> Kanaké is one of the most powerful archetypes of the Melanesian World. He is the ancestor, the first-born. He is the arrow that marks the roof tip, the central mast, the sanctuary of the great house. He is the word which makes men exist. This same word establishes the system of organization which governs relations between men and between them and the geographical and mythical environment. (Tjibaou & Missote, 1975: 5).

That Kanaké, the ancestor, the cultural symbol and metaphor be transformed into Kanaky, the political project and country to be, was inevitable. Jean-Marie envisaged it. It was simply that cultural goals were necessary preconditions to political goals. At the same time, the instruments for achieving political goals – political parties – were "...never more than crutches which allow the guts of the Earth to express themselves" (Tjibaou *in* Rollat, 1989: 158).

The framework of Jean-Marie's philosophy was set out clearly in this play. It was inspired by the dramatic confrontation of two civilizations. It acquired substance in the many speeches, writings and interviews that followed. It can be articulated around four themes: *l'être, la parole, le temps* and *la terre* – the being, the word, the time and the land.

L'être

"I am never me. Me, that is related to the individual. I am always someone *in relation to*" (Tjibaou, 1981: 86). This affirmation permeates, explicitly or implicitly, everything that Jean-Marie said and did. It was no doubt accentuated by his chiefly origins, hence the awareness that the chief is the symbol of the community, that his authority is derived from the ancestors and that one of his roles is to intercede between the living and the dead. Yet this affirmation was further reinforced by Jean-Marie's deep understanding of Melanesian society, his capacity to analyse it in anthropological terms and his awareness of the profound cleavage between Melanesian and European societies with respect to the status and role of the person. His thoughts on the subject are best developed in a lecture he gave at the University of Geneva in 1981, "*Etre Mélanésien aujourd'hui*" (Tjibaou and Missotte, 1981).

It is inconceivable to think of the person as an individual for both biological and cultural reasons. Biologically, the person is a body, and the body cannot be isolated. The body is blood, and the blood is that of the mother. Hence, that aspect of the person belongs to the maternal uncles and due respect must be given to this dimension. The person is also a part of a society and must develop ties with both maternal and paternal kin and with the ancestors. In consequence, to succeed in life is to give, to give generously and everywhere, in order to strengthen one's insertion in the community and, by extension, to strengthen the community itself.

Hence, the features of Melanesian society which set it apart from European, or capitalist, society: of consulting, proceeding by consensus and talking things out. Of sharing rather than accumulating wealth, of placing the interests of the community before those of the individual. To be successful, to acquire prestige, it is not sufficient just to accumulate wealth:

> In our system, if you do that...you become small, because you do not have any relationships. You are obliged to cut yourself off from the community.
>
> Prestige is to give, to give in abundance and to give everywhere. (Tjibaou, 1981: 87-88).

La parole

"Je parle comme les idées me viennent..."; "I speak as the ideas come to me...." Many of those who knew Jean-Marie refer in their testimonies, written after his death, not only to his charismatic personality, but to the sound of his voice: "...the sound which rises or falls, the elocution, the articulation, the hesitations...the silences" (Violette, 1989: 6).

Hesitations and silence were a fundamental part of his discourse, as they are of any Melanesian discourse, because the words are measured, pregnant and come from afar. A French journalist and friend observed: "...the word sounded always exactly right because it was the expression of a long internal maturation" (Besset, 1989: 21). He continues, by citing Jean-Marie: "The Kanak discourse is not a thesis, antithesis, synthesis. It consists of repeating to convince, to impregnate the entrails of the word, to make the word penetrate the whole body." In this profoundly Melanesian sense, Jean-Marie Tjibaou was an *homme de parole,* a man of honour, who did not speak lightly or in vain, who used images rather than concepts, and for whom the mixing of silences and of speech allowed feelings and concerns to go beyond the confines of mere language.

He was also a customary chief. As a chief he was the word, the venerated son of the ancestors, the central pole of the *grande case,* he who speaks in the name of all the members of his tribe, who expresses their consensus, their unity of thought and action, passes on the answers that the ancestors had found to those fundamental questions about life on earth: who are we? where are we going? what will become of us? where do we come from?

Le temps

In French it is possible to distinguish between *le temps* and *l'heure*. Both are translated as 'time' in English; yet, the distinction was a fundamental one for Jean-Marie and he exploited it constantly:

> ...the manner in which time is perceived and experienced. That, I would say for Melanesians, in the tribes, is not a matter of concern. One doesn't speak of time. Yes, one speaks of seasons. But not of chronological time (*l'heure*)....Chronological time is a modern phenomenon....Time is the rhythm of nature....It is the plants which assume the role of the hands of the clock.
>
> For the people, in traditional Melanesian society, yams determine the overall calendar, running through the entire year (Tjibaou, 1981: 90-91).

If nature determines the rhythm of people's lives in traditional society, so industrial society establishes a fundamentally different rhythm, based on a concern with profitability:

> It is a new phenomenon in the rhythm of work, but also in the rhythm of life, in the rhythm of thought. It obliges us to rethink the world. One plans, and one has the impression that one will impose its rhythm on the world....It is like day and night, when compared with traditional society (Tjibaou, 1981: 91).

It is not simply that the rhythm changes, but the system of values as well. As time is progressively sliced into smaller and smaller parts and goals change, so the Melanesian and the European worlds are further distanced from each other, and the difficulties of insertion of Melanesians in the work world are accentuated. For the Melanesian, time is experienced, for the European, it is objectified, intellectualized, measured and given an economic value: "...Kanak time is above all experienced, according to the rhythm of nature, of warmth and of cold, of yams, of old age and youth, and the event which renews alliances warms up the community and allows it to develop" (Tjibaou, 1976: 285).

So, Jean-Marie distinguished between "short" and "long" time. There is the short, ephemeral, urgent time of Europeans, of Western civilization, the hands of their clocks hastening forward under the pressure of considerations of profit and of political and economic mastery of the environment and its resources. In contrast, there is the long time of the Melanesians, which is marked by continuity, which finds its roots in the "time beyond time" of the great myths, which is inscribed in the histories of the clans through the genealogical record, which is "inhabited" rather than "imposed", and which is focused on the great social events which give life and meaning to the cycle of birth, marriage and death:

> Without a doubt, the three events...constitute the warm periods of socialised time. At the beginning and at the end, they are inscribed in time, but within they are the warmth, the fervour, the solace and the experience of fraternity tested. In experiencing these temporal events, the Kanak gains access to the total universe which makes him exist and exist fully (Tjibaou, 1976: 292).

It is such a configuration of time which gives roots, permanence and the sense of belonging to a "thousand year civilization".

La terre

After the pain of a weekend mourning in Nouméa, the bodies of Jean-Marie Tjibaou and Yewéiné Yewéiné were taken to the airport of Magenta for their last voyage to their tribal home. As the planes left and the two companions were separated, Franck Wahuzue, friend and adviser of Yéyé ventured: "Jean-Marie returns to the earth. Yéweiné to the earth." (Couhe, 1989:17).

The earth, land, the native soil, heritage. Again the English language accommodates with difficulty a term which finds its roots in peasant France and which became an integral part of Jean-Marie's vocabulary: *terroir* – the specific corner of the earth to which one belongs, the place of the ancestors, the place of one's people. There is, of course, a word for it in Bislama – *manples* – as there is in any Pacific language.

For Jean-Marie, the individual, the group can exist only in reference to a specific place. Genealogy and history are rooted there. That place is the repository of the archives of the group. It explains, justifies and gives meaning to the existence of the cycle of birth and death and of each individual who is born to it. Without it "...one has no history. One is a citizen of the world and of nowhere":

> Land alienation and transfers of ownership have not only displaced tribes, but have fundamentally shattered them. A clan which loses its territory is a clan which loses its personality. It loses its burial ground, its sacred places, its geographical and sociological reference points. Its entire universe is disturbed, its network of relations with its allies, together with the related protocol which is thrown into a state of confusion (Tjibaou, 1976: 285).

If the land anchors the group, so it determines the group's relationship to the cosmos. Here again, Jean-Marie is clear, the Judaeo-Christian vision of domination of the Earth makes no sense to Melanesian society:

> In our system, man is not the master. He is an element of the world. He is among the plants. There is a plant which is his totem. Among the animals, there is an animal which is his totem, which is the totem of another clan. And it is a completely different philosophy which is connected to this. We belong to the world, to the world of the living, to the world of nature, to the world of the trees, the plants, the stones, and we must respect it (Tjibaou, 1981: 89).

Jean-Marie's ideas may be perceived as ranging from landscape to ecology, terms which are an integral part of the professional baggage of the geographer but which are in no way mere objects of interest here. Rather, they highlight the fundamental indivisibility of the Melanesian universe. Space, or place, was of no concern to Jean-Marie as an objective reality. His was an indivisible world of sensations expressed in a dense network of relations among man, land, myths and gods. It is a world steeped in experiences binding earthly man to the spiritual realm. "The tribal territory thus presents itself as an enormous stage in a never ending theatre, with each actor being attributed a specific role and place" (Tjibaou, 1986: 285).

The Nature and Importance of Tradition

All spheres of human experience are interwoven into something which Jean-Marie describes as tradition or custom. Yet, if he devoted a large part of his adult life to this journey into his own and his people's past, it was not to deify tradition or to withdraw into some mythical Eden, but to identify clearly those cultural references which make the Kanak what they are today: their conception of mankind, their relationship to the environment, to the cosmos and to the rest of the world. It was:

> Not to return to the past to stay there, but in order to acquire the strength and the landmarks capable of supporting our discourse in the present and for the future. Our ancestors are not the Gaels or the direct descendants of Mozart, and in order to participate in history, we must first become people rooted in our fundamental specificity. And for us to open up to the modern world, we must invent new forms (Tjibaou, 1981: 2).

For Jean-Marie, yesterday was a part of today, and today is a part of tomorrow. It is necessary for collective experience to be perennially renewed. It is society, culture, that provide the human being with needs and aspirations; society is at once created by man and creates man in its turn. If the purpose of culture is to prepare the individual and the community to confront the future, so the particular challenge of Kanak society is to accommodate to modernity without losing its soul: "To inscribe the tribe in the city, the traditional in the modern world" (Tjibaou *in* Togna, 1993:4).

The challenge is an enormous one: to create a cultural environment which "integrates modernity into the inspiration that comes from the ancestors". In that way, and in that way alone, it is possible to exercise control over one's destiny. It is all the more challenging because, in drawing on the accumulated wisdom of his ancestors, Jean-Marie was also concerned to criticize the West and propose an alternate vision of the future, inspired by his people's experience:

> We are well-placed in Melanesia to appreciate that one is advancing towards a global death-trap. The West is like a crazy machine, they've got to the point where they are trying to brake it with their feet....We don't want to return to the past, we want to find a new direction. Our first objective is to find and express at the institutional level the Kanak art of living. People have been to school. When they return to the tribe, they don't know how to do anything, they are lazy, handicapped. The school manufactures workers for the Common Market, it standardizes people, it teaches that they must go to Nouméa where people become savages, where nature is dirty and dead. We need to re-evaluate the very organisation of life in a context in which the only option offered by the West is industrialization (Tjibaou *in* Chesneaux, 1989: 25).

Here Jean-Marie's thoughts plunge deeply into the experience of the world's newly independent nations and broach the universal question, thereby reaching out to the future world of us all: *"We need to re-evaluate the very organisation of life in a context in which the only option offered by the West is industrialization."* He was fully conscious that it was vital for the Kanaks to appropriate the economy as a nation (or institutionalised body), in order to benefit fully from its wealth and achieve material independence, but it was even more important for them to appropriate it as a people (or culture), to achieve spiritual independence. "But if we take over the economy we must be very careful not to become ourselves a people colonised by the economy: that is to say one must not consider paid work as a unique source of pride for mankind" (Tjibaou *in* Rollat, 1989: 204). Surely, in this sense, the Kanak way of life and Melanesian civilization as a whole have a crucial message to offer to Western civilization in its race to self-destruction?

Generosity and Dialogue

This, then, brings me back to that necessary question as to whether Jean-Marie Tjibaou spoke only for his own people, his own 'parish'; whether he was a partisan, a sectarian person concerned only with the promotion of the interests of the Kanaks at the expense of all others they would meet in their quest for self-determination.

It is a fundamental question, in part for political reasons. What kind of future might other Pacific Islanders – Wallisians, Tahitians, Ni-Vanuatu – and other peoples – Indonesians, Caldoches, Arabs, Antillais, Pieds-Noirs or Metropolitan French – expect in an independent Kanaky? What is the relevance of his message for Fiji and for other Pacific Island countries? It is also a fundamental question for philosophical, for moral reasons.

In a sense, the answer pervades the portrait I have drawn thus far of Jean-Marie. It found constant expression in his choices and his acts. It marked in an unequivocal manner the beginning and end of that brief period during which he occupied the centre stage: 1975 to 1989.

Let me return to his play *Kanaké* which was divided into three acts. The first, 'Boenando', revolves around a traditional yam festival. It evokes the spirit and values of Melanesian society. In the second act, 'Conquest', the ceremony is brutally disturbed by the coming of soldiers, missionaries and traders. Forced labour, alcohol, confrontation, the loss of tribal land and, more important, the systematic destruction of the Kanak spiritual order are the direct consequence of their presence. In the third act, 'Sharing of the

Yams', the Melanesians and the Europeans turn to each other anew. They tear off their masks, ceasing thereby to be puppets and becoming authentic human beings. They make offerings to each other in the customary manner, thereby confirming the desire to share the wealth of their respective nations and, gathered in a large circle, the master of ceremonies announces:

> Let the sacred conch shells resound in order that the spirits of our ancestors be appeased!
>
> I now tear from the ground the KAROTI [tree of mourning] in order that no hatred, no bitterness bar the pathway to our future!
>
> Let each one of us tear from his heart the tree of his discord!
>
> Our ancestors threw into the water the tree of mourning, we throw it into the fire, because the fire purifies, it brings light and warmth. And we want the hatred to be burnt, the way of our future to be clear and the circle which we open to all other peoples to be fraternal.
>
> Such is the call I make" (Tjibaou & Missotte, 1984: 32).

This spirit of sharing found repeated expression in the gestures Jean-Marie Tjibaou made throughout his life: the desire that Mélanésia 2000 be followed by another festival, Calédonie 2000, where Kanak and Caldoche cultures would share the same stage; the 1983 proposal for electoral reform leading to independence, which would grant the right to vote to Kanaks and to all the 'victims of history' (descendants of common law prisoners, deportees and the first settlers); the draft Constitution for an Independent, Secular and Socialist Kanaky, based on the principle of a national and multiracial society, respect of individual and collective liberties and recognition of the Universal Declaration of Human Rights, to mention only these few examples.

Jean-Marie had incredible faith in, and respect for, his fellow man, this in spite of the fact of his people having been deceived time and again for more than 140 years.

On 26 June 1988 Jean-Marie Tjibaou, president of the FLNKS, shook the hand of Jacques Lafleur, his counterpart for the RPCR, and Michel Rocard, prime minister of France, thereby marking the signing of the Accords de Matignon. It was, in Jean-Marie's own words:

> ...a handshake tough to manage for Monsieur Lafleur as well as for me. At the end of the painful events which our country experienced,

> it was difficult to imagine that one could, one day, envisage doing something together, envisage a common future. The gesture has been criticised, rejected in both places, but for many it represents a wish. I think it is important for the future....
>
> Irrespective of the colour of our skin, we must all be treated quite simply as members of humanity.
>
> Monsieur Lafleur said "One must be able to share and, perhaps, pardon...."
>
> "Share the present", but the present is the expression, the accepting of each other, to accept that we are of different cultures and to promote these cultures (Tjibaou *in* Bensa, 1990: 176).

It was, of course, a gesture too painful for some to bear. Jean-Marie had thereby relegated all possibility of achieving independence for his people to 1998. Nevertheless, he had brought his people, his island, back from the brink of civil war:

> Insist on the "long" time (patience), save lives and indelible wounds, prepare the future without being intoxicated by militaristic passions, guarantee the pluri-ethnicity of the archipelago, consolidate the economy in order to avoid falling into a new dependency (Besset, 1989: 14).

Jean-Marie had opted once again for the Melanesian values of peaceful negotiation, for faith and respect of his adversaries of the moment, for patience and for a strategy of constructing a post-independent Kanaky ten years before there was any possibility of it being declared. It was all the more necessary to construct the post-independent Kanaky because of Jean-Marie's careful reading of the fate of much of the Third World, notably of Africa, condemned by a new economic imperialism to an even more tragic form of dependency and marginality than during the colonial era. That battle-cry of the 1950s of a distant continent, "First give ye the political kingdom and all else will follow", rang hollow in his ears. The counsel of his lifelong Ni-Vanuatu friend Father Gérard Leymang, whom he had first met in the Seminary at Païta and who despaired at the bankruptcy of his own country, was not on any account to be ignored: "We screwed up our independence because we hadn't prepared it. Don't do like us" (Leymang *in* Rollat, 1989: 267). The yet-to-be independent Kanaky must serve as a model to the rest of the Pacific with all its peoples working together: "...to make this country the one which one dreams of inhabiting because it is the most beautiful, the most developed, the most attractive of all the Pacific" (Tjibaou *in* Bensa, 1990: 179).

For Djubelly Wea, the pain of the Ouvéa massacre was too great to bear. No compromise, no further sacrifice was possible and he had no choice but to assassinate Jean-Marie Tjibaou. "Vive l'indépendance" were his last, desperate words.

By Way of Conclusion

Jean-Marie's analysis of his own civilization, of its drama and of its needs resembles that of many other indigenous peoples across the world. Nevertheless, it rises above the clamour to redress past wrongs on one fundamental ground. It does not demand retribution.

Jean-Marie proposed a fundamentally generous and welcoming discourse that was born, no doubt, of his personality and his experience. He had a Christian faith which transcended the institution that is the Church, and he possessed the ancestral secrets and wisdom of his people. In his daily life and in his career, he navigated constantly and confidently between Melanesian and Western civilizations, striving to blend one into the other. A humanist with a profound faith in the intelligence of mankind, he benefited immensely from a university education and five years spent as an ordained priest. At the same time, Jean-Marie never lost sight of his peasant roots or of the fact that he belonged to the family of people rooted in an infinity of cultural experiences spanning the earth. Jean-Marie Tjibaou was a Kanak. Kanaks are Melanesians, kindred spirits of those who inhabit a vast arc of islands stretching from New Guinea to Fiji. Melanesians are Oceanians, a broad alliance of ancient civilizations which span the Pacific Ocean. Oceanians are brothers to all mankind. History had destined the Kanaks to share their land with strangers. Jean-Marie wanted these strangers to share his country with his people.

He fully recognized that in each people there is a mix of the particular and the universal, of the momentary and the eternal. Each dimension gives strength and meaning to our existence. One cannot exist without the other. Cultures and civilizations cannot exist without dialogue. Without self-respect, there is no dialogue. Without dialogue, there can be no rebirth.

Jean-Marie grasped and respected the full sense of the Melanesian values of exchange and interaction. He invited other peoples to understand and respect them and, hopefully, appreciate their merits in a harsh, industrialized world. He was committed to the independence of his country and, above all, of his people. He was, at the same time, concerned to help construct the future world, his world and our world: "People must be well-educated for them to be intelligent and creative. So that they can say they are missionaries and that they must be messengers for the generations to come, the standard-bearers for the safeguard of the planet" (Tjibaou *in* Bellow, 1989b: 29).

He knew the spiritual void of the West and its distant peasant roots. He also knew that:

> It is possible to create the most profitable economic systems in the world, but we are not robots designed to live at ease in these systems. There is a human dimension to our existence which means that, even with the most modern, the most protective, the most satisfying of comforts, we are always a mass of transcending needs and desires...striving to be better, if not indeed to become something more, something else: and that is inscribed in what we call our culture" (Tjibaou *in* Bensa, 1990: 179).

Perhaps it was his condition of being a colonized man which made Jean-Marie so acutely aware of this essential dimension of the human condition. Whatever, he has gone, a victim of having extended his hand in friendship and solidarity. But his words, his people, his civilization remain. Should we not listen to them and reflect?

Notes

1 "Les mots, en effet, ne seraient-ils pas les données premières de la rêverie géographique?" (Meunier, 1993: 11). This and all other quotations in the text have been translated from the French by Eric Waddell.

2. Alain Rollat's book, *Tjibaou le Kanak*, was brought to my attention after I had completed the first draft of this paper. A number of minor modifications and additions have been made to the text as a result of it.

3. A term widely used to describe the European settlers of New Caledonia, thereby distinguishing them from both the Melanesian population and the metropolitan French who are only temporary residents.

Chapter 6
Reflections on Socio-Economic Change in Rural Fiji

John Overton

A Personal Introduction to Rural Fiji

The study of geography brings together a local context, local research and the experience of the researcher. As a new arrival to Fiji in 1985 I brought only the latter, and that was rather limited. My previous work in Kenya had focused on the early colonial period and the ways in which the colonial state had reshaped the spatial economy of the country, separating and regulating the interactions between European settlers and Africans. Land use and land tenure was a central concern. One interesting aspect of that context, though one which my work did not cover directly, was the emergence of an African entrepreneurial group, the basis of today's élite. Within the interstices of the colonial economy, they had sought and often found opportunities in land and livestock accumulation, cash cropping and business activity.

Studies of these changes seemed to provide a link between the past and the present and insight into the processes of socio-economic differentiation. Although influenced by the neo-Marxist concern for class formation, the work was firmly rooted in the peculiar political and cultural contexts of colonial Kenya. There was opportunity for geographers to begin to appreciate how the dynamics of social change had impact upon spatial organization and interaction (and vice-versa).

There was potential for similar studies in Fiji. Ward (1986, 1987) and Brookfield (1988) had suggested evidence of emerging inequality in rural Fiji, and much more research could be done to see what were the long-term processes of change in the village. Influential for me also was the environment of the University of the South Pacific (USP). The busy teaching schedules, the discussions with diverse and highly stimulating groups of students, and the ability to get into the field meant that my education in the local context was rapid. Being at USP was instrumental in my involvement in a major rural survey of rice farmers in the Central Division conducted for the Ministry of Primary Industries. It also allowed me to visit villages that would eventually become study sites.

My first real introduction to village Fiji was at Draubuta in the Rewa delta of Viti Levu. My guide was Josefa Raibosa, a student who became my field assistant in Draubuta and Lomaivuna. In 1985 there was no road to Draubuta and the village was reached by punt across the Wainibokasi River. Jo and his wife Komera lived in the village behind which was the grave of Jo's uncle, Rusiate Nayacakalou. Nayacakalou had included Draubuta, his home village, in his studies in the 1950s.

Draubuta is steeped in history. An old village site, surrounded by a ring ditch, lay some distance from the present village; here an attack by Ratu Seru Cakobau was repulsed during the course of his long running battle with the people of Rewa. The bush seemed alive with small garden plots, wild yam groves, sacred *yavu* (old house foundations) and a host of trees and plants with historical, medicinal or nutritional value. On the cleared land, there were large areas of *dalo* (taro) and cassava and fields of rice planted both by villagers and the Indian tenants who leased some village land. In the village there were many who commuted daily to work in Suva or Nausori; others had large gardens of cash crops; and others seemed to have a largely semi-subsistence existence. Although there was no electricity reticulation to the village, one household had a portable generator, video set and stereo and this equipment seemed to circulate through neighbours and kin.

The village was a vibrant place, its economy was diverse and its society seemingly mobile. Custom, language and traditional status remained the cornerstones of village society but much else seemed modified and dynamic. My first visit to Draubuta spurred me to reorient my research interests towards Fiji and more contemporary aspects of change.

The Draubuta introduction started my Fijian research in earnest. Thereafter, and following a move to the Australian National University in 1986, I was able to develop work in a number of village and settlement scheme sites that formed the basis of a study of land tenure and differentiation in rural Fiji (Overton, 1987, 1988a, 1989, 1992a, 1992c, 1993). Yet, despite this continuing involvement, I am still very much of an outsider in rural Fiji: still vastly ignorant of so much of the culture, history, language and daily practices within villages but hoping to bring some wider perspectives to the interpretation of change. In trying to rectify this position, it was crucial to know what had been written before.

Modernizing Societies: The 'Colonial' Period

Any research on rural Fiji has the advantage of a near 40-year span of activity. Before 1970, much of this work was carried out by academics from overseas. It was 'colonial', not in any pejorative sense of the word, but because it was conducted when Fiji was still a colony. That meant that researchers worked through a mostly expatriate bureaucracy, with whom they had close ties and from whom they received assistance and guidance. Some of the work, such as the Spate Report (Spate, 1959), was also a response to the needs of an administration facing impending decolonization and working to accelerate the development of the local economy and society. It was sound research built upon solid empirical work but informed by theory.

One of the earliest, most influential and still most valuable work was conducted by a Fijian anthropologist, Rusiate Nayacakalou. Although his major work on village Fiji was not published until after his death (Nayacakalou, 1975, 1978), his surveys in a number of villages in the mid-1950s were well known. Nayacakalou accompanied and assisted Spate during his tour of Fijian villages in 1958. His work was notable for his intimate knowledge of village life, his meticulous surveys and his ability to address the broader question of tradition versus modernity. It was contemporaneous with the research of the renowned anthropologist Sahlins, whose 1962 study of the island of Moala not only provided another fascinating detailed examination of village Fiji but also pointed to ways in which village and island life was being slowly but fundamentally transformed.

The Spate Report proved a catalyst for much of the work done by expatriate geographers and others. Spate was called on to investigate the problems and prospects of the Fijian people and he identified some of the key elements of change in villages: the development of co-operatives, signs of entrepreneurial activity and, critically, the growing number of *galala* (independent Fijian farmers living separate from villages and pursuing commercial agriculture). In this group and others Spate saw the elements of a new Fijian society, one conscious of *vaka Viti*, its cultural and communal heritage, but less bound by what Spate saw as the burden of its obligations. The answer, he recommended, lay in a change from communalism to individualism.

Though eschewing an explicitly theoretical framework, Spate's work was not out of step with much development theory, especially the emerging interest in modernization theory then current in the social sciences. Yet it was left to others in the 1960s to make the open move to theoretical interpretations of rural Fiji. Belshaw (1964) picked up on many of the features Spate had noted. Watters (1969) attempted to show how such evidence could be interpreted as a process of modernization: the gradual weakening of the bonds of communalism and tradition in favour of new values, institutions and goals that reflected a more materialist and individualist way of life. Though aware of the costs of such changes, Belshaw and Watters (and Spate before them) saw them as beneficial: changes which would improve the material standards of living of Fijians and make it possible for them to achieve further improvements on their own. Socio-economic change was desirable; differentiation (in the sense that new classes would emerge in rural areas) was essential. These Fiji studies were not unique. Elsewhere in the Pacific, and often with a strong link to the Australian National University where Spate worked, there were similar studies by Brookfield, Howlett, Lea, Finney and others which analysed the nature of transition.

Spate's influence went further. Instead of merely talking to 'important people', Spate toured numerous villages. Although, because of his status, he was guided toward the village leaders and elders (and rarely the women), he set a precedent of field-work, of seeking an understanding of processes of change in the villages and of appreciating the variety of responses throughout the Fijian countryside. His research assistant and doctoral student, Roger Frazer, applied these lessons when he went on to produce a very detailed study of Ra Province (Frazer, 1961, 1973). Ward (1965), Watters (1969) and Anderson (1974) also based their work on a number of rural case studies, allowing them not only to understand the common features and processes at work but also to develop a notion of transition across time and space.

Although this work before 1970 was carried out largely by non-Fijians and although the theoretical foundations and some of the conclusions reached were the subject of later criticism (for example Crocombe, 1971), they remain extremely valuable pieces of work and, for one new to Fiji in 1985, they provided essential reading.

Class and Economic Change: The 'Neo-Colonial' Period

The burst of activity by expatriate geographers on Fiji in the early to mid-1960s was followed by a relative hiatus. When the return came, it was with quite different theoretical perspectives. This group of studies might be termed 'neo-colonial'. The researchers were again expatriate, but they were working now within independent Fiji, sometimes as consultants on major projects. They overlapped with the 'post-colonial' work from local institutions but continued to bring wider perspectives to the study of Fiji, linking Fiji studies to broad theoretical debates and current issues. They were not 'neo-colonial' in the sense that they attempted to control local research from outside, though sometimes they explored what might be termed 'neo-colonial' economic activities, such as foreign-owned tourism enterprises (Britton, 1983) or, less specifically, the plantation sector (Brookfield, 1985).

A major research effort was the eastern islands project. Harold Brookfield headed a large team which included a number of geographers prominent in the region, such as Bedford, Bayliss-Smith, McLean, Latham, Haynes, Hardaker, Campbell and Muriel Brookfield. Their project was funded by the United Nations Educational, Scientific and Cultural Organization (UNESCO) and the United Nations Fund for Population Activities (UNFPA) under the international 'Man and the Biosphere' programme and focused on island ecosystems in the eastern regions of Fiji (Taveuni, Lomaiviti and Lau). It was an impressive study, involving a large interdisciplinary team and much primary field-work in areas not often studied by the previous generation of researchers. Although socio-economic change was not an explicit focus of the work, much that was eventually written dwelt on this issue. A number of working papers and minor reports presented the results of important local case studies on the islands (Bayliss-Smith, 1976, 1978; Bedford et al., 1978; Brookfield, 1979). The main report (UNESCO/UNFPA, 1977) covered a range of matters concerned with the ecological and economic bases of the region and identified its position on the periphery as an important planning issue.

Perhaps the most important academic product of the project did not appear until 11 years after the main report (Bayliss-Smith et al., 1988). By this time the theoretical interest had shifted markedly. The most important new element in the book was the interest in emerging patterns of differentiation (mainly by class or ethnicity) and the use of political economy as a conceptual framework for analysis. The team recognized that new forms of differences were appearing in the region, whether through evidence of poverty and vulnerability, unequal distribution of land or the ability of some with 'high rank and status' to gain economic advantage. The book also explored the dimensions of regional inequalities though, in a departure from a conventional view of core-periphery relationships, concluded that the eastern islands of Fiji were a sort of 'pampered periphery' able to exploit the national political roles of their leaders and channel state resources in their direction. To me, this book remains one of the best, if unfortunately most neglected, analyses of contemporary social, economic and environmental change in Fiji.

Such concern for inequality has also affected a number of other, more recent studies by geographers in Fiji. One of the most important of these was the later work of Gerard Ward. Ward returned to Fiji as part of the Fiji Employment and Development Mission (Bienefeld, 1984), and his working papers for the project formed the basis or a number of publications that concentrated on land issues. His work for the mission involved a resurvey of some of the village case studies he had worked in the late 1950s (Ward, 1965, 1986). This allowed Ward to comment on some of the longer-standing processes of change, especially with regard to land tenure and the emergence of land accumulation by a few in the villages engaged in cash cropping or livestock farming. As the 'land frontier' closed in Fiji, with little suitable new land available for agricultural resettlement, village resources, especially land, were being distributed less equitably and commercial relations of production (land rents, wage labour and commodity exchange) were replacing old systems of exchange based on reciprocity. These were potentially potent forces in the creation of a new rural society in Fiji: one marked more by class, cash and individual accumulation than by kin affiliation, communal redistribution and subsistence. Even if such a society was not yet dominant, or even evident, in Fijian villages, the forces for such a transformation were in place.

Ward's work was paralleled by a number of others. Britton's study of the Fiji tourism industry (1983) did not focus on the rural sector, but the conclusions concerning the dominance of foreign and local élite capital, increased spatial concentration and marginalization of the poor from the industry again mirrored the concern in the 1980s for inequality and poverty. Sofer's doctoral research took him to village sites on Kadavu and Viti Levu (Sofer, 1988). He also noted the growing gap between centre and periphery and the dominance of urban-based institutions (in government, transport and marketing) over the rural economy. Rutz (1978) has also undertaken significant anthropological research on agriculture and land in rural Fiji.

My own work fitted within this approach with the aim of analysing the nature and dynamics of socio-economic and spatial differentiation in rural Fiji. As with the others, I was able to note the ways in which new forms of economic organization (wage labouring, military employment and new forms of cash cropping, such as rice and ginger) were affecting material standards of living in the villages and settlement schemes and reforming patterns of inequality. Like Ward, I was able to draw on earlier studies for baseline data, thanks to Nayacakalou and Lasaqa. Land was at the heart. On the settlement schemes of Waibau and Lomaivuna, leases were being used in numerous ways to extend ownership and participation in ginger farming (Overton, 1988b). In the villages, those engaged in rice farming seemed to be securing tracts of the limited areas of good land whilst others found it difficult to gain access to land.

Nevertheless, I was also struck with the forces of community. People were successful in straddling the cash and the communal worlds (perhaps less of a contradiction than had been suggested by earlier writers). The community, especially in places, such as Draubuta, seemed to be able to limit individual accumulation of land: my data showed that inequality in land holding amongst the *mataqali* (sub-clan) had in fact decreased since the Nayacakalou and Lasaqa studies (Overton, 1992a). Villages were much more than just centres for subsistence or commercial agriculture: they performed a number of economic functions in the wider economy, as 'retirement homes', dormitory suburbs for urban workers, barracks for the military reservists and a 'safety net' for those who failed to prosper in the urban economy.

In all, we had looked anew at rural Fiji influenced, if often only mildly and implicitly, by neo-Marxist theories of underdevelopment and class formation. It was an approach which often looked at the same processes of change observed by researchers in the 1950s and 1960s but, whereas they saw things such as individualism, cash cropping and urbanization as signs of a largely benign and desirable process of modernization, we were rather more sceptical of other possible results including social stratification, poverty and cultural disintegration. Some of us were also disturbed by the coups of 1987 which we saw, probably far too superficially, as a dramatic and reactionary response to inequality and the repression of some forces which might promote equitable and gradual change (Overton and Ward, 1989; Overton, 1992b). Again, perhaps, naïveté and idealism overshadowed an incomplete understanding of the complexity of Fijian social and political affiliation and action.

The University of the South Pacific and the 'Post-Colonial' Period

Overlapping the work of these non-Fijian researchers was the development of a body of work emanating from Fiji and involving Fijian residents and citizens. Some of this came from regional institutions, such as the South Pacific Commission or, more recently, the South Pacific Regional Environment Programme; some came from people working in the bureaucracy; and some individuals working in a variety of places in and outside Fiji. The most important local contribution, though, has been from USP.

There were important antecedents for the work at USP. First was the contribution of Fijians who had received tertiary education overseas but who conducted research at home. Nayacakalou (1975) and Lasaqa (1984) were vital in this respect, adding new insights for the academic world from their intimate local knowledge and giving new levels of understanding for their own people from their academic training. Unfortunately for USP, both found other roles in the bureaucracy in Fiji and their potential involvement in teaching and research in USP were lost even if their work was well-known there.

Since the founding of geography at USP, the study of rural Fiji has proceeded apace. Prem Prasad (1984), Rajesh Chandra (1980) and Randy Thaman (1982; Thaman & Clarke, 1983) have published on a wide variety of local topics. Bill Clarke did much to foster this interest, bringing his experience from earlier work in Papua New Guinea and addressing some issues of broad environmental concern (1971, 1977, 1990; Clarke & Morrison, 1987). In general, what has marked this USP-based research from that of outsiders has been its orientation towards applied rural geography and issues-oriented work. It has attempted to inform local debates on issues such as land degradation, land tenure or dietary change rather than contribute to theoretical discourse on social transformation, for example.

Another virtue of the USP approach was the involvement of students in publication. A number of students at USP have used the concepts and skills they learned to describe and interpret their own world in new ways. For me, an illustration of this was Mesake Tukai's essay on Cautata village (1988), but many others before and since have had their work published: Ponter (1986), Tubuna (1985), Eaton (1988), Ali (1988a, 1988b) to name but a few. Now it seems there is more emphasis on graduate theses, reflecting the higher number of students going on to advanced studies.

Such studies warrant more attention than is possible here. All this work by Fiji's people has added a different dimension to the interpretation of change in rural Fiji. First, there has been intimate local knowledge. Research that is conducted in the Fijian or Hindi language, that draws directly on the personal histories and experiences of local people, and that often integrates society, land and economy with culture, history and religion has a quite different 'texture' to that conducted by outsiders. Too often, many of us have attempted to reduce the elements of village life to distinct, measurable and autonomous components, when in reality many practices can be understood only within the totality of the cultural context.

A second major contribution of the local perspective has been the focusing on issues of local concern rather than always on abstract global theories. Local scholars have not eschewed grand theory; rather, they have been able to direct their work and its interpretation to matters that are of importance to Pacific people. What may be perceived by outsiders as an attachment to the 'green' theories of development (development from below, basic needs, sustainability, etc.) is probably more an appreciation of the way that ideas about rural change have to be oriented toward implementation and participation at the village level if they are to be of any value in the Pacific.

So the 'post-colonial' study of rural Fiji has been a valuable counterbalance to the previous dominance of research by outsiders. It has strengthened the importance of appreciating local context and questioned the application of general theories. Most of all though, it has involved Pacific people in the study and improvement of their own lives as never before, either through the participation of people themselves in the work or merely in talking to researchers in their own language and with a deep shared understanding.

Conclusions

The past 40 years have seen a series of methodological and theoretical approaches to the study of rural Fiji. 'Big theory', whether modernization, Marxism or sustainability, has guided the interests and conclusions of several waves of researchers. Whilst reliance on detailed village-level field surveys has continued, the manner in which this has been carried out has shifted subtly toward more direct involvement of local researchers and the resurvey of earlier studies to gain a better appreciation of change in the past 30 or so years. Since the founding of USP, research has increased, not only through the direct involvement of USP staff and students but also through the contact made with visiting researchers.

Throughout, though with different emphases, there has been the interchange of approaches and interpretations. It is perhaps too much of a generalization to say that the expatriate scholars have brought the wider perspectives and theoretical interests and the local scholars have grounded their work much more solidly in local context and relevance, for there have been notable exceptions on either side. Yet in that interchange surely lies the heart of good research: work that is informed by broad issues and questions yet based on intimate local knowledge and context.

Perhaps such an ideal can be achieved at the individual level only through the emergence of another Nayacakalou or Lasaqa. In a corporate sense, USP has been, and will continue to be, central. Having been a temporary teacher at USP and, more often, a visiting researcher, I am convinced that it is in the cross-fertilization that USP offers – an institution open to the world but committed to its place in the Pacific – that future research on the rural Pacific can best be grounded. For there is still much to be done to monitor, describe and analyse the transformation of rural geographies in Fiji and elsewhere. As yet we know little about women in rural Fiji, apart from Chung's pioneering work on fertility change (1991). There are regions, such as Vanua Levu, which have been little studied. For such a large industry, the sugar sector seems relatively neglected. Add to these continuing shifts in theoretical concerns, and the study of rural Fiji should continue as a fascinating and fertile ground for research.

Chapter 7

A Scatter of Islands: Reminiscences from Tonga, Rarotonga, Niue, and Fiji

A. Crosbie Walsh

I cannot rid myself of a sneaking feeling that to write something autobiographical is to claim a measure of greatness, but my sole claim is that for periods of time over the past 30 years or so I have lived, taught and studied in four quite different Pacific Island countries and visited a number more. To have been invited to share, through writing, some of the ideas and experiences gleaned over these years in what Albert Wendt vividly called "so vast, so fabulously varied a scatter of islands, nations, cultures, mythologies and myths, so dazzling a creature" (1976: 49) is an opportunity that could not be missed, especially because the social scientist in me has too often, over these years, held me back from saying what I really felt.

Viewed in retrospect, I have too often been torn between assuming that 'thinking' is superior to 'feeling' while, at the same time, vaguely recognizing that each is indispensable to the refinement of the other. Analysis, I was taught, demands 'detached objectivity', yet life suggests such analyses are often culturally biased and sterile; in identifying 'fact', they often miss the 'heart' of the 'matter'. Truly great creative thinking is not detached, when the occasion demands, from feeling and purpose. Or as Wendt continued, "Oceania deserves more than an attempt at mundane fact; only the imagination in free flight can hope--if not to contain her--to grasp some of her shape, plumage, and pain" (1976: 49).

Somewhere through the tangle of words which follow there are threads of personal philosophy which, although lacking the internal consistency necessary to give the philosophy a name with a -ity or -ism suffix, are nonetheless important and consistent for me. Philosophy colours and creates our individual perceptions of reality, shapes our thoughts and feeling, makes us the sort of person we are, and determines our approach to everything we do, be it teaching, interaction with students and colleagues, research, publication: all activities in which the academic claims to be 'objective'.

Why I came to teach in the Pacific Islands can be traced to philosophy. The geography influences came from three people at the Victoria University of Wellington: founding Professor Keith Buchanan, an erudite radical humanist, with a sound English liberal education, significant research and publications on West Africa, a keen interest in the Chinese 'experiment', and, like me, a passion for causes, some of them already lost; Harvey Franklin, demanding, incisive almost to the point of cruelty, but ultimately liberating (I smarted for a long time after he accused me of intellectual dishonesty for the position I had taken in an assignment on Soviet Central Asia); and Ray Watters, warm, bungling, hot from recent research on modernization in Fiji, often not well prepared for post-graduate seminars but always enthusiastic, keen to encourage discussion, and gently critical of our arguments. Ray's story of how he finally retrieved field notes which had fallen from his back trouser pocket after a hurried dash one night to a Fiji village pit latrine, a story replete with references to torches, spears and 'stalagmites', deserves entry in the annals of research during the colonial era. Along with other such stories, it added a sense of 'being there' to our desk-bound Pacific studies.

There were personal reasons, too, for my interest in the Pacific. New Zealand in the late 1950s was a country which had not yet accepted its multicultural heritage. It was unsure of itself as a nation. Although, at one level, everything that was supposedly worthwhile started and stopped in the Mother Country; at another level, Pommies (and I was one of them) were not welcomed, especially when they proved argumentative and drew comparisons to how things were done at 'home'. The Land of the Long White Cloud was very White. What Ron Crocombe (1992) calls the third (Pacific Islander) phase of immigrants had not arrived. There were few Pacific Islanders then, even along Auckland's Karangahape Road. As for Maori, 100 years after the advent of colonialism, they were assumed to be (still) dying out or (almost) assimilated, their cultural heritage irrelevant to modern living, even for them. Maori were seen to be either happy-go-lucky buffoons and content with their lot, or lazy, ungrateful drifters.

University studies were often no more enlightened. My Honours' history assignment on the Treaty of Waitangi, for example, produced a lecturer's retort that the treaty was irrelevant because it had no basis in law. The same lecturer (who taught me of European happenings in the Pacific under the guise of Pacific History) held that while the Maori had myth and legend, they had no history. Oral history was not history. Only the *Pakeha* (Caucasian) had History. This from an educated and relatively liberal woman who, I am pleased to say, some years later (but too late for me) changed her mind. New Zealand was assumed to have no racial problems, and those who said it had were 'trouble-makers'.

All this was very difficult for me to grasp. My wife was Maori. Neither she nor her family fitted the stereotypes. Somehow, in a rather muddled sort of way, I reasoned that if our children were to grow up proud of being part-Maori, and able to speak Maori, we had to leave this unhealthy environment and retreat to somewhere where Maori language and culture were dominant. So it came to be that in 1960 I applied for a teaching job at Tereora College, Rarotonga.

I got the job, but the only accommodation available for at least a year was at the Otera Rarotonga whose tariff would nearly equal my salary. New Zealand's Island building programme had been redirected from building houses in Rarotonga to Niue, where two successive hurricanes (not cyclones in those days) had destroyed almost all the housing. I was not to visit Rarotonga or Niue for another ten years.

I applied instead for Tonga High School, assuming that Tongan language and culture were much closer to Maori than they proved to be. How different my life would have been but for the Niue hurricanes I do not know. So much of what we do seems to be just sheer luck: a door closes, we will never know the rooms it guards, and another opens revealing rooms we otherwise would not have known.

Tonga 1962-1966

The passport entry reads: "Permission has been granted for Bearer to Reside in Tonga for three years from 15 January 1962."

I was up before dawn as the *Tofua* wound its way through the reefs guarding the Nuku'alofa waterfront, though I never did get photos of the Norfolk pines along the Palace foreshore, or the town as it came into view, or the people I met on those first few days after arrival when everything was fresh and exciting. I had bought a new camera (and new shorts, short-sleeved shirts and white long socks: the *Palangi* [Caucasian] uniform) on the day we spent in Suva, and I had failed to wind on the film correctly.

We were to spend five years, not three, in Tonga and two of our four children were born there in the old Vaiola Hospital. Tonga's unique urban land tenure (and lack of 'development' at that time) inhibited the emergence of social areas. For neighbours, we had representatives of most strata of society. To our right, my *Palangi* headmasters. We had three in five years, each reversing the educational philosophy and practice of the other. Not an easy situation for a young First Assistant or a staff, both Tongan and European, equally young and inexperienced, who had to explain the changing modus operandi to parents and students. To our left, two neighbours, eye specialist Taumoepeau and Noble Luani and their families. I had early instruction from my 4-year-old daughter on how best to learn Tongan when she invited a Taumoepeau daughter to stay for a bath with "*Kaukau*?" (bath?) while I was still struggling with *Oku ke fiema'u...* (Do you want to ...). Language is essentially oral and situational; my learning was too much from books.

Behind was the *fale Tonga* (traditional oval Tongan house, usually at least partly built of traditional materials) of recent migrants from Vava'u we never got to know, and across the road a *fale papa* (wooden house, generally rectangular), home of Big Manu, fiddler, worker for the Free Wesleyan Church, and his small son, Little Manu. Their bicycle made quite a sight as they cycled along Mateialona Road, identically dressed in blue shirts and *vala* (wrap, lavalava). Across the road to the left, Adolf Johanson, manager of the Produce Board when bananas for New Zealand were Tonga's chief export earner, and his wife Ruby and family, part-Tongans, with whom we became close friends. Most of our friends were part-Tongan, or mixes like our family, and I owe a lot to them for insights into Tonga which would, I think, have been denied but for these connections.

Much of what I learnt, however, focused on the school and it was the school, or rather my place within it, which determined my standing in the *hou'eiki* (chief) and commoner Tongan, and local and expatriate *Palangi*, communities.

As might be expected, our lives touched only lightly on those of royalty and the nobility. Prince Tu'ipelehake was once a guest in our home. (He was on time much to the chagrin of our *Palangi* guests who arrived late. So much for Tongan—and *Palangi*—time!); and the King admitted to reading my MA thesis. On separate occasions, I had lengthy social sessions with Fusitu'a and a young Crown Prince Tupouto'a.

The Tongans who were our friends were mainly colleagues from school and others whose English was far better than our Tongan. Relations with other Tongans were not easy. Both sides had to work at it. Language, of course, was the main barrier. Despite many hours with Churchward's *Dictionary* and Shumway's *Grammar*, my Tongan never really advanced to the take-off stage, but it did cause many laughs as readers familiar with the importance of the glottal stop in Tongan words may well imagine.

Sometimes, though, we do not need spoken language. On arriving in Tonga, I had abandoned ideas of researching Maori migration to Wellington for my MA thesis for obvious reasons, and started, during weekends and school breaks, to work on urbanization and migration in Tonga. I was accompanied during field-work in Ha'apai by Paul Havea who introduced me to his cousin Kolongo, saying I was *faingofua* (easy to be with). We never spoke much to each other, but a sort of mystic bond was forged which lasted for several years. When I revisited Tonga in 1971, Kolongo heard on the radio of my arrival and came down from Ha'apai to meet me. We spent the evening in each other's company. Little was said but the meeting meant a great deal.

There were two distinct groups of Europeans in Nuku'alofa: local Europeans, mainly men, some of whom had married locally, and transient Europeans, such as teachers like me, whom the local Europeans tolerated just to bring up numbers. Local Europeans and many Part-Tongans seemed to be a class on their own, sandwiched, as it were, in this highly stratified society between the unreachable and the untouchable. While many were comfortable with this role, some were touchy and others, to maintain their perceived place in society, were downright racist. I was surprised to learn that having a Tongan wife was no insurance against such attitudes.

There were three clubs in Tonga in those days. We joined the Yacht Club (which had a Commodore but no yachts) because all the family could join in. The other clubs were essentially male social drinking places. The most prestigious club was the Nuku'alofa Club, started in 1914 just before the outbreak of World War I. The then English treasurer apparently continued to send overdue subscription reminders to German and Austrian members in internment in New Zealand until 1917 when they were finally expelled from the Club. They were not to be readmitted until 1927, though invitations to their daughters to attend the annual ball were dispatched (and ignored) from the end of the war in 1918. One incident I recall at the Nuku'alofa Club (membership limited to Europeans or people of European descent, Nobles and Cabinet Ministers) was when I announced that I had also joined the Tonga Club (membership open but with only a handful of Europeans) because I wanted to meet more Tongans. One member, a trades foreman from New Zealand who, significantly, later married a Tongan, retorted, "I would not join that club. I would have to drink with my workers." I wondered why I was drinking with him!

I think the five years I spent as First Assistant (and teacher of geography, English and history) at Tonga High School were probably the most important general experience of my adult life. They provided the first real test of my theories on teaching, and my attitudes to many things in life. For the first time, I had some authority to influence the lives of a significant number of others. It was a learning situation that I am not altogether proud of today although, thankfully, former students, like most of us reminiscing, mainly recall the good times. I only fully realized the immensity of this experience and its impact on me when I attended a school reunion in Auckland last year. After 25 years, I could still recall the names and younger faces of all my ex-students present, an incredible feat for I'm generally not very good with names. There is no doubt Tonga changed me far more than I changed any Tongan.

I arrived as a liberal educationalist, opposed to corporal punishment, any form of rote learning, hierarchical authority, the school tradition, religious observation, and militaristic practices. I left, having caned more students (many for speaking Tongan) than I care to remember; having used rote learning as an essential part of preparations for the all-important School Certificate exams; having endorsed a prefect hierarchy and created a tradition of records and achievements through which to instill pride in the school; having resurrected monthly church parades, and morning prayers at formal school assemblies, and having insisted on military-style drill in preparation for marching to the Opening of Parliament. I was learning that what is right in one place is not necessarily right in others, and in doing so I lost a little bit of the cultural arrogance with which I had unwittingly arrived.

At the same time, in the best liberal tradition of educating the whole person, I took a close personal interest in the students and their families, seeking to build both their confidence in me as the teacher and in their own ultimate success. Students often remember their teacher's favourite saying. Mine apparently was "God helps those who help themselves." The school motto is *"Ki He Lelei Taha"* (to do the best; to do one's best). Some students took this to mean they were the best; I said it meant they were to do their best. To succeed, one needs determination not just to pass, but to excel. By hook or by crook, I was determined Tonga High School students were going to do just that.

Special difficulties were standing in the way of learning. The boys in particular were very shy, which was not helped by others teasing them. Yet they had to learn English, hence my caning them for speaking Tongan and my constant insistence in class that they speak up often and clearly. For the School Certificate English exam, we had to learn about poetry and

Plate 7.1. Tonga High School geography field trip to ʻEua Island, 1964. Following the eruption of Niuafoʻou in (Tin Can Island) 1946, evacuated villagers from Angaha took their church bells to the resettled village, also called Angaha, on ʻEua.

drama. We wrote 'creative' English as Konai Helu Thaman recently reminded me and published it in the newly founded annual school magazine, printed by students on an old French missionary press purchased from the Catholic Bishop.

Our success in examinations gradually broke down parental opposition to a number of other new educational practices which departed from the type of education they had experienced as youngsters. Previously, parents had seen acting as entertaining but not really educational, while activities such as the introduction of Tongan language and culture classes and geography field trips were total wastes of time. In my view, everyday Tongan was not good enough. Our students needed to be at least as well educated in things Tongan as students in the more Tongan-orientated secondary schools. They needed to be competent in, and proud of, things Tongan, and they needed a much better knowledge of, and commitment to, the Tonga outside Nuku'alofa. They also needed to develop study skills based on observation and personal interpretation.

Field trips to 'Eua and the Northern Islands were thus not merely introductions to aspects of Tongan history and to mountains, vulcanism, streams and erosion not present on Tongatapu, or even to new geographic skills: field trips were also a shared and relatively lengthy exposure to the other Tonga to which their *Palangi* education (and probable future employment) denied them. They were attempts to temper the latent elitism evident in much secondary—and tertiary—education in Tonga as in many countries. Although at that time I was more than a little critical of Futa Helu and his foundling 'Atenisi University, in retrospect I think we had both identified what we perceived to be similar shortcomings in Tongan educational practice for, of our former students who remain in Tonga today, several are outspoken in the current democracy debate.

Before leaving Tonga I should say something of my research there because it was this, and the teaching, which mapped much of my subsequent career path.

Tonga in the early 1960s was an exciting place to be. These were the years when New Zealand archaeologists Jack Golson, Roger Green, Janet Davidson and Les Groube were following up earlier leads on Lapita pottery. Australian historian Noel Rutherford spoke discretely of the voyeurism of former missionary and prime minister, the Rev. Shirley Baker. American ethnomusicologist Adrienne Kaeppler was recording near forgotten *lakalaka* (action song performed standing up) and *ma'ulu'ulu* (action song performed sitting down) while demonstrating the still evident role of song-dance in preserving the social order. Danish archaeologist Jens Poulsen was digging up *kaloa'a* (shellfish, large bivalve) and *to'o* (shellfish, small bivalve) from a 2,000-year-old midden site. Even amateurs had their say with Mervyn Holmes-Libbis, who worked for Radio ZCO, finding 'astronomical' signs on the top of the *Ha'amonga* (the 13th century stone trilithon).

Somewhat less exciting perhaps, because they were of the present, Australian agricultural economist Brian Hardaker was studying coconut production, his fellow countryman geographer Alaric Maude was studying population and land use, and I was studying migration and urbanization. The King (you will recall he had read my thesis) was later to observe that Maude's thesis (Maude, 1965) was longer than mine.

Very little in my university training prepared me for my first major research exercise. Theories and survey techniques arising from Western experience were mostly either irrelevant or impossible to operationalize. My supervisor insisted I read a book, I think by Gibbs, on urbanization to provide a theoretical base for my study. What a disappointment when it finally arrived: Chicago (sic!) and much Western urbanization theory were just not relevant to a study of Nuku'alofa with its 9,000 or so souls. Lacking appropriate theoretical tools, most early Pacific urban studies were essentially descriptive. Dependency and articulation theories, and the plethora of useful Third World urban studies now available, had not yet arrived on the scene.

There were few established parameters for the study. Record cards of the kingdom's first accurate census had been mislaid (I later found them in the Premier's garage, some punch holes gnawed through by silverfish), and there was no direct information on internal migration.[1] There was not even a map of the town adequate to my purpose, and its internal and external boundaries were disputed by its three Town Officers (who were paid according to the population living in their part of town) and Lands and Survey. Basic measures, such as size, density and growth rates, possible spatial differentiation within the town, and differences in migration rates from different parts of the Kingdom, were thus difficult to determine.

I started at the beginning, mapping every building in the town, calculating the incidence of each housing type (to be used as a measure of urbanism) and counting, with Alaric's help and in his lounge, the 56,838 cards which represented the people of Tonga in 1956, and sorting with needle and by age, sex, occupation, village and island of origin, the 9,202 cards representing those who were resident in Nuku'alofa. This work, together with interviews in the Northern Islands and with migrants in town, took up many evenings and weekends and all school holidays. Sometime in late 1963 I proudly announced to Alaric that the work was finished. All I had to do was write it up. He replied (and I have repeated his phrase to university students many times since): "You have only just begun."

Nevertheless, it was finally finished, thanks to those I interviewed and to friends, colleagues and students, all Tongan, who helped at every stage (Walsh, 1964). Two years later I left Tonga. Another *Palangi* 'expert' had been launched on a new career path—with a little bit of help from his friends.

New Zealand 1967-1971

For two years I taught at a country secondary school in the lower North Island. I was instrumental in starting a kindergarten for Maori children in the town and a Maori Club at school. Things were still not good racially. Few teachers were interested in things Maori or, indeed, in Maori children. The Maori renaissance was still a few years away. In this environment of mutual disinterest, Maori children soon became disciplinary problems and under-achievers. These were the parents of today's Maori children.

Something of the same view existed at Wellington Teachers' College where I spent the next two years (I was invited to apply for the job after senior staff heard me talk to their students on Tonga!), but there, at least, the social studies staff were sensitive to the need for bicultural education, and none more so than geographer Des Kelly who had taught for a number of years at Levuka Public School. During my time in Wellington I wrote two educational books. One, based on parts of my Nuku'alofa thesis, tried to demonstrate relatively profound concepts by relating them to children's experiences (Walsh, 1972b). Randy Thaman, a Peace Corps volunteer, who I was to meet again at the University of the South Pacific (USP), helped me with the photographs. The other was a simple statistical account of several aspects of contemporary Maori life which, one critic claimed, brought "some long overdue objectivity to the subject" (Walsh, 1971).

The two writings which probably caused my life to take another turn (because they kept me in touch with academia, not always easy for a secondary school teacher) were an historical overview of Tongan migration (Walsh, 1970) and a paper on Nuku'alofa in which I found certain aspects of Tongan urbanism to tally with Harvey Franklin's views of the peasantry in modern Europe (Walsh, 1969). The latter was my first conscious attempt to use theory as a tool for analysis, and it led, indirectly, to my appointment to a geography position at Massey University which, in turn, led to brief visits to Rarotonga in 1971 to resurvey land use changes noted by an earlier researcher and to Niue in 1972 where I studied land use and migration, and later to Fiji and Papua New Guinea.

Rarotonga and Niue 1971-1972

Of my Rarotonga research, which was never published, little needs to be said, but it did strike me that the use of the term 'agriculture' or 'horticulture' to describe much Rarotonga land use was misleading. Big citrus growers like the Napa family in Arorangi were horticulturists, but most growers had a far smaller commitment, and for them different expectations and policy seemed necessary. The apparent disinterest of small, part-time growers just could not be explained away by claiming they were not 'economic men', one of the ethnocentric in-ideas of the time.

Land use mapping in Rarotonga was easy, a short climb producing panoramic views of semi-permanent land use. The mapping of the large, flat, wooded, raised atoll of Niue was far more difficult and some ingenuity was needed. The available aerial photographs were old, and cloud covered much of the prints. On the ground, numerous small, scattered areas of shifting cultivation occurred inland off small tracks, and visibility rarely exceeded a hundred or so metres. Observation was possible only over short distances at ground level and, of necessity, recordings had to be somewhat crude. I equipped myself with a compass, a motorbike, and with the help of village policemen (who were responsible for ensuring all villagers had adequate crops planted), and a smattering of Niuean to indicate whether there were ('*Fai*?') or were not ('*Aifai*?') plantings to the left or right of the track, I plotted from the bike's odometer the location and size of most cultivations belonging to *magafaoa* (extended family; familial landholding unit) in the island's 14 villages. The map was as accurate as resources and occasion permitted. Niue had requested a land potential map; it got (through no fault of mine) a land use map. The map was duly published--at some cost to the New Zealand government--and never, to my knowledge, used.[2]

Two useful things did come out of this first visit to Niue. First, in trying to estimate the volume of produce grown in typical plots, I sampled areas where both traditional and modern methods of cultivation were used at several locations. My findings were that cultivation methods using traditional slash and burn and the digging stick, though more labour intensive, were no less productive and generally less damaging to Niue's fragile environment than the introduced 'plough' method which required the clearing of larger areas and monocultivation which, in turn, produced higher soil alkalinity, lower soil moisture retention and extensive areas of weeds (Walsh, 1972a).

The study of emigration, the second useful thing, was timely in that it recorded the end of the ship era. It was the first study of modern Pacific international migration (Walsh & Trlin, 1973). Hannan International Airport, opened during my stay, was soon to be the conduit through which far higher levels of emigration would occur as some 3,000 of Niue's near 5,000 people sought a perceived better life in New Zealand. The study comprised an examination of official records (name, sex, age, village, and destination of passengers kept in books in the police office), a survey of prospective migrants, and a statistical analysis by village of variables such as land holdings, wage income and remittances which I thought might help to explain village migration level differentials. In a later study, I used census material to estimate the impact of emigration on the economic and social viability of different types of households in villages typified by higher and lower levels of migration, and I sought to establish a means of predicting future levels of migration from the familial composition of past migration (Walsh, 1978). It still troubles me that so few people seem to have read these writings. The moral, if I may be permitted a little cynicism, is do not publish in Pacific regional or government reports or non-mainstream local journals. If you think you are on to a good idea, get it published in 'important' academic journals in the West, or at least in Australia. It is then more likely to be noticed at home in New Zealand and the Pacific.

Fiji 1974-1976

In 1974 I went on a 3-year secondment as Head of Geography (later Geography and Population Studies) to the USP, Laucala Campus. Besides a general desire to return to the Pacific, I had two purposes in mind. First, I wanted to recharge my intellectual and experiential batteries by working in an environment where the Pacific was the main focus (it had, and still has, the barest of footholds in New Zealand geography departments) and the presence of John Harre as Head of the School of Social and Economic Development (SSED) and Ron Crocombe as Professor of Pacific Studies, whose works I had read and admired, seemed to guarantee this. Second, I had a dislike of Indians (a not uncommon attitude held by Europeans seeking to protect Pacific indigenes from every race except their own), and I did not want to be like this. Although knowing the attitude to be irrational (one cannot believe in the equality of all races, then arrange them preferentially) I knew I could not dispel the idea *in vacuo*. I had to be exposed to a significant Indian presence. Fiji was the place to be!

I must confess to not getting off to a particularly good start at the USP. Previous communist sympathies (I'm still very much a socialist) had complicated my work permit application, causing me to arrive after classes had started.

Those early days would have been very difficult were it not for the wholehearted support of the other two geographers in the 'department', American Randy Thaman (whose wife, Konai, I had taught in Tonga), loud, lovable, enthusiastic, a veritable dynamo of a man, and Prem Prasad, the kind, gentle, conscientious Indian I needed to meet. Later we were joined for one year by John McKinnon, a good teacher and stimulating academic fresh from PhD studies in the Solomons. Together we made a very good team.

The programme we thrashed out in discussion then, with its balance between physical and human geography, progression from global to local, emphasis on the practical, and application to development, is not too different, I understand, from the USP geography programme today. I should note also that it was our insistence on being researchers as well as teachers which probably retained geography its place in the SSED. For quite some time there were rumours we would be moved to the School of Education, which was viewed at that time as very much a training place for secondary school teachers. Had we moved, we would have lost our central place in the social sciences, and today's geography at the USP would have been a very different beast.

Field-work was for me, as it had been in Tonga, an essential part of learning, and at university level good student field-work lends itself to publication. This was the origin of two (I'm sorry to say, short-lived) serial publications, *Basic Research in Pacific Islands Geography*, with major contributions from Raijieli Racule, Kamla Reddy, Dennis Oliver and Rajesh Chandra, and *Student Research Exercises*, a less pretentious series, with a major piece by Juliet Yee and Saroona Narain. My second year students studied seller place of residence, ethnicity and produce in the Suva market;

Navua before the expected impact of developments at Pacific Harbour; and urban and rural Fijian and Indian attitudes towards family planning in the Nadi area. Third year students had individual research assignments and were involved in social area studies of parts of Suva. Their 'random' sampling of Tamavua provided something of a surprise. The ethnicity of those interviewed replicated that of the interviewers, a most unlikely coincidence given the dominance of Europeans and Indians in Tamavua and the high proportion of Fijians and small proportion of Europeans in the class. In explanation, I was told Tamavua's Europeans and Indians owned too many ferocious dogs. So much for random sampling!

One piece of unpublished student research which deserves mention was that of Sister Catherine Jones who examined 1975 arrival and departure records to determine the ethnicity, occupation, residence and purpose of travel of probable emigrants. Although even then a delicate topic, it was an opportunity to demonstrate spatial differentials in the impact of emigration, and the importance of region and locality in planning processes typically dominated by national and macro-analyses. Regrettably, government planners continue to undervalue the geographic dimension.

My own researches included an ethnic dimension. First was a provincial analysis of Fijian, Indian and Other migration from 1966 census data, the first census with place of birth information for all ethnic groups. In this study, the migration origin, composition and destination of the major ethnic groups were shown to be quite different. Like so many things in plural Fiji, actual bi- (or multi-) modal distributions could not be reduced to a meaningful national average. An oral adaptation of this paper was given to students at the first Pacific Week introduced by Vice-Chancellor James Maraj who decreed that all disciplines for at least this one week should teach Pacifica, an unnecessary admonition for geography. In the talk, which was taped for University Extension purposes and later broadcast in part without my knowledge on Radio Fiji, I said that Fiji could ill afford the brain drain which was taking skilled Fiji citizens overseas (Canada had recently relaxed its immigration regulations and the first wave of Indo-Fijian migrants had departed by boat for Vancouver). I also said that the University should be teaching race relations. The broadcast caused a furore. Prime Minister Ratu Mara's office rang the Vice-Chancellor who rang Ahmed Ali, Acting Head of School, who, to his credit, said he would oppose my deportation (sic!), and my phone rang hot with a mix of congratulatory and cautionary calls. I could not quite understand what all the fuss was about until it was explained to me later by a local European at a cocktail party. Although I had said nothing which many others did not know, I had said it publicly. All things were not well in the nascent Republic of Fiji.

The other work which had an ethnic dimension was my doctoral thesis which, in looking at urban squatting within the larger setting of Fiji and Suva urbanization, looked especially closely at the condition of the Fijian and Indian poor and their strategies for survival in Suva's squatter settlements. I believe the findings, which are based on sample surveys of squatter settlements (for which I must thank senior students at the USP, more closely supervised after my experience with the Tamavua study!), were considerably strengthened by my being able to use, as control groups, Housing Authority and Squatter settlements data obtained from 1976 Census household schedules. This raises another matter of importance to academic research in the Pacific, and an opportunity to comment on a relationship between academic researchers and government departments.

Access to census material (on the understanding that I respect its confidentiality) was granted by Government Statistician Ratilal Lodhia. I took it as a thank you for work undertaken gratis for the 1976 Census. In preparation for the 1966 Census, Auckland University geographer Gerry Bloomfield had defined urban census areas (Bloomfield, 1967). The task, undertaken by Netherlands Universities Fund for International Cooperation (NUFFIC)-funded demographer Martin Bakker (who was attached to geography) and I in 1975, was to update Bloomfield's work by redefining Fiji's 13 urban area boundaries, and the enumeration areas within them.

Looking back, there were four lessons to be learnt from our work, and the first was that Bloomfield had done a remarkably good job thanks largely, I suspect, to his geography training. The second lesson was never again to do this sort of work for nothing. Far from helping Fiji, as we had hoped, it guaranteed that parts of our work would be ignored. Officials seem unable to distinguish cost from value, often thinking that a cheap or costless exercise is also near valueless. So, do not blame the overseas experts who charge high fees. Part of the problem lies with local administrators. The third lesson was that census work is quickly forgotten. Once politicians know numbers in their electorates and macro-planners have statistics on which to base their macro-plans, funding, personnel and interest dry up. If one has not got one's report recommendations accepted by then (and we had not), they are likely to be forgotten forever. The fourth lesson is that, to complete quality work within the time available, one needs a very clear set of objectives, a strict timetable, and a high standard of teamwork. On the face of it, perfectionist Martin and hyper-activist me might seem an unlikely team, but it was precisely this antithesis which produced an efficient synthesis. While, for example, I was impatient with Martin, standing in the middle of a cane field two miles south of Nadi township, seeking to establish an urban area boundary based on a 6-figure grid reference (and all we could see was cane!), he slowed me down and caused me to question, verify and confirm far more than I was accustomed. We finished the work on time and were reasonably pleased with the result (Bakker & Walsh, 1976).

Another programme associated with the Department of Geography at the time was the Canadian International Development Agency (CIDA)-funded comparative study of food distribution in New Hebrides (Vanuatu), Fiji and Tonga led by Gerry Ward and Terry McGee from the Australian National University (McGee, 1975). Geography facilitated this study in the face of some opposition from others in SSED who considered it an exercise in 'academic imperialism' from which the USP and the Pacific would derive no benefit. The critics were wrong for the association brought a number of benefits.

I have the Fiji coordinator, Mike Baxter, to thank for my final choice of thesis topic ("Do something small, Croz. It will grow, and it's only for a ticket"). He was right about it growing; theses do mushroom, but it was more than a ticket: I learnt a lot from the exercise. Rajesh Chandra's academic career started with his involvement in the programme (Chandra, 1977, 1980). Students in the three island groups researched also gained income and experience from helping with the surveys. In Fiji alone, over 60 students put in some 4,000 hours of work on the project. It could also be argued that sociologist Epeli Hau'ofa's present association with the USP can be traced to the days when he was co-ordinator of the Tonga part of the programme (Hau'ofa, 1989), and that Sitiveni Halapua's first step to becoming Director of the Pacific Islands Development Program at the East-West Center, Hawaii, was taken when he was Epeli's assistant.

Further fragments of memory return: of Viliami Alofi, Isireli Koyamaibole, William Whippy and other men pushing the USP van (with some help from the women) through a mile of Navua flood waters on an 8-hour trip back from Nadi; of Sister Catherine unpiously sipping beer at a midnight feast to the obvious surprise of fellow students; of Preliminary

Geography teacher, Charles Rhodes, trying to get past a student roadblock during the USP Traffic Survey in 1975; of staff and students being turned out of the Fijian Hotel at Sigatoka because of an earlier USP study (not by a geographer) which the proprietors did not like; of the reported expression on the faces of two young Indians when they realized that Kelera Cavu, the woman they had said was too old to be a student, also spoke Hindi; of a young, unbearded Rajesh Chandra complaining about an 'only B+ grade' mark for an assignment (B+ was a very good grade from me); of Randy Thaman's front lawn dug up for his very first vegetable garden in Fiji (I never knew what his landlord said); of male students in the SE243 Population and Development class claiming female students would want the same number of children as them, and of the subsequent hand count which produced a 6-children average for the men and only a 3-children average for the women; of Saras Achari, Amita Singh and other young Indian female students, after some hesitation, politely sipping *yaqona* (a drink made from the pounded roots of *Piper methysticum,* the Polynesian *kava*) in a Fijian village; and of the USP staff and senior students of many religious persuasions enjoying *jelebi* and *ladu* (Indian sweetmeats served on happy occasions) at Diwali, the Hindu festival of lights which celebrates the victory of good over evil. Happy memories.

I left Fiji at the end of 1976, my intellectual and experiential batteries fully recharged, and with a healthy respect for all its races. Like the TV programme of the time, my mission was accomplished. In subsequent years I was to undertake a study for the Economic and Social Commission for Asia and the Pacific (ESCAP) on migration, urbanization and development which was to take me to other South Pacific countries (Walsh, 1982). Only Papua New Guinea remained. My brief visit to the University of Papua New Guinea in 1979 and 2-year secondment there in 1982 benefited greatly from earlier Pacific experiences, but that is another story and another scatter of islands.

Notes

1. Tupouniua (1956). Data on an individual were recorded on a card with punch holes along all edges. To count males, for example, one held a bundle of cards in one's hand and pushed a wire rod through the hole allocated to sex; if the hole had been punched (the code for males) cards

would drop out, leaving the remaining (unpunched hole) cards all female. One then hand-counted both piles of cards of male and female totals. Even the simplest tabulation, as can be imagined, took a long time. Mathematical calculations were done on my slide rule or on the Facit calculator owned by H.M. Treasury. It was a clumsy device requiring a handle to be turned so many times, one way for multiplication and addition, the other way for division and subtraction. Younger researchers of the Computer Age just do not know what they have missed!

2. 1973 Land Use Map of Niue Island, 1:30,000, Department of Lands and Survey, Wellington, 146/5.

Chapter 8

To Micronesia via Suva: A Tale of Two Universities and their Regions

Harley I. Manner

Introduction

Since its establishment in the 1960s, the University of the South Pacific (USP) has forged an international reputation as the major institution of higher education, research and service in the South Pacific region. The Department of Geography, as a part of the School of Social and Economic Development (SSED), has played a major role in the training of Pacific Island students. To do this, the department has attracted many well-known scholars of the Pacific region to its Suva campus. Although the university offers centrality and accessibility to the islands of the Pacific for the purposes of service and research, many faculty have joined USP because of commitment to the process of social and economic development, and because the university and the department has fostered an integrative approach to basic and applied geographical research and teaching (Forster et al., 1983).

This approach is also evident in the geography courses taught at the university. Thus, whether the question is human-environment interactions of traditional societies and cultures, the impact of economic growth and development on transitional societies, urbanization, development, geomorphology or island biogeography, geography at USP has recognized and fostered an integrative yet human approach to the discipline. In this brief narrative, I trace my development as a geographer, and what geography at USP taught me. I am suggesting that it has given me an even greater appreciation of the role of people in their environment, a lesson which I try to apply in my present position in Micronesia at the University of Guam (UOG).

Geography pre-USP

As an undergraduate, I studied geography at the University of Hawai'i, and, like many such students in the United States, the countries of the South Pacific were places I knew about only from postage stamps, regional courses on Australia, New Zealand, and the Pacific, and friends who had migrated to Hawaii for work, education, or pleasure. The insularity of the Hawaiian Islands was also a constraining factor. Unlike our counterparts in Europe and on the U.S. mainland, travel to other states and nation-states was expensive and difficult. Because of this fact, as well as the insularity of our minds, the other countries of the Pacific were places to visit in the distant future. Although the Peace Corps offered us opportunities for volunteer work in foreign countries, it was not an option that I wanted to pursue. Too many of us were concerned with part-time jobs, completing our degrees, and other activities relevant to undergraduate life. Research was something we did in libraries and laboratories; field research was something that only archaeologists did in Egypt. Even as developing geographers, field research was an almost totally alien idea, not completely understood or valued by undergraduates. Few of us considered geography as a career opportunity. Rather, it was an interesting degree option and nothing more.

I received my bachelor's degree in 1965 and, after a short hiatus, began work towards a master's degree. As a graduate student, I concentrated on physical geography as my systematic specialization, and the Pacific Islands as my regional specialization. In 1967 I travelled with my mentor, the late Professor John M. Street, to conduct field research on subsistence agriculture in the Mareng territory of the Western Highlands of Papua New Guinea. This field study was the first of many that I would eventually take in the Pacific Islands. Our trip was a geographer's dream and included short visits to islands where traditional agriculture was still practised. En route from Hawaii to Papua New Guinea, we visited Tahiti, New Zealand, Fiji, the former Condominium of the New Hebrides, and the former British Solomon Islands Protectorate before landing at Madang. By this time I had a better understanding of the nature and significance of research, a better view of traditional agriculture in the Pacific and of peoples' interactions with their environments. Our research was an extension of a larger project on the Human Ecology of the New Guinea Rain Forest in which Street, W.C. Clarke, R. Rappaport, A.P. Vayda and others were concerned with the effectiveness of the Mareng agricultural system in the maintenance of ecosystem quality. This project resulted in the generation of an incredible amount of information on a small group of people. Some products of this project were Rappaport's (1967) *Pigs For the Ancestors* and Clarke's (1971) *Place and People: an Ecology of a New Guinea Community.* The main focus of my research was the effects of the Mareng system of slash and burn agriculture on the the physical and chemical properties of soils, much in the vein of Nye and Greenland's (1960) *The Soil Under Shifting Cultivation.* I spent one year in the field and returned to Hawaii where I spent one year in the soils laboratory analysing soils from forest, grassland and subsistence gardens of different stages of production. The result was a master's degree in geography. Although I should have known better, the USP was still unknown to me.

In 1972, I again travelled to the Mareng territory to conduct field studies for my doctorate. As during my earlier field study, my research was an extension of the work which I started during my master's program. Most of my efforts were directed to the analysis of the structural and functional aspects of the tropical, montane rainforest ecosystem as affected by Mareng shifting cultivation. In particular, I was concerned with the role of human activities in the transformation of forest to grassland. I collected a large body of biomass and species composition data from the range of Mareng primary and secondary forests, gardens and grasslands.

During this study period, Clarke accompanied by the late P. Straatmans, visited me in the field. Such visitors always brought with them a sense of reality that one can lose studying in an isolated area, far from home and friends. To break the excitement (and monotony) of field-work, I took infrequent breaks from Marengdom; on one such trip, I nearly froze and starved to death eating small, white potatoes with Eric Waddell in the Enga Highlands. After his sojourn with the Enga, Waddell would write *The Mound Builders* (1972), spend almost 20 years in Canada and, as did Clarke, take the position of Professor of Geography at USP.

After a year in the field, I returned to Hawaii and began the task of analysing the data that I had collected. The late Prem Prasad was a fellow graduate student in geography at the University of Hawai'i and on educational leave from USP. Prasad would later become chair on his return to USP in 1971. In 1974 I took a teaching position at Bucknell University, a small liberal arts institution in Pennsylvania which proved physically and mentally too cold and too remote for someone from the Pacific Islands. Too few students and faculty understood the tropics and the interaction between people and place, and the Pacific was too far from their cultural and economic universe. The focus of their attention was, typically, the urban centres of the U.S. East Coast, Europe and, to a lesser extent, South America and Africa. As an enchanting vacation spot, the Pacific Islands were too far west of Miami and the Bahamas. They felt that the Pacific had too few people and cities and too little economic dynamism to be of geographical consequence. (As I write this, I am mindful of the recession in the United States and the prominent role that the Pacific (Rim) countries are expected to have in the forthcoming 'Pacific Century'.) It did not help matters that the only other geographer there had little comprehension of the world west of the Mississippi River. Despite these shortcomings, I completed my doctorate in 1976. In the late spring of 1979, however, I responded to an advertisement announcing a lecturer's position in geography at USP which appeared in, of all places, the *New York Times.* To my good fortune, USP responded positively to my application.

June 1979-November 1985

Although I had previous field experience in Papua New Guinea and other parts of the South Pacific prior to 1979, and was born and raised in Hawaii, I was not mentally prepared for living in 'the real Pacific'. Perhaps this lack of preparation was due to my perceptions of field research as distinct from employment. As a geographer, one was expected to endure the hardships of field-work for which the reward would be a more comfortable working/living environment sometime later. In 1967 and 1972, Mareng in Papua New Guinea, was an extremely difficult and isolated field-work site: it was a day's walk from the nearest airstrip; I battled malaria three times; supermarkets, flush toilets and electricity were unknown there; and I could count the number of English language speakers on one hand. Perhaps my understanding of the 'real Pacific' was coloured by the fact that Hawaii touted itself as the 'hub' of the Pacific, as far as U.S. military-strategic and economic interests were concerned and as a bridge to Asia and the rest of the Pacific. Didn't Hawaii have the East-West Center for Technical and Cultural Interchange, a Center for Pacific Islands Studies, and internationally renowned faculty at the University of Hawai'i? Nevertheless, the concerns of life in Hawaii were far removed from the realities of life in the South Pacific. Those of the mainland United States were even further removed.

I arrived in Fiji about the middle of June 1979, two to three weeks after the USP semester had started, uncertain as to what I was to teach, what the university and its faculty was like, and still wondering why I had taken the position there.

These uncertainties and fears were quickly dispelled, as grinning from ear to ear, and dressed in his best shorts and zories (some things never change), Randy Thaman met me at Nausori Airport. We recognized each other as kindred geographers even though we had not previously met. On the drive from Nausori to Laucala Bay and during the weeks that followed, Thaman explained the role and mission of USP and geography's place in the university. He kept on saying that he now had someone with whom he could "talk" geography. In 1979 the Department of Geography and SSED were housed in a large, rambling, wooden, hot and humid, former cafeteria building. The focus of SSED was "oriented particularly towards a critical understanding of the development process and its implications" (USP, 1984: 162) for the Pacific Islands through its preliminary, foundation and degree programmes. The SSED degree programmes provided courses for students who had specific vocational aspirations, and a more liberal arts education "as a background to a wide range of employment" (USP, 1984: 163). Structurally and functionally, USP in 1979 was a far cry from the hallowed, ivy-covered, red brick walls of private, liberal arts colleges on one hand, and open admissions universities in the United States (including Hawai'i) on the other, where a tertiary education was either expected or, in other cases, more or less taken for granted. At USP, education which served national and regional interests was paramount and was reflected mainly by the quality and commitment of the students and staff. Admission to USP was selective and highly competitive as most countries of the region were economically disadvantaged.

I remember many other things about my first day on campus, even though I had arrived on a 'red eye' flight from Hawaii the night before. David Jones, as Head of Geography, invited me home to a lunch consisting mainly of fishbone soup. More important, geography was a prominent and well-respected discipline in the school, the university, and the region. It had five active and committed scholars, unlike my previous position where two geographers were surrounded by three hostile geologists. Perhaps, of all the things that I remember best was the polyglot of languages spoken on campus, and, while English was the standard language of instruction and discourse, it was a second or third language for most students and some faculty. By contrast, I was fluent only in one.

The years flowed by, and I took root...and learned much. Geography at USP, in particular its faculty and students, and the practice of geography in the region, taught me three important lessons.

First, geography in the Pacific is very much a living, human oriented discipline, particularly in the area of human interactions with environment, or what some people generally refer to as cultural ecology. During my first semester there, I was assigned the task of teaching the first-year course in cultural geography. Although I was not overwhelmed by the material, having taken undergraduate courses in that area, it was a challenge as most of my training had been in physical geography. My task was made easier because of the tremendous support that Randy Thaman and the other faculty gave me. Randy took it upon himself to school me into the philosophy of education at USP and its concerns as well as those of the Pacific Islands, perhaps because of mutual interests in traditional subsistence systems. It became apparent to me that a very human oriented approach to geographical education and geography as a discipline was necessary as a significant proportion of our students came from the villages, remote islands, and more rural parts of the Pacific and perhaps understood the relevance of the traditional ways of doing things and the importance of the environment to their being. Even students from the urbanized parts of the islands had relatives in the countryside and had a closer affinity with the natural environment than most of us schooled in the West. Most, if not all students had a deep sense of their traditional cultures, which they were very willing to share.

The second lesson follows from the first. It is a reinforcement of the importance and value of many traditional methods of resource use and management which I learned first from study in the Mareng some 20 years ago. Basically, the Mareng and many peoples in the Pacific have developed, and still to a large extent practise, fairly conservative systems of resource use and management. I am not arguing for the mythic, Rousseauian ideal of man living in harmony with his environment, as there are many examples of their environmental mismanagement. Unfortunately, many of these environmentally sensitive methods of resource exploitation and human adaptation to environment are being abandoned or replaced by more modernized, yet perhaps non-sustainable ways of doing things. Put another way, the many *pasin bilong tumbuna* (traditional ways of doing things) have been labelled as primitive and old-fashioned, to be discarded in favour of *pasin bilong white man.* What is unfortunate is that this belief is part of the ideology of many Pacific Islanders, and for which there is little scientific basis. For example, the ecologically sound practice of forest fallowing in slash and burn agricultural systems is giving way to less sustainable annual and multi-cropping systems, often in response to population and other socio-economic pressures.

Of course, there are other reasons for change. For example, the literature indicates that on many atolls of Micronesia, the systems of pit taro cultivation are being abandoned because of depopulation, damage and destruction of the pits during World War II, damage to gardens by pigs, and changing aspirations. The depopulation of the atolls because of migration to more urban centres in the Pacific and elsewhere will likewise affect the viability of these systems. I think that the loss of these adaptive ways of subsistence, while inevitable, will mean a world of lessened diversity and that too, I think, will be a loss. I also find it ironic that many western trained scientists are now re-examining sustainable, traditional systems of subsistence of the Pacific and elsewhere in the tropics for application in the developed world (see Clarke, this volume).

The third lesson of my USP experiences centres on the question of who should be the beneficiaries of our teaching, research and service activities. For me, USP and the South Pacific region created a professionally very advantageous, exciting, yet humbling experience. Too often, because of our levels of academic achievement, the salaries and the deference that people pay us, we develop a 'big headedness' or a heightened sense of self. We become too self-important, and we forget that we are transients in service to the countries of the region. Our research, for example, is often conducted for the purpose of enhancing our professional careers and, although this is a necessity at USP, given that tenure does not exist, such research may not best serve the immediate interests of the region and its peoples. I am not arguing that such research not be done, but that we are the servants of the university region and its peoples. Often we pay too little attention to the people and place in which we work; our focus is often too egocentric. We analyse their systems for application in our own worlds, and often without any thought of just compensation. I have often thought about these questions, particularly on field trips with students to a village or the rural countryside, where traditional customs and values dictate that visitors be accorded a hospitality that often cannot, or is not, fully or even partly reciprocated.

Post-USP

I left USP near the end of 1985 in order to take a position in the College of Arts and Sciences at the University of Guam. From here I continue to study the patterns and processes of human interaction with their physical environment. Much of my recent work has focused on the systems of subsistence and resource management of Micronesia, in particular atoll

Micronesia, where the conditions for living are extremely harsh. Yet people do live there, and they have developed sustainable systems of resource use, well adapted to their island environments. What is striking is the lack of basic and applied geographical research on the subject, particularly by geographers.

In part, this lack of interest, hence information, can be traced to the restrictive policies of the U.S. Navy between 1945 and 1963. During this period people wishing to travel between Micronesia and the rest of the world needed security clearance from the U.S. naval authorities.

Between 1900 and 1945, Micronesia's environments and cultures were intensively studied by German and Japanese scientists. The ethnographies compiled by the Germans during this period contain a wealth of information, but too many of the cultures have undergone significant changes, while others face extinction. Some very basic physical and cultural geographical facts about these islands are also in doubt as they have not been systematically studied. In 1989, for example, I described a kind of taro islet agriculture practised on Puluwat Atoll (see Plate 8.1). Previous studies had indicated only 46 vascular plant species for the atoll; I recorded 184 species (Manner & Mallon, 1989).

I can readily understand why the Puluwatese may not want to inform the world of what seems to be a very sustainable system of agriculture, but I am somewhat puzzled as to why this system of resource management has escaped recognition by western trained scientists. Given the isolation and difficulty of reaching the atoll, I can easily understand the large difference in the number of plant species. For example, my time and research activities on Puluwat Atoll resulted from the fact that I was stranded there for five weeks. My companion, Dr. Mary Spencer, and I had gone there by tuna boat belonging to the neighbouring island of Tamatam in order to supervise a Puluwatese student, Ermel Mallon, on a summer research project. We were to stay on the atoll for four days, but unbeknownst to us, relationships between the Puluwatese and their atoll neighbours were strained and led to the extended stay there. To make a long story short, the Puluwatese were loath for us to leave, especially on a Tamatam boat, and they convinced us to extend our stay on the atoll. We did so because our Puluwatese hosts said that the inter-island ship would arrive there the following week. One week became five. I practise patience, learned which of the six to eight ways of preparing breadfruit were constipative, which plants were used to relieve constipation, and came to the conclusion that Puluwat Atoll in 1989 was even more isolated than Mareng, Papua New Guinea in 1972.

Plate 8.1. *Maa* (taro islet) from Puluwat Atoll. *Maa* are formed in freshwater depressions to grow taro (*Colocasia esculenta* and *Cyrtosperma chamissonis*), sugar-cane, vegetables and ornamentals. The islets are formed with entirely organic materials.

Plate 8.2. World War II landing barge used for the hydroponic cultivation of taro (*Colocasia esculenta*) on Ulithi Atoll, Yap State, Federated States of Micronesia. As salt-water inundation of taro swamps is a problem on many atolls, the landing barge is a useful adaptation for an otherwise solid waste problem. Ulithi Atoll was a major U.S. staging area during World War II.

If the research results from the Puluwatese study are any indication, I am sure that much remains to be found on the other atolls and islands of Micronesia as Pacific Islanders are keen at experimenting. An illustration of their ingenuity in adapting to harsh environments and making use of material resources is shown in Plate 8.2 from Ulithi Atoll in Yap State, Federated States of Micronesia.

As the major institution of higher education in the western Pacific, the UOG has a mission not unlike that of the USP. Stated simply, the UOG is charged with providing higher education for the people of Guam and the Western Pacific Island communities through its teaching, research and service activities. It has:

1. Undergraduate programs that build upon the Western Pacific's unique and varied cultural traditions and offer career opportunities, together with a fundamental arts education;
2. Research and graduate programs that are responsive to the specific needs of Guam and other Western Pacific island communities and contribute to their economic growth and stability; and,
3. Community service programs that promote intercultural interaction, societal development, and personal improvement (UOG, 1990: 3).

Unlike the USP, where research and service are high priority activities, the same has not been true of the UOG. For example, an unstated condition of my hire at UOG was that I would serve as a model of a teaching faculty who did research because research productivity in the College of Arts and Sciences was low. Second, the average teaching load per faculty member in the college was four courses per semester. Third, there was a physical and, to some extent a perceptual, distinction between the research faculty, housed mainly in the research institutes, and the teaching faculty. Fourth, the University Research Council's budget for faculty generated research projects was US$10,000, limited to individual grants up to $1,500, and hardly used. (At USP, the budget was $50,000, and there was eager competition.) The situation has changed considerably since 1986. Many older faculty have retired and academics with a commitment to research and regional service have replaced them. Today, the University Research Council's budget has increased to $20,000 per annum (at USP, it is now $70,000). The College of Arts and Sciences now has a procedure for faculty assignments for research and service. Faculty granted a research or service assignment teach fewer than four courses per semester.

Despite the UOG's regional mission, the relatively low cost of tuition, the (albeit, now lessened) availability of student grants, loans, and work-study programmes, the Republic of the Marshall Islands has joined the more expensive USP and the Federated States of Micronesia is sending some of its scholarship students there. These developments suggest that the UOG has not offered the full range of programmes requested by all the islands of Micronesia. Indeed, unlike USP, UOG does not offer certificate and diploma programs; its liberal arts curriculum is comparable to that found in other U.S. small to mid-sized universities, but with regional and cultural course substitutions where applicable. The UOG response to the above defects has led to some soul searching but little else.

It is debatable whether or not the development of certificate and diploma programmes and a more regionally applicable curriculum will attract more students from the other islands of Micronesia. First, such developments would increase the financial stress on currently existing programmes at UOG and result in less effectiveness and a decline in the quality of offerings. Second, the number of students attracted to such programmes may be insufficient to be more economically viable. Of approximately 3,000 on-campus students, 11% are from the other islands of Micronesia (not Guam). Third, Micronesian student preparation for university courses is extremely poor. More than 75% of Micronesian students are admitted to the UOG with English proficiency skills of seventh grade or less. To rectify this inadequacy, such students often spend three years in remedial English programmes before qualifying for entry into degree courses. Less than 25% of all students initially enrolled in the remedial English programmes pass to take the required first-year course in English. The fourth reason is associated with the political agreements between the United States and the nation-states in Micronesia. As a result of the Compact of Free Association between the United States and the Federated States of Micronesia (FSM), and that between the United States and the Republic of the Marshall Islands, citizens of those states now can freely migrate to the United States and its possessions. Prior to the signing of these agreements, migration was mainly for temporary reasons, such as education. An estimated 6,000 citizens of the Federated States of Micronesia now reside on Guam as a consequence of the compacts. Fifth, and a consequence of the compacts, federal grants for education to the Federated States of Micronesia were drastically reduced, and the Federated States of Micronesia unintentionally failed to secure Pell grants, the major source of Micronesian student study awards.

The results of these actions are twofold. First, with less funding to the education departments of the Federated States of Micronesia, students will graduate from secondary schools with even less preparation for university work. Second, their opportunities for grants, scholarships and other funds for university education will be even more limited.

The above summary is symptomatic of a much larger problem of neglect and underdevelopment in Micronesia. Although much of Micronesia was a trusteeship (created by the United Nations) of the United States for approximately 50 years, some authors have generously suggested that this "American Lake" in the Pacific is an example of benign neglect. Others have suggested that Micronesia exemplifies the worst-case scenario of institutionalizing dependency through the provision of poorly planned social welfare programs and less than adequate socio-economic development projects.In almost all respects, the Federated States of Micronesia, Palau, and the Marshall Islands are developing countries. An idea of the magnitude of the problem can be seen in Table 8.1 which lists some demographic and socio-economic data for the Pacific Islands. The problems of development and growth in Micronesia are not unlike that of the rest of the South Pacific.

Except for Nauru, all countries in the South Pacific have a negative trade balance. This is a result of the cost differentials between the export of limited quantities of relatively low valued natural resources and the importation of more costly basic and manufactured goods. For the Federated States of Micronesia, the ratio of imports to exports in 1989 was 10.3:1 or US$72,724,000 to US$7,065,000 (The National Planner, 1991) which was partly offset by U.S. aid and grants, and remittances from abroad. Although pelagic fish exports, particularly of tuna, may offset trade imbalances, the opportunities for a more diversified economy are limited and such development has been hindered by a lack of supporting infrastructure (for example, inadequate transport and storage facilities), capital, technology, distance from metropolitan markets, changing socio-economic aspirations, fluctuations and vagaries of the world market, and disruption and destruction during World War II, to name a few. When coupled with the high rates of population growth (for example, 4.2% in the Marshall Islands and 2.9% in the Federated States of Micronesia), one can only imagine even greater pressure on limited natural resources and poorly developed social-economic infrastructure in the future. As the development plan for the Federated States of Micronesia suggests, population growth "even at an overall rate of less than 1% per year, will place severe strains on the nation" (The National Planner, 1991: 42), and make it difficult to transform the Federated States of Micronesia from what has been described as "a largely consumption-

Table 8.1. Some Socio-economic characteristics of the South Pacific region

Country	Land Area (km²)	1990 Mid-year Est. Pop.	1990 Pop. Density	Annual Growth Rate (%)	Gross Domestic Product (A$ '000)	Per Capita (A$)	1989 Year (A$'000)	1989 Exports (A$'000)	1989 Imports (A$'000)	Balance	Chief Exports
A. Samoa	200	46800	234	3.6	260417	6663	1985	384371	472396	(88025)	Fish and other sea foods
CNMI	471	44200	94	8.9	355972	11558	1985	163093	392151	(229058)	Clothing
Cooks	237	16900	71	-0.2	65053	3943	1987	3535	55362	(51827)	Fruit & juices, copra, pearl shells
FSM	701	101200	144	4.0*	117044	1372	1983	----	----	----	Fish, coconut prod., pepper, handicrafts
Fiji	18272	725000	40	1.9	1580870	2181	1990	544463	759784	(215321)	Sugar, coconut oil, gold, timber
Fr. Poly.	3521	196300	56	2.7	3875976	19745	1990	110840	985634	(874786)	Coconut oil, cultured pearls, vanilla
Guam	541	133400	247	2.2	1513369	12334	1986	----	----	----	Re-exports, fish
Kiribati	690	71800	104	2.3	44930	654	1988	6435	28596	(22161)	Copra, fish, seaweed
Marshalls	181	46200	255	4.2	52682	1514	1984	----	----	----	Coconut products, fish, handicrafts
Nauru	21	9300	443	2.3	----	----	----	101052	17564	83488	Phosphate
New Cale.	19103	167600	9	2.0	2641153	16354	1988	837634	952774	(115140)	Nickel, coffee
Niue	259	2500	10	-5.3	4347	1553	1984	67	----	----	Copra, fruit, vegetables, sorting goods
Palau	488	15200	31	2.3	----	----	----	----	----	----	Fish, trochus shells, handicrafts
PNG	462243	3528500	8	1.6	4853623	1376	1990	1773434	1853129	(79695)	Minerals, wood, coffee, timber
Pitcairn	5	100	20	0.0	----	----	----	----	----	----	Stamps & coins, handicrafts
Solomons	27556	324000	12	3.7	222153	725	1988	96319	145768	(49449)	Fish, timber, copra, shells, palm oil
Tokelau	10	1800	180	1.5	----	----	----	----	----	----	Copra, handicrafts
Tonga	747	96300	129	0.5	119800	1256	1988	----	----	----	Coconut oil, spices, fruit
Tuvalu	26	10200	392	4.1	7595	767	1989	----	5170	(5170)	Copra, cinematographic film
Vanuatu	12190	146400	12	2.4	183899	1283	1989	28798	88562	(59764)	Copra, beef, cocoa, timber
Wallis/Futuna	255	13700	54	1.3	----	----	----	----	----	----	Trochus shells (1981)
W. Samoa	2935	157700	54	0.1	147767	939	1987	16015	96487	(80472)	Copra, wood, cocoa, taro, beverages

* According to the *Second National Development Plan 1992-1996* of the Federated States of Micronesia, the growth rate is listed as 2.9% 1973-1985/89. All data in this table are taken from SPC, 1992.

Abbreviations: $A = Australian; ---- = Not available; Est. = estimated; Pop. = population.

Sources: Anon., 1991c; SPC, 1992; Douglas & Douglas, 1987.

driven economy into a production-based economy" (Bank of Hawaii, 1989:9).

One response to the above problems and changing Micronesian social-economic aspirations has been internal and external migration--internal migration from outer islands and rural villages to rapidly developing urban cores in Micronesia, and emigration to the United States and its territories. In some cases, this rural to urban and outer- to inner-island migration has created less than desirable socio-economic-health situations in the urban areas of Micronesia. For example, Ebeye Islet in the Marshall Islands, which serves as a residence for the civilian Marshallese work force at nearby Kwajalein Atoll, has a population density of 22,956 people per square kilometre (Office of Planning and Statistics, 1990), and all the attendant social and public health problems that accompany such overcrowding. The more than 6,000 citizens of the Federated States of Micronesia and the Marshall Islands who have migrated to Guam for reasons of work and other opportunities have strained the Territory's social welfare, health and educational infrastructure. Little is known of the effects such migration has had on the cultural ecologies of depopulated home islands and atolls, and unfortunately, too few will care.

I write these seemingly random thoughts and facts on Micronesia to suggest that the problems of geographical inquiry in "American" Micronesia are not too dissimilar from those of the rest of the South Pacific. Yet, in contrast to the USP region where geographers have been in the forefront of research and service, much remains to be done here. There are a few constraints which I am trying to overcome. For one, at the UOG, geography is an under-represented and, most likely, a misunderstood field of study. Until first semester 1993 I was the only geographer in the College of Arts and Sciences, my predecessor having been transferred to the Micronesian Area Research Centre. Through my efforts, a second geographer has been hired, and plans for a geography major are in the early stages of development. I hope that this addition will increase the discipline's visibility throughout the university campus and, through research and service, address the problems of social, economic, and environmental change in Micronesia. I now have someone with whom I can talk Geography.

Conclusion

Because of the lessons and experiences gained at USP, my study and practice of geography became a living, human-oriented discipline. Many of my efforts in service and research are aimed to serve regional interests, although they are still based in appropriate, although less important, theoretical frameworks. I think that my work today has more direct application to meeting the realities of island life and the pressures and impacts of socio-economic change. Even more important, people are more than a biotic component in a system. They have faces, they have names, and, more often than not, their systems of subsistence work because of their understanding of ecological processes, concepts, and consequences, while we in the more modernized world find difficulty living with these same concepts. Perhaps everyone needs a Mareng or a Puluwat experience (or a South Pacific or Micronesia experience), to realize that some things (never) change.

Chapter 9

Pioneering Geography at the University of the South Pacific: Personal Reminiscences

Geography helped me appreciate difference. It made me more sensitive towards those who think and act differently from me and to appreciate places different from those with which I am familiar. Geography also provided me with the tools needed to analyse and evaluate the natural world. My own cultural traditions taught me the interconnectedness and dynamism of time and place. Such knowledge is context specific; geography provided me with a larger picture – a global perspective. Geography is both challenging and humanizing.

Konai Helu Thaman

Some years after I left the University of the South Pacific, I encountered a former student who was spending a semester at the East-West Center in Honolulu. When she reminded me that she had taken my Man and Environment course, I asked her if she got anything from it. Her reply was, "Yes, one thing – there is no such thing as a free lunch".

John Bigay

I arrived in Suva in January 1970. The university had been established some two years earlier though, as I found, it did not begin functioning fully with an array of degree courses until 1970. Everything was new, everything was beginning. The campus had no purpose-built buildings; all were either converted or unconverted remnants of the old New Zealand Air Force base. We made do. I recall lecturing in a hut with holes in its floor and having to place a table so as to avoid an unintended disappearance. When Queen Elizabeth came to present the university with its charter, the only building able to house the ceremony was the old sea plane hangar inhabited by the School of Natural Resources and mynah birds. To scare away the latter, explosive charges were detonated and so protected the assembly from unwanted contributions to the ceremony. The humid heat of the hangar was considered another problem. An ingenious young architect suggested cutting a hole in the hangar wall, placing a pile of ice in it and blowing the cooled air over the regal dais with a fan. It worked, and I shall never forget walking encumbered in academic robes in a procession past the Tip Top ice-cream van as it unloaded the ice.

Our resources were meagre in the extreme. The map collection was almost non-existent. I wrote to as many national map agencies around the world as I could contact. The replies were interesting. I recall a characteristically elegant response from Paris. The French sent a set of beautiful maps of one area at all the scales they produced. The Canadians were the most generous allowing me to select a sizeable sample of large-scale maps representative of Canada. The Indian Survey with the Indian penchant for bureaucracy (a relic of the British raj) did not reply for months. When a letter arrived (with a reference six digits long), it told me my request had been passed to another department. However, a gift of maps did arrive eventually, and I was duly grateful. The Japanese did not reply.

The shortage of books which affected all disciplines was a more serious problem. The Inter-University Council in London made me a grant of 500 pounds sterling to buy geography books for the university library. From New Zealand, the university received a large consignment of tea chests filled with second-hand books. Many of the university staff joined in the sorting of university level books from those more suitable for schools. Though many books were battered, this gift was much appreciated both in the university and in the schools of Fiji. The book and journal shortage remained. I remember serving on the finance committee when several of us took the Vice-Chancellor to task for having spent more on mowing the campus grass than on books.

A major problem was the shortage of staff for, although student numbers were small, a coverage of specialities was essential if teaching at university level was to be offered and significant research carried out. New Zealand, in particular, did much to help in this respect as qualified indigenous staff were too few to fill the need at this stage and the governments of the region's developing countries had equally urgent needs for local qualified people. Geography lost the services of one of the few Fijian PhDs, when Dr. Isireli Lasaqa, a man whom I regarded most highly and who had first taught geography in the university, entered the highest ranks of government service when Fiji became independent in the latter part of 1970.

The newness of the university and its small size meant that I, as a senior member of the academic staff and with experience of setting up a university in West Africa, found myself much involved in university administration and planning. I served on numerous committees and chaired several of them. I played a major part in the design of the committee structure, was involved in the incorporation of the theological college within the university and served as a member of the University Council. Together with staff and students, I produced a code of conduct designed for a multi-racial residential university, a code agreed by students and administered by them. Geography and geographers were making a contribution to the wider functioning of the university in its early years.

The involvement of academic staff had to be wide-ranging and total. This commitment was a more essential part of the creation of a new university than the erection of new buildings however much they may be appreciated today. The university was new born. It had no tradition, yet a tradition could not be a ready-made manufactured one. It had to grow from the circumstances of the university, the people of the region and the university's role in the region. The contribution of academics to the emergence of the tradition and reputation of the University of the South Pacific was to maintain standards of scholarship at an international level and to participate in the affairs of the region. The university could not remain aloof.

As a geographer, I was called upon to serve outside the confines of the campus essentially as an economic adviser to the government of Fiji. I recall advising on the question of the nationalization of the gold mining industry and upon matters arising from proposed prices and incomes policy. The experience which I found the most demanding yet the most satisfying was my service as a member of the 3-man Board of Inquiry set up to assess the impact of the dock strike of 1971 on the country's economic development plans. Subsequently, I took part in seminars of employers and trade union leaders which were designed to improve industrial relations in Fiji. As a geographer, I was therefore privileged to participate not only in the affairs of the university at the highest level but also in issues important to Fiji as a newly independent country. Of course, I was not alone in this; for example, several of us on the university staff participated in a course designed to prepare the senior civil servants for the tasks they would perform in the administration of independent Fiji. USP has a major part to play in the developing nations of the South Pacific which it serves provided that it listens as well as speaks.

Not all at USP was sweetness and light in the early 1970s. Universities are notorious for their internal schisms as their many prima donnas give voice, and USP was no exception. It is perhaps an essential part of the process of forging custom and practice. Even academics mellow. USP was and is a real place.

The memories which survive reflect my enormous affection for Fiji and its peoples. Recollections of the beauty of the country still move me almost to tears. The warmth and friendship of the students I knew remains unforgotten. Fiji will be with me always.

Edward Simpson

I believe that geography has never been more relevant to our region. Current global and regional concerns about the environment and development dictate that future generations of Pacific Islanders return and rediscover the holistic world views of their ancestors and the interconnectedness of physical and cultural phenomena which they understood and used to guide the way they lived and related to their environments.

Konai Helu Thaman

Chapter 10

International Aid in the Pacific: What Is in It for Us?

Lionel Gibson

Development Assistance in the Pacific Islands

The last quarter century has seen the aid process in the Pacific undergo a number of interesting and important changes. This era has seen the development of formal aid programmes in the Pacific by official donors (both bilateral and multilateral) as well as by voluntary organizations. Commensurate with these changes has been the development of an aid donor bureaucracy with all the associated administrative and political paraphernalia.

At the recipient end of the equation the last quarter century has seen the expansion of Pacific Island governments, a process which has often been partly or virtually completely funded by development assistance (Nauru is the notable exception). In attempts supposedly to realize their development objectives, Pacific Island governments have relied heavily on aid monies, particularly for capital expenditure. At the level of non-governmental organizations too, there is evidence of increases in aid spending, particularly by agencies which have begun to mirror closely their governmental and intergovernmental counterparts.

Aid levels in the Pacific now stand at amounts which, in some cases, some commentators consider to border on the absurd. On average, Pacific Islanders now receive the equivalent in aid of more than A$1,000 each per year. Although the U.S. and French dependencies receive inordinately large amounts of development assistance, they no longer head the list of aid recipients. This dubious honour goes to Niue and Tokelau with per capita aid receipts standing at around A$4,000 (SPC, 1993). Gone forever into the realms of Pacific legend is the romantic image of "subsistence affluence". Indeed, one could be excused for wondering how Pacific societies ever survived before the advent of development assistance.

This paper presents a brief review of official development assistance in the Pacific Islands in the context of both aid theory and the aid process in the international arena. This paper considers some of the more important questions surrounding development assistance, indeed development itself. Particular attention is paid to the result of the aid process on the majority of Pacific Islanders and their lack of participation in the development assistance process.

Setting the Stage: the Beginning of the End

The aid process is a comparatively recent arrival on the world stage. The first official development assistance programme was the much heralded Marshall Plan initiated by the United States in 1948. The programme for the reconstruction of Europe was in some ways a unique occurrence. In other ways, this plan was to set the stage for a performance that not only continues, but now stretches from Eastern Europe to the most isolated parts of the Pacific Islands.

The Marshall Plan was unique in three ways other than simply being the first programme of its kind: it was a resounding success; it finished ahead of schedule; and it was completed under budget. In 1947 the architects of the Plan had envisaged that the reconstruction process should take four years and should cost no more than US$17 billion. Incredibly, by 1951, Europe's overall production was up 37% from its 1947 level; steel production doubled between 1947 and 1951; inflation was under control; progress was alive and well in Europe and North America. The plan was brought to a successful conclusion nine months ahead of schedule at a cost of US$13 billion. One would have to search long and hard today to find an aid project which displays all of these qualities.

Despite its apparent uniqueness, the Marshall Plan heralded the beginning of a global process and an almost ubiquitous development ideology. It was here that the motivations for, and the aims of, aid donation were articulated in all their ambiguity (in the case of the former) and paradoxically, in all their clarity (in the case of the latter). General George Marshall could say on the eve of the reconstruction of Europe:

> Our policy is directed...against hunger, poverty, desperation and chaos. Its purpose should be the revival of a working economy in the world so as to permit the emergence of political and social conditions in which free institutions can exist (Hunger Project, 1985: 217).

Although having an obvious humanitarian element, political motives – preventing the spread of communism – were uppermost in the minds of the architects of the Marshall Plan. More than this, though, the notion of humanity was one that saw development within the narrow strictures of economic growth and modernization. This concept of development has shown an incredible resilience in the face of a rather poor track record and despite the constant parade of new development fashions.

On 20 January 1949 President Harry Truman announced the United States' "bold new programme for making the benefits of our scientific advances and industrial progress available for the improvement and growth of underdeveloped areas" (Esteva, 1992: 6). If this signalled the birth of the development era (and some would say of the Third World itself), the Marshall Plan had, two years earlier, created the mechanism by which this new development was to be funded and implemented and had pre-empted the motives and objectives of this world-wide programme.

The birth of official development assistance in 1947 in Europe initiated the aid process throughout the Third World. Asia, Latin America, Africa and the Pacific Islands have all become more or less dependent on aid for the provision of not only funding, but also direction for their various development efforts. Unlike Europe, however, these development efforts have not been as successful in the Third World. The rewards of development in the South have proved to be a rather cruel and distorted reflection of not only what had earlier occurred in Europe and North America, but also of the hopes of development practitioners in donor and recipient countries. One cannot help but be reminded of the rather harsh words of Frantz Fanon: "From Paris, from London, from Amsterdam we would utter the words 'Parthenon! Brotherhood!' and somewhere in Africa or Asia lips would open '...thenon!...therhood!' It was the golden age" (Fanon, 1961:7).

The development assistance process, whether in the Pacific Islands or elsewhere in the Third World, has retained its concern for development as defined largely outside the real life experiences of those who live on the periphery. Whilst development assistance theory has changed in the post-war period and whilst the aid debate has raged incessantly, the views of the majority of those actually within the Third World (not merely near or concerned with it) have rarely, if ever, been seriously taken into account.

Aid Theory in the Pacific: Going Around in Circles

In terms of how development commentators have viewed aid in the Pacific, the region has behaved like a microcosm of the rest of the Third World. The prevalent views of aid held by donors and recipients alike have changed almost in symmetry with changes that have taken place at the international level.

The periods immediately prior to and following independence saw aid being regarded as a tool to generate economic growth to modernize Pacific economies and cultures. Consequently, aid programmes tended to concentrate on infrastructural projects and those designed to increase production and productivity in rural areas. Although not on the same scale, the Pacific went through its own form of a green revolution with technical and financial solutions being sought for development problems that involved an intricate web of physical and human interactions.

The second stage of post-independence thinking witnessed a modification in the 'aid for economic growth' doctrine. Both recipients and donors during this period spoke of the need to concentrate on the quality rather than the quantity of growth.

This heralded the period that has variously been called 'growth plus redistribution', 'growth with equity' or 'growth with social justice'. Official commentators stressed the importance of reducing inequalities between social groups as well as between regions. Aid, it was felt, should play an integral part in this process.

The third phase of development thinking evolved from general disillusionment with economic growth models, whether they were dressed up in redistribution rhetoric or not. During this period mainstream development thought began to be infiltrated with views which had hitherto existed only on the periphery of development theory. Ideas of bottom-up development or development from below as well as concerns for appropriate and intermediate technology began to be served on the development table.

Coupled with these, and with the support of large aid donor agencies – such as the World Bank – came policies which aimed to reduce poverty and inequality (particularly in rural areas) rather than to increase production and wealth. Needless to say these policies, in the hands of the large aid donors, neatly avoided sensitive political and social issues, such as land reform, land tenure and social structure, preferring to concentrate on poverty targetting, training and credit access to disadvantaged groups on the periphery of Pacific societies.

The last few years have witnessed a dramatic swing in development theory and policy. No more do we hear cries of rural development for peripheral groups. No more is there concern to fund projects which try to reduce poverty and inequality at regional or social levels. We live now with a development paradigm which stresses growth, but growth with a difference. Economic planners on both sides of the aid equation (the givers and the takers) are pressing for industrial export-led growth in economies which respond to the market: economies, in other words, which encourage competition at both intra-national and international levels. The general feeling is that the Pacific must now face some hard truths about the world economy of which it is an inextricable part. The best way to do this, it is believed, is to increase efficiencies of local institutions and processes through the avenue of competition. 'Structural adjustment' is the current buzzword on the lips of donors and recipients alike. If countries of the region improve efficiency by allowing their economies to become more responsive to the demands of the market, then development will take place. Development is here seen as necessarily requiring economic (export-led) growth on the old assumption that a bigger cake means more to share. It is assumed that the mysterious market mechanism will ensure that the fruits of development will be distributed equitably.

The Aid Debate: Much Ado About Nothing

The long-standing debate between proponents and opponents of the aid process has gone hand in hand with the ebb and flow of aid theory. The debate has often acted as the ideological market place where representatives of particular points of view have attempted to sell their wares. In this arena, careers have been made, passions have been aroused, arguments have been strident. In this arena, the voices representing the views of the majority of Third Worlders have been largely silent.

The aid debate consists basically of proponents and opponents of the development assistance process. Proponents of development assistance tend to be people involved in the process in official capacities: members of international donor organizations as well as recipient government personnel see aid as an essential component of development. This avenue, they argue, fills the necessary gaps in Third World economies. The savings, foreign exchange and technology voids are bridged by aid flows allowing economic development to progress unabated (Todaro, 1989).

Opponents of the process abound, and they come from both sides of the political spectrum. From the far Right, aid is held to be ineffective as a means of promoting economic growth or of ensuring democracy or freedom. Aid is seen as "merely a system of gifts" which is "more nearly akin to doles than to subsidies" (Bauer, 1976: 96). Official development assistance, this group argues, is wasted in the sense that it supports the consumptive and military needs of authoritarian states rather than the productive (private) sectors of recipient economies.

Commentators from the Left allege that aid reinforces patterns of dependence, perpetuates neo-colonial relations and exploits in that it is intrinsically designed to benefit the ruling classes in aid-giving and aid-receiving nations. Development assistance is therefore viewed rather sceptically as a form of imperialism (Hayter & Watson, 1985) or as "a sophisticated instrument of control" (Weissman, 1974: 11). One of the more ardent yet articulate statements from this school of thought neatly summarizes its stance thus: "...foreign assistance fails to help the poor because it is of necessity based on one fundamental fallacy: that aid can reach the powerless even though channelled through the powerful" (Lappe et al., 1980: 10).

Juxtaposed to, and often indistiguishable from, these more ideological concerns is the argument concerning the motives behind aid donation. This debate is often conceptualized in terms of a dichotomy between the cynical and the credulous. Cynics see the motives behind aid donation as being self-interested, being driven by reasons of economic gain, political compliance or benign international behaviour. More optimistic and usually 'official' commentators argue that aid stems from humanitarian concern that donor institutions have for the fate of their fellow humans. The political or economic spin-offs of the aid process, it is believed, are incidental, not core determinants of development assistance.

The debate on motives, as well established as it is, does, when reduced to first principles, seem rather redundant. To focus, as the debate has done, on why aid is given is to beg the more critical questions. One should really ask questions about the results of the process regardless of whether the motives are pure or pragmatic. Does official development assistance lead in some way to development for the recipients or not? One commentator has noted:

> It is certainly true that rich countries' motives are mixed, and that foreign policy and export interests play their part. One would be amazed if it were otherwise....The question surely is not whether the aid givers' motives are entirely pure, but whether in any given situation, the combination of interests at work will promote trends which are advantageous or disadvantageous to those whom the critical observer would like to see benefited (White, 1974: 21).

Development: Finding Meaning in the Meaningless

It is often said that there are as many definitions of development as people in the field. This, along with the looseness with which the term is often used, are primary contributors to the rather amorphous nature of the term. It is difficult to disagree with cynics who regard development in the same way as truth: the more one delves into its meaning, the closer one gets to discovering that, at its very core, there is simply a vacuum. Despite the twin problems of the lack of clarity and the multitude of connotations, it is here argued that development as an end (as opposed to a means) does have certain characteristics that people, whether they be from the Left or Right of the political spectrum, can agree on.

Rostow and Marx, it could be argued, would probably have agreed that the end of the development process should be to make people happy. This may sound trite, but behind the stages of growth and stages of history models lay a belief that somewhere at the end of everything lay Utopia, whether capitalist or communist, a place where people had dignity, a place where they felt good about themselves, a place, to paraphrase one commentator, where people could eat, enjoy material prosperity (however defined), relate to others and think continually about their existence (Tuan, 1989).

Development, if it aims to enable people to enjoy the good life, must surely involve the recipients of the process themselves in defining the limits of the process and in constructing a new paradigm which belongs not in Washington or New York, but to the recipients whether they be in an isolated coastal village or in an overcrowded squatter settlement.

Aid and Development in the Pacific: One Step Forward, Two Steps Back

Whatever one's belief concerning why aid donation takes place, the result of aid is, to say the least, less than impressive. Of course, there is evidence (usually physical) of the fruits of development assistance. Most of the main highways in the Pacific Islands, many hospitals, schools, power plants, indeed the University of the South Pacific itself, are testimony to the munificence of the aid process. Yet, physical infrastructure does not constitute development in any meaningful sense, particularly when these amenities are not available to all sections of the community.

Even within the confines of neo-classical economics, the aid record is poor. Development assistance has not been able to generate self-sustaining growth (with or without redistribution). The fact that aid levels show no sign of falling is an indication of the lack of economic self-sustainability. Furthermore, trade deficits (usually with the largest bilateral aid donors) are on the increase throughout the region. Even Fiji, New Caledonia and French Polynesia, three of the more sophisticated economies, have trade deficits of about A$250 million, A$500 million and A$1 billion respectively (SPC, 1993).

Trade figures would be even more grim if many Pacific Island countries did not have the luxury of preferential trade agreements which have given them access and guaranteed them prices which they would not have otherwise received under conditions of open competition. It is significant that in the euphoria of structural adjustment (no longer is it called austerity programming), Pacific Island governments are in danger of allowing the removal of what is now considered to be a bastion of the dreaded disease called protectionism. Exports from the region may soon have to take their chances alongside other Third World (particularly Asian) goods for access to Pacific Rim markets.

Economic growth, too, has been rather erratic, to say the least, in the islands. As producers of mainly low value, high bulk primary products for export, Pacific economies have been able to secure only a small share of the enormous growth in world trade. Market expansion in primary goods has proved limited, particularly in comparison with the exponential growth in demand for manufactured goods. When this structural problem is coupled with unpredictable weather conditions and a disappointing growth in tourism, the roots of economic stagnation become apparent.

One does not have to look very far to uncover evidence that aid is simply not moving the Pacific towards realizing the 'good life'. Materially, although 'scientific' evidence is lacking, information strongly suggests that Pacific Islanders are experiencing declining living standards and a resulting increase in poverty, however it is defined (Bryant, 1993). Community safety nets that existed as poverty buffers prior to the development era no longer function efficiently. It is a wicked irony to see development workers from outside the region teaching Pacific Islanders the benefits of community care.

The list of societal ills in the Pacific is virtually endless. Urbanization has fuelled urban unemployment, which has exacerbated urban poverty. Informal sectors throughout the urban Pacific have mushroomed. It is perhaps just as well that they have for, as elsewhere in the Third World, they are proving invaluable to the continued survival of urban systems. Urban housing authorities have proved incapable of coping with increased demands.

To this somewhat dire recipe could be added the breakdown of social controls, the trading of Pacific culture for a surreal version of popular western culture, the increase in violent crime, a general decline in the standard of health of Pacific Islanders and the alarming rate of environmental degradation. 'Paradise' has not only been postponed but it is in grave danger of perishing altogether beneath the weight of the development process.

Aid and Development as the Problem: Modernization and Monoliths

It would be rash to suggest that the ills of Pacific Islands development are solely results of the development assistance process. Nonetheless, aid has acted at the cutting edge of development theory and policy. Aid has provided the financial and practical thrust of the development effort throughout the region. More than this, development assistance has performed an important ideological function. 'Growth', 'growth with redistribution' and now 'industrial-led free-market growth' are more than merely economic catchwords. They carry with them a whole set of values which have been neatly described by Keyfitz as "the middle-class style". This consists of:

> ...cooled homes equipped with television sets and refrigerators, transport by automobile and procurement of foodstuffs and other supplies in self-service supermarkets. It is found most typically in cities with paved streets....The press and other media have...local, national and worldwide politics; urban crime; and other problems like the cost of living to arouse its mass public....there is a worldwide middle-class – right down to such matters as when to eat one's three meals, the way to set a table for dinner, what to do on workdays and how to spend one's weekend (Keyfitz, 1982: 651).

These values, along with the substantive development assistance, have precipitated the development problems that now confront the Pacific.

Development thinking, of which development assistance is an inextricable part, has also been at the forefront of development problems. Despite the shifts in development priorities, one important thing has remained the same. With each turn came a single answer. When economic growth did not work well, then growth plus redistribution was the panacea. If the last 25 years of maldevelopment have taught the Pacific any lessons, perhaps one of the more important ones is that monolithic solutions and complex problems are mutually exclusive.

Ways Forward: off with the Blinkers and off the High Horses

Whatever our politcal biases, if development is to make people genuinely happy by providing for their material and non-material needs, we have to recognize that the process (in this context, the aid process) must be multi-faceted. Complex problems require imaginative and sophisticated solutions. The University of the South Pacific has an important role to play in all of this. It is an institution that has an enormous breadth of disciplines and of contacts with the islands. It is therefore in a unique position to be a leader in interdisciplinary development work. True welfare is much too important to be left in the hands of economists. People's feelings and dignity cannot be neatly held as constants to maintain equilibrium in economic theory. It is to the discipline's great credit that the Department of Geography at this university has been engaged in interdisciplinary work for some considerable time.

The answers to the region's development problems will not be found solely within the university. People must participate. Not just the well-educated or the rich and powerful, but the most marginalized members as well. For those so-called backward elements, simply by the act of being on the periphery, they may be in a better position to contribute to what must be a consultative and composite way forward.

Academics, used to being the impulses of change, will have to learn the art of listening. Although, schooled in all the methods of rigorous and logical analysis, they may also need to learn to dream. Berger is right when he says that we need to bring together the attitudes of hard-nosed analysis and the utopian imagination in a new paradigm based on the precept of hard-nosed utopianism (Berger, 1976). Perhaps then, and only then, will we be able to move towards a Pacific in which aid contributes to a process that satisfies ordinary peoples' material needs yet also gives them the dignity and freedom to question and change the conditions of their existence.

Chapter 11

What Future Pacific Cities? The Challenge in Managing Urban Environments

Jenny J. Bryant-Tokalau

Introduction

> ...home grown pollution has spiralled. A number of lagoons, especially in Micronesia, have become no-go zones where swimming, washing and even canoeing is barred by health inspectors until rehabilitation programmes can be put in place. The Port Moresby public water supply, when it is available, is no longer safe for drinking. Population and space pressures have lead to ever shorter crop rotations on smaller islands....Land degradation is thus common, with top soil washing down rivers and into the sea" (Callick, 1993: 6)

This scenario, taken from population projections in the first part of the Pacific 2010 project (Cole, 1993) highlights growing concern about the future of Pacific nations. The doomsday scenario outlined by Callick is a generation away--but it is not very far in the future if such issues as population growth, environmental degradation, land distribution and tenure and employment opportunities are not urgently addressed. Unsafe drinking water supplies, polluted lagoons and massive loss of top soil are current realities in the Pacific.

This paper explores the future of Pacific urban areas. Although the Pacific has been referred to as "a sea of islands" (Hau'ofa, 1993), upon those islands is a growing concentration of populations in urban areas which are, in some cases, microcosms of towns and cities in the higher population centres of Asia. Although Pacific populations are small, the speeds at which they are growing and the densities in relation to land area should be of considerable concern. Of particular concern in this paper is the environmental degradation which accompanies urban growth. In the majority of developing countries, around 35% of the population lacks access to adequate sanitation. Most developing cities lack environmental infrastructure and services, such as water supply, sanitation and solid waste disposal. Degradation of soil, fresh water, coastal and land-based food supplies and the deterioration of housing and other services are common. In all cases, the poor are most affected by this deterioration. In the Pacific, the impacts of urban growth, although on a smaller scale, are very similar to those throughout the Third World. For example, in Kiribati, only 44% of the population has access to safe water; in Papua New Guinea, 43% lack access to adequate sanitation (Table 11.1; Bakker, 1990; Bryant, 1993; SPREP, 1992a; Ward, 1993).

Table 11.1. Access to water and sanitation in the urban Pacific.

Country	Access to safe water %	Access to sanitation %
Fiji	69	91
Kiribati	44	99
Papua New Guinea	25	57
Solomon Islands	--	73
Tonga	99	88
Vanuatu	61	87
Western Samoa	69	99

Access means percentage of total population served.
Source: World Bank, 1990.

Cities are stimulating places and the centres of education, discourse, government and many other activities in which all societies wish to participate. The problems arise when urban centres place excessive demands on their environments and population (Hardoy et al., 1992). Good planning and recognition of the relationships among the human inhabitants, their well-being and the physical environment are what should be causing reassessment of the nature of Pacific urban areas, not a halt to their very existence. Urban centres, whether within the Pacific countries or on the Pacific rim in Australia, New Zealand or the United States, are now a fact of life and influence most Pacific Islanders.

Pacific Urbanization

In 1984 geographer John Connell stated that it is no longer possible to regard Pacific Islanders as solely rural people. Connell's evidence for this statement was based on the fact that in the 1980s only in Melanesia and the smallest states were less than one quarter of the population living in urban areas, and in five countries more than 50% of the population was urban. By the early 1990s only Papua New Guinea, Solomon Islands, Vanuatu, Western Samoa and Niue had less than 25% of their population living in urban areas, and seven countries were more than 50% urban (Table 11.2). In addition, Solomon Islands will have 26% of its population living in urban areas by the year 2006 (McMurray, 1993b: 103), and Papua New Guinea will have 33% urban by 2005, based on current urban growth rates (McMurray, 1993a: 63).

Projections for Vanuatu are lower as fertility in Port Vila is assumed to be less than in rural areas (Arif, 1993), presumably because the urban population is exhibiting increasing permanence (Connell & Lea, 1993). Arif's estimate gives Port Vila's growth rate as 1.4% per year (Arif, 1993: 89); others place it at 4.5% or even higher (SPREP, 1992a: 268, quoting World Bank social indicators, and Bule, 1990). If the South Pacific Regional Environment Programme (SPREP) and Bule are correct, Vanuatu will also be more than 25% urbanized by the turn of the century.

The other two nations with lower proportions of the population urbanized, Western Samoa and Niue, both exhibit high rates of emigration with the majority of their populations living overseas, largely in urban areas. Having said that, however, the definition of urbanization, and the recently changing economic circumstances in Western Samoa in particular (with the establishment of factories employing large numbers of women) make the calculation of the urban population difficult as it is obviously changing rapidly. Indeed, some projections place Western Samoa's urban population at 25.5% by the year 2000 (United Nations, 1991). Where to draw the urban boundary there is a matter of much debate because of the land tenure system and the fact that urban migration is placing a great deal of pressure on the traditional villages which are part of Apia, the capital (Jessop-Tuimaleali'ifano, 1990; Thomas, 1987). It is possible that with return migration, particularly from New Zealand with its increasing unemployment levels, notably amongst Maori and Pacific Islanders, pressure on Apia will increase as returnees seek work in the urban area.

Despite the fact that definitions of what is urban or rural are problematic in the Pacific (Bryant, 1993; Chapman, 1991), there is no doubt that the numbers of people and areas of land affected by urban growth and its functions are growing. The situation of Melanesia is outlined above.

Table 11.2. Urbanization in the Pacific

Country	Main urban centre	Total population urbanized	Average urban growth rate P.A.%
American Samoa	Pagopago	40	1.6
Cook Islands	Avarua	27	-2.8
Fiji	Suva	43.4	2.4
Fr. Polynesia	Papeete	59	2.9
Fed. States of Micronesia	Kolonia	26	2.6
Guam	Agaña	91	2.1
Kiribati	S. Tarawa	35.5	3.2
Marshall Is.	Majuro	66	3.4
Nauru	Nauru	100	1.4
New Caledonia	Noumea	80	4.1
Niue	Alofi	21	-0.7
No. Marianas	Saipan	94	3.2
Palau	Koror	68	-0.06
Papua New Guinea	Port Moresby	15.5	4.4
Solomon Is.	Honiara	20.3	5.3
Tonga	Nuku'alofa	30	2.1
Tuvalu	Funafuti	43	9.1
Vanuatu	Port Vila	22.7	4.5
Western Samoa	Apia	21	0.9

Sources: Bakker, 1990; Bedford, 1987; Connell & Lea, 1993; King, 1992

Elsewhere in the Pacific, the number of those for whom urban living has become a way of life is growing. In Fiji for example, in 1986, 39.4% of the population was urban. By 1990 that figure had reached 43% (SPREP, 1992a). In other small island countries, such as Kiribati, Tuvalu and the Marshall Islands, the proportion of the population urbanized is particularly significant, not only because of the limited land areas involved, but also because of the annual urban growth rate and the pressure on the physical and human environments.

The variety of island types in the Pacific makes generalization impossible about the current state - and future of - the urban areas. Isolated, low lying, densely settled atolls with few natural resources contrast with urban centres surrounded by large hinterlands with access to agriculture, mining and other major income earning opportunities, and with a web of communication and transport networks which keep them constantly in touch with the Pacific Rim. The presence of resources, however, does not mean full realization of development goals, nor necessarily a high degree of urbanization. In such countries as Papua New Guinea and Solomon Islands levels of urbanization remain low. Fiji, on the other hand, has realized a great deal of its potential; but then its location and historical circumstances have assisted in taking advantage of options. For many Pacific countries development options are thought to be few (Ward, 1993).

The impacts of migration, such as that from outer islands to centres and that from interiors to coasts, include pressure on land ownership and access, the breakdown and challenging of traditional patterns of behaviour and major political upheavals. These are likely to continue, particularly with higher levels of education and the alienation of people from their land, overcrowding of housing, greater competition for education and health care, and deterioration in basic services provision. Despite government schemes for repatriating people to rural areas, not everyone has a rural village or settlement to which to return; so, the issues facing urban settlements will continue to grow. Urban poverty is becoming increasingly obvious. Several studies have been undertaken in recent years which demonstrate that the urban areas of the South Pacific are manifesting life-styles which were unheard of as recently as 20 years ago (Barr, 1990; Bryant, 1992a, 1993; Connell, 1984; Slatter, 1991).

Although it is possible to be too negative about the Pacific future, to the extent that academic observers are in danger of perpetuating a mood of hopelessness (Hau'ofa, 1993), it is also vital that people recognize the trends occurring in Pacific cities. Unchecked, the urban areas, whether large or small, are in danger of manifesting low living standards from which the majority wish to escape. This paper examines the environmental degradation occurring in Pacific urban areas and outlines some possible management strategies.

The State of Pacific Urban Environments

The environmental problems facing densely settled urban areas in the Pacific have been partially documented (e.g. Bryant, 1992b, 1993; Connell, 1984; Reti, 1990). Some areas are characterized by overcrowded, substandard and often informal housing, a concentration in diseases related to poor and unsanitary living conditions, such as respiratory illnesses, tuberculosis, cholera and other gastro-intestinal complaints, polluted water supply and the ever-present difficulty of human waste disposal, particularly on low-lying atolls. Urban growth also has an impact on the availability of land for market gardening, the supply of wood for fuel (where available at all) and the question of how and where to dispose of rubbish, both industrial and household.

Other issues becoming more obvious in urban areas are those of traffic emissions in several cities, industrial effluents, and the impacts of construction activities on shorelines, therefore on lagoons, reefs, shellfish and water supplies. These problems tend to affect poorer urban dwellers more than the wealthier groups, because their settlements are normally located on marginal land close to industries or rubbish dumps. Most recently, knowledge of the possible consequences of global warming and subsequent sea-level rise has meant that Pacific Island governments are now paying very close attention to a whole range of environmental issues. The impact of sea-level rise, if it occurs at all, will be gradual; nevertheless, it may be particularly grave for low-lying coral atolls. Not only could this mean that settlements may have to be moved to higher land (if that is possible), but also it could lead to the development of a class of 'environmental refugees' which will have significant consequences for urban centres in the Pacific and Pacific Rim countries.

Throughout the Pacific, there is further evidence of environmental degradation in urban areas. In South Tarawa, Kiribati, for example, a shortage of sanitary facilities and overcrowded housing are leading to pollution of the ground-water lens which provides fresh water. Coastal erosion has increased, partly due to the construction of causeways built to link islands on atolls (Sullivan & Gibson, 1990). Outbreaks of ciguatera (fish poisoning) have also been linked to physical changes to habitats. The fact that there was no ciguatera on some atolls but there were heavy outbreaks after causeway construction is circumstantial evidence of the impacts of such alterations on marine environments and human health (Carpenter & Maragos, 1989).

Major Areas of Concern

The crucial areas of urban environmental degradation relate to water supply, waste disposal (household and solid as well as industrial and haz-

ardous), land use, and the impacts of all of these on human populations. The small coastal land areas on which most Pacific urban areas are built are coming under increasing strain.

Water supply and waste disposal

The nature of the atoll countries, with limited or no ground-water reserves and their dependency on marine and limited terrestrial resources, makes them very vulnerable to the problems of waste disposal. Toxic and hazardous wastes are particular issues in industrializing countries, but the disposal of solid and liquid wastes, especially domestic garbage and human excreta, causes the greatest problem. As urbanization increases in the Pacific, the pollution of ground water is likely to increase as well. South Tarawa and Funafuti provide two examples of severe pollution from inadequate disposal of human waste, leading to outbreaks of cholera and other gastro-intestinal diseases. Ground-water pollution and the contamination of shellfish by micro-organisms from excrement cause a range of health problems including skin and eye disorders, as well as gastro-intestinal illnesses.

For example, on the island of Kosrae, Federated States of Micronesia, 87% of the drinking water supply is piped from streams and considered to be unsafe. In addition, 70% of houses have poor drainage. In Pohnpei, 9% of houses have no toilets but share with others. Where there are sewerage systems, they are poorly constructed and there are leaks into the water supply (UNICEF, 1991). In Tuvalu, the septic tank designs were found to be inappropriate to local conditions. With rising sea levels, coral atolls and limestone islands will face a rise in the water table, thus surface flooding which will make certain methods of waste disposal inappropriate and unhealthy.

The disposal of waste is a problem in all urban centres. In Suva septic tank effluents cannot percolate properly as much of the area is underlain by marl, or soapstone. The high annual rainfall of around 3,000 millimetres (mm) and low evaporation (around 1,300mm) causes frequent saturation which prevents oxygen penetration. This means that the septic tanks work slowly and inefficiently. Therefore, seepage of sewage waste into Suva's water bodies is widespread (Chape & Watling, 1992).

Sewerage systems are expensive and in countries where earnings are low and overall budgets are stretched and are partly dependent upon foreign aid, the provision of sewerage treatment plants is not a high priority. If a community cannot afford to construct a sewerage plant, then it is unlikely that it can afford to operate and maintain one (Carew-Reid, 1989). This must surely call into question the wisdom of aid money being spent purely on the provision of such plants. Waste disposal has an obvious impact on human health. Although people in most Pacific countries appear to be well nourished and healthy, the increasing incidences of cholera and other gastro-intestinal diseases are major cause for concern with faecal coniform levels exceeding World Health Organization (WHO) recommended levels contributing to outbreaks of cholera, typhoid and hepatitis.

Solid and industrial waste disposal

Solid waste disposal is also a problem in urban areas. Kolonia, Pohnpei, for example, has no organized garbage collection, forcing residents to dispose of rubbish in their backyards or privately haul it to a dumping site. Problems of diarrhoea, parasites and other infections are rife (UNICEF, 1991). Garbage collection services which do exist in Pacific towns do not serve the entire urban population, notably fringe and squatter settlements. The people living in these settlements generally burn their rubbish (thereby creating air pollution and fire hazards) or dump it on the roadside or into the sea. Recycling and waste reduction programmes are very limited.

Organic wastes are also by-products of manufacturing in the Pacific. Most countries have food and beverage factories; some have fish canneries, sugar mills and sawmills. As pointed out by Carew-Reid (1989), the amount of organic waste discharged by these factories can equal or exceed that amount of human waste produced in a town. The long-term impacts of such wastes are not fully understood, but it is certain that, depending on the concentration of the effluent, they will affect nearshore marine organisms and human health. Such wastes use a great deal of the oxygen naturally occurring in the water, causing stress to other organisms (Holthus, 1990).

A great deal of solid waste must be disposed of in urban areas. Packaging—especially cans, glass and plastic bags—is visible evidence of the lack of recycling in most parts of the Pacific. The main exception is some former American territories where aluminium cans are either shipped overseas for recycling or used for reef building. The dangers of solid waste are everywhere evident. The thousands of plastic bags on Suva beaches alone have not only spoiled what was an attractive environment for tourists, but also are known to strangle sea creatures on which depends the livelihood of many urban poor.

On high islands of the Pacific, many waste disposal sites are located in valleys, near coastal waters and streams. Some marine organisms are sensitive to chemical pollutants even at low concentrations. Surveys have shown that trace compounds in landfill gases, for example, include very volatile and harmful organic compounds, such as vinyl chloride, benzene and methylene (Stone, 1990). The common method of burning or incineration of waste causes further problems of atmospheric pollution which is not only irritating but also dangerous. Land shortage is a major problem for most islands, but particularly for atolls. As a result, dump sites are frequently located in flood prone areas or on highly porous soils, leading to easy contamination of ground water (Ogawa, 1990).

Other Major Problems

Issues of atmospheric and underground nuclear testing, industrial wastes, including heavy metals, as well as atmospheric, land and water pollution in its various forms, have been discussed in detail elsewhere (Bryant, 1993). There is potential for extremely severe contamination and nutrient overloading of water courses and coastal waters by a number of industrial wastes, as well as the outputs of major resource extraction activities such as mining. Urban centres also face new hazards from major fires, particularly in towns where fire prevention services are ill-equipped.

Human Settlements, Congestion and Environmental Problems

Increasing urbanization in the Pacific is undoubtedly leading to congestion of human settlements and of transport routes, as more private vehicles run on the limited number of roads. The environmental consequences include contamination of water supply, lack of access to sanitation, atmospheric pollution from vehicle emissions and the consequent health problems for urban dwellers, particularly for the poor. Respiratory illnesses, gastro-intestinal complaints, and child malnutrition are all increasing in Pacific cities.

For example, 20% of Fiji's urban families live in a single room. It is estimated that more than 25% of Vanuatu's urban population lives in slum or squatter camps. In some areas of Port Vila there are population densities of over 19,000 persons per square kilometre (km^2) (Bule, 1990), and the municipal rubbish dump is already saturated and causing contamination of shellfish (Vanuatu Government, 1991). Apia has major problems of drainage and water supply; as a result, gastrointestinal diseases and skin conditions have noticeably increased (Western Samoan Government, 1991).

In Fiji where 43% of the population lives in urban areas, it is estimated that, because of the current shortage, the urban housing stock will have to increase by 19,000 units in the next 15 years to provide for even a modest population growth. The current pressure on land is obviously placing a strain on urban infrastructure and causing problems, such as bush and mangrove clearing as the poor search for firewood, with obvious consequences for soil erosion and species loss.

Sixty-six per cent of the Marshall Islands' entire population now lives in the two urban centres of Majuro and Ebeye. The density of Ebeye is reputed to be one of the highest in the world at 22,956 per km^2. The Majuro Atoll density is 2,025 per km^2, but in the Delap-Uliga-Djarrit area it is 11,090 per km^2 (SPREP, 1992b). The pressures of life under such densities have been documented by a number of researchers as well as by the Republic of the Marshall Islands. They include problems of communicable diseases, high infant mortality, increasing marginalization of women, nutritional problems and severe unemployment (Connell, 1984; Republic of the Marshall Islands, 1990).

The Marshall Islands exhibits perhaps the most devastating results of overcrowded living conditions and the impacts for the population in Pacific urban areas. Despite a per capita health expenditure of US$115, the fertility rate of 244 live births per 1,000 per year is the highest in the Pacific. The total fertility rate is 7.23 (among the highest in the world) meaning that the average woman will have more than 7 children during her life. The crude annual birth rate is 49.2 children per 1,000 (only 9 African countries exceed this rate). The Infant Mortality Rate (IMR) of 63 per 1,000 live births is among the highest in the Pacific (Kiribati is higher). Worse is the IMR for mothers aged 15 to 19, of 106 per 1,000 live births. Thirty per cent of the urban population over 15 years has diabetes, and more than 11% of children are under weight. One third of all deaths are of children under the age of 5; these are largely due to respiratory infections, gastrointestinal illnesses and malnutrition (Republic of the Marshall Islands, 1990).

Environmental degradation and human health and productivity

Most analyses of the state of health of urban populations, as related to environmental degradation have been carried out by public health departments, although until recently few countries recognized the inextricable links between environmental degradation and human productivity. Some major studies in the region have been concerned with changing patterns of nutrition of urban people and the impacts on child and maternal health in particular (Thaman, 1988b). The recent series of reports by the United Nations Children's Fund (UNICEF) on the situation of children and women in the Pacific Islands has highlighted the major problems faced by urbanizing people, as diets change, gardening land is lost, water supplies become stressed and contaminated, and sewage systems are inadequate. The issues of rising unemployment and the competition for land are adding to the stresses of urban life.

As demonstrated by the case of Marshall Islands, there is no doubt about the interconnectedness of health, population, and the environment of urban habitats in the Pacific. The diseases most prevalent are those related to living conditions--gastrointestinal, respiratory, and mosquito-borne infections; nutritional diseases; and communicable diseases, such as cholera and tuberculosis. Overcrowded living conditions and lack of adequate services and infrastructure contribute to these issues of environmental health, thus towards the ability of affected populations to participate fully in education, employment and other aspects of development (Robertson, 1988).

The provision of clean water and sanitation are fundamental to improved urban health and productivity, yet a significant proportion of urban dwellers are living in marginal locations with inadequate garbage disposal, fresh water and sanitation (Table 11.1). Although the figures indicate that Pacific urban dwellers are on the whole well served by water and sanitation, the evidence of contagious illness presented here and in the 1991 UNICEF reports demonstrates that conditions for urban dwellers are declining.

Responses to Urban Environmental Degradation: Sustainable Development?

If cities cannot provide the basic needs for a growing proportion of the population and face deteriorating environments, then they are clearly not 'sustainable'. The use of resources and the contamination of water supplies cannot continue unabated. Urban areas, therefore entire countries and the Pacific region, are about to face some extremely serious and explosive situations. The role of the inhabitants as participants in the urban environment and in trying to deal with the increasing stresses is crucial to the future of the cities of the Pacific.

Urban environments are not yet viewed as a major priority in the region, with countries until recently being heavily dependent on natural resources of the forests, mines and oceans. The 1992 United Nations Conference on Environment and Development (UNCED), with its stress on the interdependence of poverty and the environment, as well as recent studies by the Economic and Social Commission for Asia and the Pacific (ESCAP) (Bryant, 1992a,b), UNICEF and the United Nations Development Programme (UNDP) are changing their emphasis however. Organizations, such as SPREP, have also expressed some concern at the deteriorating urban environments. Yet, their perspective has been largely an 'ecologically sustainable' one, with minimal regard for human development and planning aspects. The SPREP Convention, with its stress on pollution and dumping and the concern expressed by most Pacific countries over waste disposal, has meant that SPREP, in its environmental monitoring and research, is increasingly involved with urban environmental assessment, particularly the problems brought about by industrialization and the dumping and leaking of toxic chemicals and heavy metals.

Part of the response to environmental deterioration has been via legislation. Throughout the Pacific, many laws, promulgated some years ago, may today be regarded as environmental but which suffer from lack of enforcement through inadequate staffing, inadequate penalties when they are enforced and lack of technical resources and funding (Chape & Watling, 1991). Legislating against poor environments is only one response to the broader problem. The laws frequently lack teeth and do not address the underlying causes.

Rather than placing the entire emphasis on legislation and central government control, it is important both to ascertain just who and what are the main agents in urban environmental degradation and to develop a strategy for involving them in approaching problems in a unified manner. There are, on one hand, the local populations who must live and work in their immediate environments, placing pressure in terms of waste disposal (both solid and human) and on the water supply and sanitation systems. On the other hand, there is the desire for greater economic development, encouraged from within and from outside the Pacific, in the form of industrialization and particularly manufacturing.

To address both issues, far better and more culturally acceptable environmental education needs to be carried out. Environmental education will be ineffective unless skilled personnel available in relevant departments monitor and assess the environmental changes taking place and if responsibility and management are not clearly defined.

In the modern Pacific urban area, pressures to find employment, thus cash incomes, are great, especially in the current period of economic downturn. The restructuring of island economies to ones which are more manufacturing and export based inevitably causes great stress on island environments. The need for cash can result in accepting developments which may be environmentally very risky (such as the disposal of toxic waste). The desire for foreign investment and the establishment of tax-free zones can lead to countries turning a blind eye to unacceptable practices. Environmental management and planning is a much broader task which needs to involve communities, good local government, private enterprise and governmental and non-governmental bodies.

The Challenge of Dealing with Urban Environmental Degradation

The Pacific has a multiplicity of ways in which it can deal with the complex issues of urban environmental degradation. In some ways, it is better placed than other regions because of the existence of regional bodies, such as the South Pacific Commission, the South Pacific Forum, the South Pacific Regional Environment Programme and the University of the South Pacific, to name a few. These bodies can provide strength and unified sharing of knowledge to the communities which are daily involved in managing urban areas.

Regional organizations are in much the same situation as international aid donors when dealing with urban environmental issues. They can make suggestions, provide expertise and funding, but, unless the local community feels that it has some say over its own local environment, little of note can be achieved. Strong local councils working with both the private sector and community groups representative of their electorate have been shown in many places to be the only effective way of dealing with local environmental issues.

The Role of Non-governmental and Community-based Organizations

Community-based organizations are common in the Pacific, ranging from environmental action and education groups to church and women's organizations and the more formal, business-associated bodies. Many of these have recently become involved in environmental work, carrying out clean-up campaigns, providing volunteers for villages and overcrowded settlements to assist in improvement of the local environments.

Most non-governmental organizations (NGOs) in the Pacific have concentrated their efforts on rural environments – deforestation, coastal erosion and the reduction of biodiversity being of major concern. Some are increasingly recognizing the importance of deteriorating urban environments, particularly those aspects which affect the urban poor.

The South Pacific Action Committee for Human Ecology and the Environment (SPACHEE), which was established and run by staff of USP's Department of Geography for some years, is a regional NGO which provides environmental educational materials to community groups and individuals. Under a United Nations Volunteers scheme, SPACHEE has recently launched a project for the urban poor where volunteers will work with squatter communities and urban villages to improve their access to water supply, housing and sanitation. SPACHEE produces and distributes regular newsletters and news alerts; it is publishing pamphlets in local languages designed to educate the public about basic environmental matters.

In the Melanesian countries, the environmental message is presented in the culturally appropriate medium of theatre such as through the Wan Smalbeg group from Vanuatu. Drama groups in some countries visit villages, schools and meetings, giving performances on environmental issues. The Vanuatu National Council of Women, along with other similar councils throughout the Pacific, is also promoting environmental care. Although most of the activities are oriented towards the degradation of the rural environments, there is increasing attention being given to urban areas.

There is a danger in depending too heavily on community based organizations to solve the problems of urban areas, particularly those problems which most affect the poor, or marginalized groups. A sad but true fact is that "in the absence of resources, most governments do not need convincing that they should do less; they will do less anyway" (Gilbert, 1992: 436).

Conclusion: A Pacific Urban Future?

In the Pacific, as elsewhere in the developing world, resources for the provision and maintenance of basic services and infrastructure in urban areas are becoming increasingly difficult to find. Although our cities and towns may be some way from the 'urban chaos' alluded to in the management of many large cities elsewhere, the poorer sections of Pacific urban populations in particular are lagging behind in access to decent housing, water, sanitation and basic health standards (Bryant, 1993; Connell & Lea, 1993).

Pacific countries are increasingly looking towards privatization to solve many of their economic problems. The bottom line of the private sector, however, is that catering adequately for the poor is difficult as they offer few economic returns. Therefore, environmental degradation, an increase in anti-social behaviour, the marginalization of groups, especially women, children and youth, will continue. If the Pacific is to avoid the 'chaos' faced by other parts of the world, then urban growth and its implications need to be firmly on the agenda of regional and national meetings. More important, long-range planning, and commitment to avoiding a future which could include massive outbreaks of disease and difficult social change, must be made.

A serious assessment of urban management practices needs to be undertaken. Basic issues, such as those outlined by the United Nations, should be taken just as seriously in smaller urban areas as in large. Improved municipal waste collection, sound waste treatment and disposal practices, some co-ordination of waste management via both government and the private sector, and the involvement of all sections of the community in the management and planning of urban areas are all fundamental to the future of Pacific cities and towns (UNDP, 1990).

Towns are certainly not the only future for all Pacific peoples, and governments are seeking ways to encourage people to remain or become more committed to their rural heritage. Towns will never disappear altogether. How to make them more healthy and less likely to marginalize increasing numbers of peoples remains the fundamental question. Ward's recent conclusion that Pacific Islanders may "choose material prosperity elsewhere, rather than accept an image of paradise or a form of aid-dependent pauperism within their home islands" (Ward, 1993: 19) is a possible future scenario for the Pacific, just as Callick's vision quoted earlier may also come to pass. The most important point to remember, however, is that many Pacific Islanders will never have the option to migrate from the region. For those people, Pacific governments, regional organizations and community groups have responsibility to face the stress upon our towns and to recognize that cities are resources needing careful management. Further, they must act rapidly. Otherwise, the human resources of Pacific nations, as expressed through people's ability to produce, consume and 'develop' will be inhibited.

Chapter 12

The Proposed Namosi Copper Mine (Fiji) in the Context of Regional Mining Practice

Frank McShane

Dedication: To my father, Frank McShane Senior

Introduction

Pacific environments, economies and societies are increasingly being asked to assimilate new initiatives as part of the demands of economic development of the Pacific region. Such development often involves alliances between private venture capital and Pacific Island governments to exploit natural renewable and non-renewable resources in order to fuel economic growth. One type of development where such liaisons are essential is in the exploitation of minerals through large-scale mining. Such developments require massive financial and technological input that is beyond the resources of most Pacific Island countries. The scale and speed of change demanded of the environment, the economy and the society of Pacific Islands by the introduction of large-scale mining are always spectacular and often overwhelming.

There is continuing and heated debate concerning the benefits of large-scale mining on Pacific high islands versus its environmental and social costs (see, for example, Emberson-Bain, 1992). Many of the conflicts associated with large-scale mining in Melanesia are linked primarily to environmental issues (Grynberg & Nouairi, 1988), particularly loss of resources, disturbance of the land and the ensuing social disruption.

Fiji could now stand on the threshold of a new era with a proposal to develop a mine in the remote Namosi Province on the main island of Viti Levu. At the time of writing, the project has reached the pre-feasibility stage. This review considers the proposal through reflection on the *Draft Environmental Inception Report* prepared by Natural Systems Research (1992), the environmental consultants to the mining company, particularly

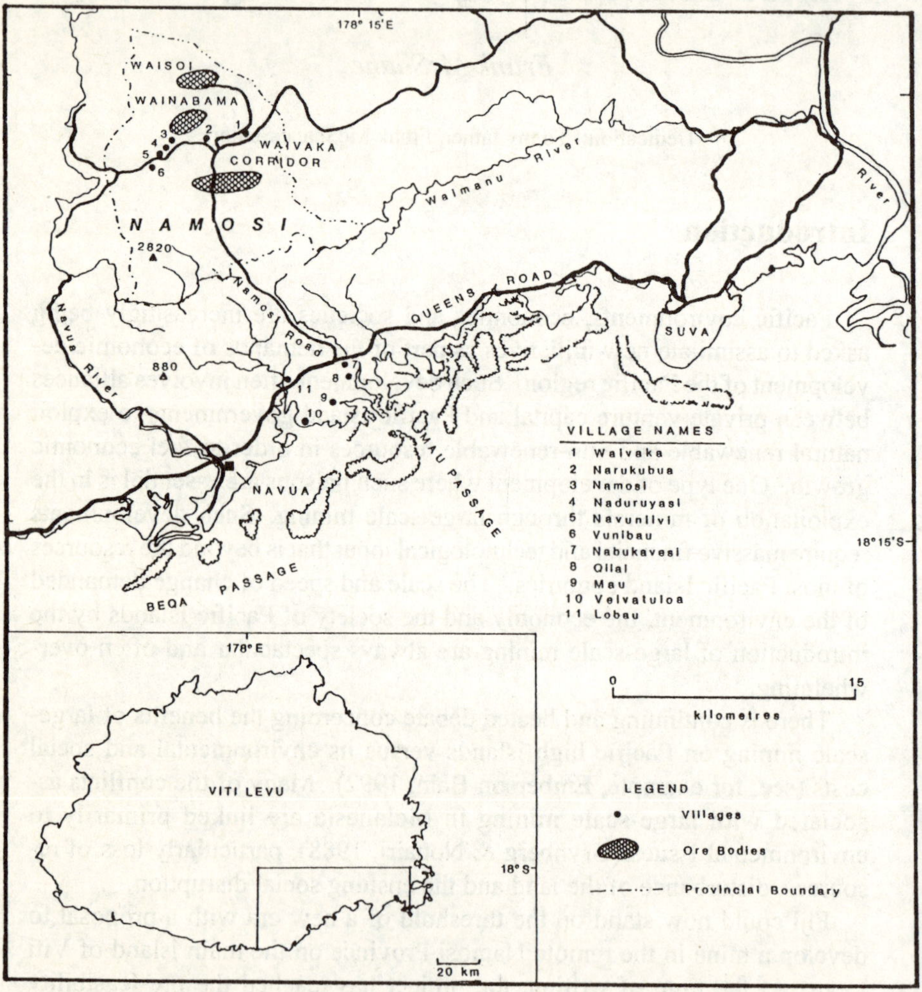

Figure 12.1. Namosi Province, showing the main ore bodies and nearby settlements. Inset shows the location of the main map within Viti Levu.

in the light of the wider debate surrounding open-cast mining on Pacific high islands.

Namosi Province

Namosi Province is located on the south-east side of the high volcanic island of Viti Levu in Fiji, sandwiched between Naitasiri and Rewa provinces to the east and Serua Province to the west, with its most southern extremity abutting the coast (Figure 12.1). The area rises to over 1,000 metres (m) in the Korobasabasaga Range. The interior of Namosi is a steep, densely wooded area of *Agathis vitiensis* (*dakua*) forest, the true botanical diversity of which has not been fully recorded (Watling & Chape, 1992).

The tropical maritime climate and south-east trade winds bring an average annual rainfall in excess of 4,000 millimetres (mm) to the Namosi area, most of which falls between December and April. Much of its interior is classified as steepland (with slopes of greater than 18°) and is particularly prone to landslides. The region is also in an area that is susceptible to other natural hazards including earthquakes and tropical cyclones.

South from the interior of Namosi, forest gradually gives way to intermediate montane vegetation, coastal mangroves and marshes, lagoons and offshore reefs. The coastal strip is characterized by developments associated with tourism. In the area behind the coastal strip, utilized land is devoted largely to the production of staples, such as taro, cassava and breadfruit; fruits, such as banana, papaya, pineapples, oranges and coconut; and *yaqona* (kava). Most of these are consumed locally and sold at markets in Suva and Navua.

The interior of the Namosi area is serviced by an unsealed road, which joins the main Suva-Nadi highway on the south coast at Nabukavesi, 24 kilometres (km) from Suva, and by the Navua River. The latter is used less for transport since the new road was constructed between 1976 and 1978 (Griffen, 1978).

The proposed mine site is located in the Waisoi area in the north of the province at the base of the Korobasabasaga mountain range known colloquially as 'The Dragon's Teeth'. There are several villages in close proximity to the proposed mine: Namosi, Narukubua, Nadruyasi, Waivaka and Waiwai, the largest of which is Namosi with a population of over 500 people. The province has a total population in excess of 5,000 people, the majority of whom live in the coastal area.

Described by Rizer et al. (1982: 309) as one of the "least developed" provinces in Fiji, Namosi has remained comparatively unaffected by its proximity to the capital, Suva. Yet today, regular carrier transport along the new road is bringing increasing reliance on the sale of cash crops and wage-earning activities in Suva. Much of the interior area away from the road remains inaccessible.

The History of Exploration at Namosi

Copper mines are amongst the largest mining developments globally. In spite of the increasing use of substitutes, copper remains a valuable commodity on the world market, the price of which is forecast to remain stable in the medium to long term (pers comm, Alan Jay, 1993). Copper mining companies sell refined copper concentrate that has been extracted from rock containing only small proportions of the element, which occurs in the natural state mainly as copper sulphides (90%) and oxides (10%) (Mezger, 1980).

At Namosi, copper occurs in association with basic volcanic rocks. A succession of mining companies have investigated the possibility of mining copper from the Waisoi Valley and Waivaka since 1912. A major exploration effort between 1978 and 1979 by Viti Copper (in a joint-venture with Anglo-American Mining, Conzinc Riotinto of Australia and Preussag AG of Germany) defined a large deposit of 480 million tons of copper at a grade of 0.48%, but this was uneconomical to exploit at the prices which prevailed at that time (Richmond, 1980).

A Special Prospecting License was granted to Placer Pacific and Placer Dome Limited in early 1992 to prospect the Namosi copper/gold porphyry. A second application was made by Placer Exploration Limited in April 1993 to prospect an area of 60,000 hectares. This area falls partly within the provinces of Namosi, Serua, Nadroga and Navosa (Anon., 1993a).

Placer Exploration Limited, Placer Pacific Namosi and Placer Namosi are part of the giant Canadian mining conglomerate Placer Dome Inc. Placer Dome is the fourth largest mining company in the world outside South Africa, with 22 subsidiary companies in 7 countries (Durr, 1990). It had sales revenues of $1.2 billion Canadian dollars and a cash flow of C$293 million in 1992 (Anon., 1993b).

Although no formal commitment to mine the copper at Namosi has been published, there are a number of reasons to believe that Placer Pacific wishes to proceed with the project. First, the company is keen to increase its "exposure to base metals" (Anon., 1989a) so that base metals will account for 40% of its revenue by 1995 (Anon., 1991a). This change in direction will involve a move away from dependence on gold and a significant increase in copper production over the next ten years (Anon., 1992). Placer would obviously like to make this move predominantly in those areas where base metals can be extracted at a lower cost per unit of metal produced. Among such areas is the South Pacific with some of the lowest cost mines of their type in the world, such as those at Misima and Porgera in Papua New Guinea. Second, the company is keen to have a large-scale copper prospect as part of its portfolio, and Namosi is its largest at present. Third, the company is spending aggressively with a F$5 million commitment given to the Fijian Government already for a pre-feasibility survey. Placer has the benefit of utilizing a long history of research on the prospect by Viti Copper in the 1980s and, partly as a result, Placer has significantly increased previous assessments of the size of the ore body. Finally, there is a general consensus that the investment climate in Fiji is preferable to many other parts of the region currently targeted for further exploration, such as Papua New Guinea.

The Economic Incentives for the Fiji Government

Incentives are also there for the government of Fiji to approve the project. The initial feasibility study carried out by Placer has shown the deposit to be 930 million tonnes (t) of copper at a grade of 0.45% (with 0.15 grams of gold per tonne) to be mined at 100,000 tonnes per day (pers comm, Alan Jay, 1993). Working with a realistic production estimate of 450t of copper a day and a price of US$2.2 per kilogram (kg) of copper, the mine would gross US$990,000 per day or US$361 million per year (F$542 million per year) minus loan repayments and operating costs over its proposed life of 27 years. This figure does not include revenues from spin-off activities, the proceeds from gold processing, or revenue from other by-products, such as molybdenum. Allowing for a tax holiday during the first ten years, it would not be unreasonable to anticipate taxable returns thereafter in the order of F$200-300 million annually for the remaining 17 years of the mine's life. This is a substantial sum in a country where the government revenue in 1992 was $548 million (Fiji Bureau of Statistics, 1993).

The development potential of the Namosi project for a small island country has not gone unnoticed. *The Weekly Hansard* for 21 April 1993 records the following comment in a Parliamentary debate:

Hon. M.V. Leweniqila (The Minister for Labour and Industrial Relations), "Mr. Speaker, we have only two major industries through

> which we are entirely dependent. First and foremost is sugar.... Number two is tourism....Namosi will bring us in an income that is much more than sugar - Government has got to be ready to prime it with thunder...so that the project could be viable."

In Parliament on 20 July 1992, Ratu Ovini Bokini, the Minister for Lands and Mineral Resources, stated that the development cost would be in excess of F$1 billion. This figure assumed production of 60,000t per day. Bearing in mind that the current proposal to mine 100,000t per day will involve higher direct costs (attributable to increasing the size of the pits, the mine infrastructure and the power supply), the total project cost may rise to F$1.4 billion. In a statement to the House on 27 April 1993, Ratu Ovini commented that the project would be

> 75% larger than the sugar industry in 1992, 10% to 15% larger than the tourist industry in 1992 and will increase the 1992 inland revenue taxes by 30% to 40%, and that the minimum expenditure commitment...for the two year Special Exploration Period (SPL) is F$5 million.

Infrastructural Requirements of the Project

Everything about the project is on an overwhelming scale. There will be two large pits dug in the Waisoi Valley, one 2km in diameter, the other 1.2km, both extending 200m below the valley floor. The development will also involve the diversion of the Waisoi Creek to prevent flooding of the mine pits and the establishment of a waste rock dump in the Waisoi Valley (Placer Pacific, 1993).

The project will make huge demands in terms of manpower and improved service infrastructure, including an 85-135 megawatt thermal-powered electricity generating station, a demand in excess of that currently supplied to the national grid at times of peak consumption. This station will be situated somewhere on the south coast. The project will also require the upgrading of the road from the south coast to Namosi village, the construction of a new port for export of the mine products, delivery of coal or oil for the power station, import of parts, machinery and fuel for the mine and other elements of the infrastructure, and the building of a camp to house 2,500 to 3,500 workers during the mine construction phase. The mine would also require a concentrator at the coast, a slurry pipeline from the crushing mill to the concentrator and a long sea outfall to carry waste tailings to the submarine slope beyond Beqa Island to the south (Figure 12.2). The operation would draw large quantities of water from the ocean near the Beqa Passage for cooling at the power station. Water would also be required in the crushing and grinding processes at the mine site and for the concentrator. This water will probably be extracted from the Waisoi Creek and others via a pumping station.

The Benefits and Costs of Large-scale Mining

The prospect at Namosi involves mining very low grade ore. As a consequence, more ore must be extracted to obtain a reasonable quantity of copper for processing. To make the project viable, the extraction of larger quantities of ore requires economies of scale that can be realized only by creating a large-scale mine. A large mine involves financial investment in infrastructure and services on a scale that is unparalleled in Fiji. Whilst the mine will consume a non-renewable resource, it will add to the capital base of the country through royalties, direct and indirect taxes, foreign exchange earnings, service industries, local business developments and new employment. In terms of benefits to the Namosi area, there is the probability of 1,000 jobs, new infrastructure including schools, roads, health services, housing and a share in the project through compensation, equity, and employment (Keith-Reid, 1993).

Large-scale mining has been a contentious issue globally for many years, and Melanesia has often been centre stage in the resulting conflict. The idle mine at Bougainville stands like an icon of another time in a decade of naïveté for Papua New Guinea. The tale of misplaced trust and mismanagement has been well told by Grynberg and Nouairi (1988) but Bougainville does not stand alone as the target for iconoclasts in Papua New Guinea. Operators of other large-scale mining developments in the country strive constantly to convince their detractors that while the mines cannot be sustainable, they can be manageable. Yet the mines at Misima and Porgera, and those proposed at Mount Kare and Lihir, have been a focus of attention and controversy since their inception.

Kau (1993) cites the examples of both Ok Tedi and Bougainville mines in Papua New Guinea to illustrate the environmental disruption caused by mining and draws a parallel between loggers of native forest, whom he refers to as "robber barons", and mining companies. Kau comments that "If BHP [a major shareholder in Ok Tedi] operated in Australia on the standards which it is allowed to in PNG it would be closed down tomorrow" (1993: 17).

Writing about mining in New Caledonia, Papua New Guinea and Nauru, Emberson-Bain (1992) catalogues a litany of undesirable consequences including, at a local level, land loss and pollution, the creation of local dependency cultures, shifts to imported foods, tensions caused by arrival of immigrant labour, health problems, the breakdown of the extended family and the erosion of women's status in the community. In the context of such issues, many aspects of the proposed Namosi development require cautious and critical analysis.

Namosi: An Environment of Concern

Hughes and Sullivan (1989) summarized the main environmental issues related to mining in the south-west Pacific Islands as follows:

(1) The capacity of the project area and its surroundings to physically accommodate the project.

(2) The capacity of the environment to assimilate wastes from the project.

(3) The effects of the project's land requirements and discharges on natural ecological values, and the subsistence and commercial resources utilised by local people.

With regard to point (1), the comparatively low population density of Namosi Province and the physical nature of the land suggest that the project could be physically accommodated. Yet Hughes and Sullivan (1992) comment that the major impact of mining projects on the land is undoubtedly the alienation of traditionally owned land, which is of paramount social and cultural importance to the landowners. Landownership and compensation in relation to Namosi are addressed in a later section.

Points (2) and (3) above are addressed in more detail in the following sections which discuss environmental issues related to the Namosi mine. The section dealing with point (3) includes comment on the draft environmental report compiled by the consultants to the mining company and a review of environmental management policies in relation to mining in Fiji.

Environmental Capacity for Waste Assimilation

Two important issues will be addressed in this section in relation to the Namosi project: the generation of waste rock and tailings and their disposal.

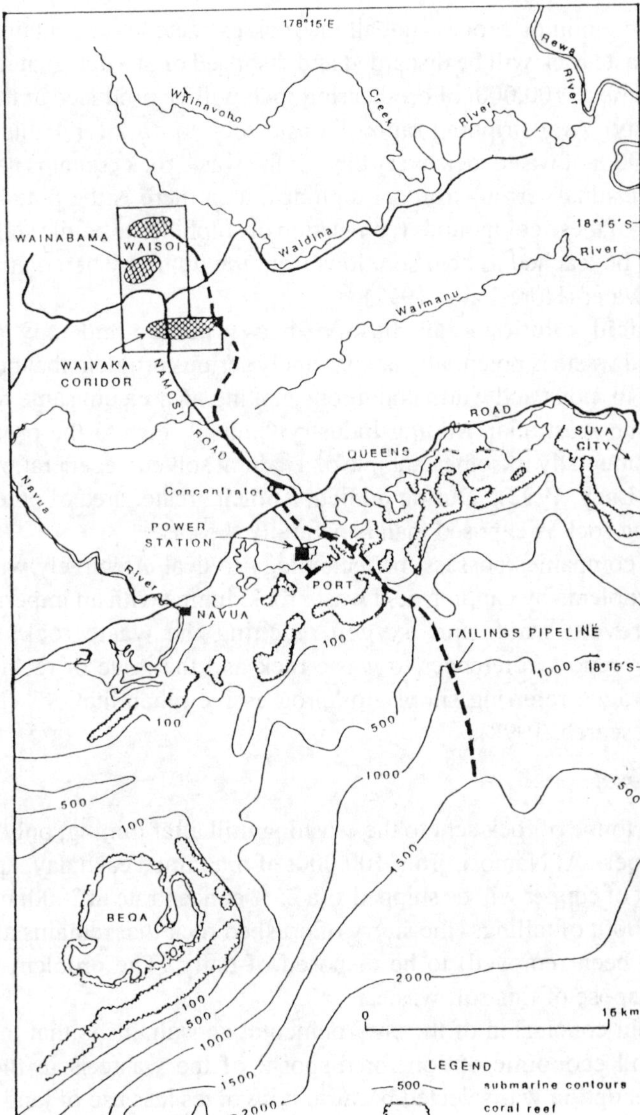

Figure 12.2. Location of the proposed tailings pipeline and other infrastructure associated with the Namosi mine.

The generation of waste rock

During the mining process not all the rock extracted will contain usable copper. Waste rock will be discarded and disposed of at a designated dump site. At Namosi, 100,000t of ore-bearing rock will be produced at the mine site each day. At a stripping ratio of waste rock to ore of 1:1 this would create 100,000t of waste rock every day. If the waste rock contains naturally occurring residual ferrous iron or sulphides, then there is the potential for oxidization of these compounds (conversion of sulphides to acidic sulphates) which may be leached as acid solutions from the dump by percolating rain or ground water (Hore-Lacy, 1992).

These acid solutions can dissolve heavy metals and may pollute rivers. Acid waste is potentially an extremely serious problem that becomes more acute in moist and warm conditions making an area unusable for generations. The Australian Mining Industry Council refer to the process as "an environmentally irksome example of a natural solvent regeneration process" (Hore-Lacy, 1992). During mining, a much greater area of potentially acid forming rock is exposed than is naturally the case.

Mining companies possess the technology to deal effectively with acid drainage problems by capping acid waste rock dumps with an impermeable layer to prevent water and oxygen reaching the waste rock. In the consultants' report, references to waste rock and the issue of reclamation are rather vague referring simply to "progressive rehabilitation" (Natural Systems Research, 1992).

Waste disposal

Of each tonne of rock sent to the crushing mill after mining, only 0.45% will be copper. At Namosi, from 100,000t of ore mined each day, approximately 450t of copper will be shipped as a 25% concentrate in 2000t batches, leaving 98,000t of tailings (the slurry of crushed rock that remains after the copper has been removed) to be disposed of daily. The problem then is where to dispose of this soft waste.

One main conclusion of the environmental consultants is that the most efficient and economic option for disposal of the waste is in the deep ocean. This option was selected because it involves less use of land, therefore less land alienation; it reduces the danger of toxic hazards on land; and it allows the natural buffering of the sea to be used to neutralize acidic tailings.

At present the proposal is to pump the waste tailings composed of sand, silt and clay grade particles offshore to a depth of 100-200m via a pipe and de-aerating tank. The tailings will exit the pipe in a submarine canyon southeast of Beqa Island and flow down the submarine slope in turbidity currents. To put the magnitude of the discharge in perspective, an interesting analogy adapted from Ellis (1989) shows that, if a large person weighs 100kg, then there are approximately 1 million large people equivalents in 100,000t of tailings waste to be disposed of each day from the mine.

Ellis (1989) states that the major impacts of submarine tailings disposal are sea bed smothering and contamination resulting in the loss of benthic fauna. The implications of this phenomenon for the Beqa area and the Navua coast depend on the role which benthic fauna play in the food chain of the near surface organisms that are utilized locally. At present relevant data are not available. It is clear that "there must be little or no risk at the disposal site of...tailings upwelling back into the shallow water....there is unfortunately virtually no environmental data in the public domain about the existing cases" (Ellis & Ellis, submitted: 4).

Should tailings disposed of at sea have an impact on the coral reefs, near what is a prime recreation spot for locals and tourists, the public outcry would seriously undermine confidence in the Namosi project. Any impact on nearshore subsistence fisheries, which have an important role for the coastal dwelling population, would also create adverse publicity.

The environmental consultants cite the operations at Island Copper mine on Vancouver Island in Canada and at another of Placer's mines at Misima (80% owned by Placer Pacific, 20% by the government of Papua New Guinea) as examples of good submarine tailings disposal practice. Of the two mines, Island Copper has the longest history of environmental monitoring and assessment. Here, mine tailings are discharged to a fjord using a siphon system to suck sea water into a de-aerating tank where it is entrained with the waste. When the tailings exit from the system in deep water, they are free of air and negatively buoyant; therefore, they sink.

The tailings at Island Copper are discharged into the calm waters of a fjord, and few impacts have been registered on local commercial marine species. Ellis (1989: 93) has stated that "in general, coastal systems recover quickly from the smothering impacts of detoxified mine waste dumped at sea once mining has ceased...a few years for abundant opportunist species, or several decades for climax organisms." Yet the situation at Island Copper is entirely different from that found in the open sea off Beqa Island, where the characteristics of the water body, the incidence of cyclonic events, the proximity of fragile reefs and tourist attractions, and the use of the area by local fishermen require consideration.

The most compelling point made by the environmental consultants in favour of submarine disposal for Namosi tailings is that it removes the necessity to build a tailings dam in a geologically unstable region, thus removing the danger of a catastrophe should the tailings dam collapse. This argument was used by Placer Pacific in Papua New Guinea when plans for the Porgera mine (25% owned and managed by Placer Pacific) in Enga Province were put forward, and by Conzinc Riotinto Australia at Bougainville. Advocates of tailings dams have argued that, if the ground were cleared to bedrock (a common enough practice in strip mining operations), then stable foundations can be laid for a tailings dam--even in such areas.

In the case of Namosi, a submarine disposal system would seem to be the environmentally friendlier option if no adverse environmental impacts occur in the overlying water column.

Effects on Subsistence and Commercial Resources

Chemical processes

Of the copper-containing ore remaining after the waste has been discarded, some will be below the cut-off grade and will be stored, perhaps for later processing should it become cost effective. The remainder is sent to the mill for crushing. After crushing the ore to a powder, the copper is separated by flotation. Flotation involves the separation of copper from the waste rock by blowing air through a liquid slurry containing a reagent, such as xanthate which allows the mineral to adhere to the air bubbles and to be collected as a froth from the top of a tank. Following flotation, the copper is refined by gravity separation to a concentrate that contains 20-30% copper. Concentrate is produced for ease of transport to the smelters. The concentrate from Namosi will be shipped abroad to be smelted and further refined prior to being turned into copper castings.

Extraction of any gold from the ore on site may involve the use of cyanide as a chemical solvent and a carbon-in-pulp adsorption system. Gold is leached from the rock by treatment in a cyanide solution and absorbed onto activated carbon circulating in a centrifuge. The gold is collected by filtering the carbon from the solution and stripping off the gold in a cyanide bath. These processes in turn generate waste water, chemicals and heavy metals, which have to be reused, recycled or disposed of.

Cyanide is a toxic ion that breaks down by oxidation on exposure to air and water after a period of weeks. Calcium hypochlorite can be used to neutralize it. When diluted, cyanide is not considered a major pollutant but in concentrated form can be hazardous. Pollution incidents involving spillage of concentrated cyanide have been documented at mining operations in Papua New Guinea, such as

> the spillage of 270 tonnes of sodium cyanide in containers from the Ok Tedi operation into the Fly River and the accidental release of 1 million litres of cyanide solution...that led to the death of crocodiles, turtles and fish throughout the lower estuary (Brodie, 1990: 17).

There are also a number of recorded incidents of cyanide contamination of water supplies associated with the U.S. mining industry, notably at Kendall Venture, Port Sunlight, Copper Elk and Atlantic mines (Pilcher, 1990).

At Namosi, the concentrator and processing equipment will be located on the coast between Navua and Suva. The potential for pollution at the processing site will be of great concern to the people of Lobau, Mau, Melimeli, Veivatuloa and Naqara in view of the potential impact on fisheries and the coast at these locations.

Increased sediment discharge

Namosi and the adjacent villages use the surrounding freshwater habitat, particularly the upper Waidina and its tributaries, as a source of fish, prawns and eels, which provide important dietary supplements for many households.

A census conducted by the Namosi Joint Venture (1979) for an environmental progress report on behalf of Viti Copper/Amax in the Namosi region found that, of 78 people questioned, 80% fished at least once a week and 51% fished 5-6 times a week. People in the downstream areas conducted more fishing trips than those upstream and the "amount of fish/prawns/eels caught was unexpectedly high" (Namosi Joint Venture, 1979: 60).

It seems reasonable to assume that any impacts from pollution at the mine site have a high probability of entering the surface water and the ground water systems. The most severe impacts would be felt downstream where freshwater resources are more heavily utilized.

The mine will extract 73 million t of rock annually which will add a significant sediment load to that produced by natural erosion in the Namosi area. At present the effects that increased sediment load introduced to the catchment area as a result of the mine will have on the use of the fisheries resource is unknown. A number of the groups surveyed by the Namosi Joint Venture attributed a decrease in fish abundance prior to the survey to a heavy build-up of sediment in the river following the 1952 hurricane (7.7%), bulldozing for the road (5.1%), and exploration drilling activities (7.7%). Some local people clearly perceive that sediment increases have an impact on the fishing resources. Such increases will be unavoidable if the mining project becomes reality.

Any increase in sediment production from Namosi will also exacerbate the flooding that affects the downstream area during tropical cyclones and other storms by filling river channels with sediment and reducing their water holding capacity.

Environmental consultants in co-operation with the Hydrological Unit of the Public Works Department are currently monitoring the sediment discharge at a number of stations within the Waidina and nearby river catchments. As anticipated, natural discharge rates and sediment loads are extremely high, particularly during cyclones. Levels of sediment discharge under the Nausori Bridge reached an estimated 25 million t in a 4-day period during Cyclone Kina in January 1993.

Potential exists for other aspects of the environment to be affected by the Namosi mine. Many of these effects are unavoidable accompaniments to the mining process; others may not be realized. The loss of native forest, the loss of soil through run-off and the addition of fine mine waste to the normally high sediment load fall into the former category. The potential for contamination of local water sources (both aquifer and surface water), pollution from the power station (including thermal pollution), contamination of the coastal area as a result of leakages during discharge and loading operations, and the environmental and social impacts of the construction of mining camps and associated infrastructure in the Waisoi Valley fall into the latter category.

The draft environmental impact study

The Namosi draft environmental impact study cites the Marcopper Mine (39% owned by Placer) at Mardinduque Island in the Philippines as an environmentally successful example of a low-grade open-cast copper mine. This mine used a shallow water coastal submarine tailings disposal system after special dispensation had apparently been given by the government of President Marcos to dump untreated mine wastes directly into the sea. This system has caused some problems. Marcopper was closed down for failing to meet pollution standards which called for a reduction of toxic material and metal levels in its tailings when subsistence fishermen complained. The company is now installing a submerged submarine tailings disposal system (Gourlay, 1992).

The Namosi environmental report cites the mine at Misima as another example of an environmentally friendly approach to open-cast mining on high islands. The Misima gold mine in the Milne Bay Province of Papua New Guinea has many similarities to the proposed mine at Namosi but produces only 16,500t of tailings per day compared with the proposed 100,000t per day at Namosi.

Some environmental costs have been associated with the Misima mine. According to Hughes (1989: 5) "soft wastes pollute the sea for 9 km along the coast" from the estuary of the main Cooktown Creek. The government of Papua New Guinea has been highly critical of operations at Misima. The Environment Minister stated that pollution from the mine had caused a shortage of drinking and cooking water in nearby creeks and posed a serious health threat. The Minister further claimed that the company had failed to honour an agreement to provide alternative sources of water (Anon., 1989c).

Environmental management in Fiji

In terms of environmental management, the sheer size of the Namosi project may warrant a critical evaluation of the adequacy of current legislation. The Prime Minister has already appointed a Cabinet Sub-Committee for the Namosi Project and the Minister for Lands and Natural Resources has appointed an Inter-Ministerial Steering Committee reporting to his Permanent Secretary to consider the implications of the mine. The resources of various government departments are also being reviewed.

> Fiji's environmental laws are many and varied, a relic of the colonial period when environmental problems were limited and clearly sectorial. At least 25 Acts have some important role to play in what is today perceived as environmental management (Watling & Chape, 1992: 128).

Although an Environmental Management Committee has been in existence since 1980 and a small Environment Unit was created in 1989, many of Fiji's environmental laws are ineffective through lack of resources for enforcement, technical expertise and funding.

The main law governing the environmental management of mines is the Mining Act (Cap.146) (Government of Fiji, 1966) which allows for compensation and restoration of land damaged by mining. The maximum fine of $200 or six months in jail is clearly inadequate. Numerous other acts (referring to water pollution, river catchment management, public health, fisheries, native land) also have implications for the environmental management of large mining projects in Fiji.

The Rivers and Streams Ordinance Act of 1882 is the main instrument for the control of river pollution. It is regarded as outdated and prone to misinterpretation. No ground water legislation exists.

Since Fiji's Development Plan 8 in 1981, there has been a specific requirement to undertake an environmental impact assessment (EIA) as a condition of every minerals exploration project. Development Plan 9 also gave a commitment to safeguard the environment and improve pollution monitoring.

Placer Pacific has undertaken to conduct an EIA. Yet Roger Moody (pers comm, 1993) of Minewatch comments that the statement contained within the preliminary study that "at any time the level of activity on environmental investigation is commensurate with Placer's confidence in the project" (Natural Systems Research, 1992: 23) is the cause of some concern as to the commitment of the company to environmental principles.

Namosi's Capacity to Accommodate the Project

The significance of land and landownership

Environmental concerns for the land are writ large in the history of mining in Melanesia. They are intimately associated with the issues of landownership and compensation; "for indigenous people, land is clearly central to social identity" (Connell & Howitt, 1991: 4). In Melanesia, culture, tradition and the requirements of subsistence living involve people intimately with the land. When the land is gone, so is the focal point of the community. Development that utilizes the land in ways other than for settlement or cultivation can be viable only if the benefits are available for future generations, or if the land can be returned to its previous state.

The macroeconomic advantages of mining promoted by governments and others may mean little to a future generation that shares few of these benefits and is landless. Filer (1990) has commented that in Bougainville the people regard the damage done to their environment as symbolic of the damage done to their society by the mine at Panguna. Hughes and Sullivan (1992: 6) state:

> Two major reasons for conflict within landowning communities and between these communities and the mining companies and governments, are the trauma that results from the permanent loss of land because of mining, and disputes about the ways in which revenue and other benefits are distributed.

Mining can affect traditional relationships with the land in a number of ways:

1) through removal of land for the open pits;
2) through changes in the use of the land and the replacement with other uses, such as construction of the work camp, roads and other infrastructure;
3) loss of the use of land and other environmental resources (ground water, rivers, forest) through pollution and other types of environmental damage;
4) appropriation of land within a lease area which may or may not be subsequently utilized but may be excluded from other uses;
5) expropriation of land (only in extreme cases and with the collusion of government).

Compensation for land lost

In Papua New Guinea, calls from local residents for more benefits and better participation in mining projects to compensate for damage to the land and natural resources have been a central theme in negotiations and a cause of conflict with mining companies. Grynberg and Nouairi (1988: 11) have commented that "to suggest...that the Bougainville crisis is simply about tailings disposal would be misleading in the extreme. The conflict arises because of the inadequate compensation for land loss". Yet Connell and Howitt (1991: 4) state that "it is too easy to argue that the 'problem' is solved by replacing rights with money."

Previous crises in the mining industry in Papua New Guinea prompted the government to give an equal share of revenues and equity in the Porgera mine to the provincial councils and the local people. The mine employs 1,587 people of whom 65% are local Engans and 13% are from other parts of Papua New Guinea. In terms of compensation for land used, Enga Province with its 6 local government councils receives K39 million plus an additional K39 million in Special Grant Support, 2.49% equity (worth K56 million) as well as compensation and provisional government grants worth K20 million. Other benefits to the local people include a sealed highway to Wabag, bridge improvements, power supplies, employment training, a hospital, primary school, secondary school and vocational centre as well as K4 million towards the construction of a new town, air services and an airstrip. At the national level, the government of Papua New Guinea receives K589 million in direct taxes and K50 million as royalties (Anon., 1989d).

Despite this compensation regime and the benefits from the mine, a dispute arose at Porgera when the Premier of the Enga Provincial Council, stated that they would not allow the project to proceed unless additional conditions were met. These conditions included: 1) the option for local people to take up an additional 20% of the mine equity; 2) assistance for local Engans to set up a public company to take advantage of 'spin-offs'; 3) the involvement of Engans in crushing and cartage of materials to and from the mine; and 4) a ban on the 'fly-in, fly-out' policy operated at the mine which deprived locals of the infrastructural improvements associated with a resident mining population (Enga Provincial Government, 1989). Further, in 1991, the Chairman of the Landowners' Committee argued that spin-offs must go to the landowners "regardless of whether we have the finance, the expertise, the reputation or the experience, then to other Engans, and then to other Papua New Guineans" (Ashton, 1991). Land disputes have also arisen among local groups; such a disagreement caused the delay of power supplies to the mine from the Hides Gas Field some 70km away (Anon., 1991b).

The land issue is complicated further because, in many Melanesian countries which have inherited colonial administrative and legal frameworks, the landowners are in reality bound by constitutional rather than traditional regulation of mineral resource rights. In Fiji for example, the landowners have customary rights to land, but the Mining Act of Fiji (Government of Fiji, 1945, 1966 and amendments) states that the ownership of minerals is vested in the state. One significant alteration to this Act incorporated in Fiji's 1990 Constitution states that

> any royalties or proceeds received by the state in respect of any minerals extracted from the land, or from the sea bed over which there exists any customary fishing rights, shall...become payable to the owners of the surface of that land or the beneficiary of the registered

> customary fishing rights...subject to the right of the State to retain such proportion of any such royalties or proceeds as may be approved by the Cabinet from time to time (Government of Fiji, 1990: 1).

The situation in Fiji

The importance of *vanua* (land) to indigenous Fijians is summarized as follows.

> The Fijian term *vanua* has physical, social and cultural dimensions which are interrelated. It does not mean only the land area one is identified with, and the vegetation animal life and other objects on it, but it also includes the social and cultural system--the people, their tradition and customs, beliefs and values....It provides a sense of identity and belonging....To most Fijians, the idea of parting with one's *vanua* or land is tantamount to parting with one's life" (Ravuvu, 1983: 70).

The attachment to land in certain areas is further enhanced by the sacred significance of some sites which are "treated with varying degrees of reverence and respect according to the influence of each site over the lives of the people who maintain them" (Ravuvu, 1983: 86).

In the past, Viti Copper negotiated financial compensation in the Namosi area for crops destroyed and rentals for areas physically occupied. Other forms of compensation included employment at the mine for local people (restricted to one male per household), purchasing of surplus crop production for the exploration camp staff, and improvement of village development through providing timber for a new school to be built, education scholarships, and funding for the road in 1976 (Richmond, 1980).

This compensation was based on activity during the exploration stage, which involved some small-scale environmental disturbance and some imposition on local people. Commenting at the time, Griffen (1978: 20) stated that "people are mainly concerned that they receive compensation from the company for the land used and that the benefits...reach all of them evenly." Should the mine proceed, compensation claims would be many magnitudes larger and allowance would have to be made for the size of such claims increasing through time as the scale of the disturbance caused by the project was progressively realized.

The people of Namosi have been negotiating with the mining company and the government through the village councils to protect their interests during the pre-feasibility stage. Each of the 15 *mataqali* (subclans) in the mining lease area has a representative on the Landowners' Committee. The committee calls meetings on a monthly or ad hoc basis. Generally, the substance of the meetings pertains to the allocation of compensation for disturbance to the local area during the exploratory drilling phase. Compensation is also discussed in relation to damage of natural resources as a result of Placer's activities (timber royalties, damages to cultivated and uncultivated land).

Should the mining go ahead, negotiations for compensation will be carried out on behalf of the landowners by the Native Land Trust Board (NLTB). Placer Pacific has prepared a Draft Compensation Agreement between the Company and the Native Land Trust Board as allowed under The Native Lands Act (Cap.133, part 3).

In the Draft Compensation Agreement, "Placer acknowledges that if the Project is developed certain traditional areas of the land, freshwater creeks and rivers, and marine environment will be affected" (Placer Pacific, 1993: 1). The company has agreed under sections 40 and 41 of The Mining Act (Cap.146) to pay compensation during the period for which it holds the Special Mining Lease to the Native Land Trust Board on behalf of the landowners for damage within the Special Prospecting Lease Area to the surface of the land including crops and trees, disturbance of surface rights of way, riverine water and related impacts.

A separate section of the document deals with compensation for the loss of economic trees and crops in accordance with the Revised Schedule (1 February 1989) compiled by the Department of Primary Industries and the Forestry Amendment Regulations (1990).

Compensation has also been proposed for the habitual users of creeks within the project area, for any water discolouration and deleterious effects to associated flora and fauna. Constant alternative sources of water will be supplied to affected villages. The statement that this supply will be installed "as far as is possible...before the creek is discoloured" (Placer Pacific, 1993: 1) seems to suggest that this will be an alternative to mitigatory action. Compensation payments will also be made under a separate category for any damage to the Rewa and Waidina rivers, but the rates of compensation have not yet been finalized.

The company has made provision within the Draft Compensation Agreement for marine compensation. This includes compensation for:

i) nuisance and interference with community access,

ii) occupation of the marine area and,

iii) damage or loss of coastal marine areas including coastal fishing access and catches.

These provisions regulate payments for:

i) areas over which construction takes place,

ii) damage of any kind to the reef,

iii) any area excluded by Placer's operations from future traditional or customary use,

iv) any marine area that cannot be returned to its original state.

Conclusion

Many environmental issues of importance to the Namosi project can be addressed by the application of good environmental and resource management techniques. The effects of others may not be adequately assessed until the mine is operational. To the villagers of Namosi, the most important issues will be related to any environmental degradation that is likely as a result of the mine and the compensation for loss of land access and resources.

Through their corporate literature, most mining companies embrace the philosophy of good corporate citizenship which refers to both a sense of stewardship of the environment and to the economic and social implications of the projects with which companies are involved. Although methods for compensating landowners for environmental and social impacts have doubtless become more elaborate, it remains to be seen whether corporations are any better equipped to empathize with those whom their decisions affect than they were in Bougainville. Many people in remote areas, although acutely aware of the progress and, in some cases the wealth, offered by certain types of large-scale development, probably remain uncomprehending of the ethos and objectives of corporate culture. As long as these differing perspectives persist among those involved in mining developments, conflict will continue to occur, each side believing that their needs and objectives have been understood by the other, yet only to be disillusioned by later events.

If the Namosi project were to proceed, it is unlikely that either Placer Pacific or the government of Fiji will make the mistakes that led to the tragic situation in Bougainville. Much has been learned and written since then. The situation in Fiji is entirely different in many respects, but the stakes are still high. Placer is thought in many circles to be of a different corporate calibre to the 'robber barons', yet the ability to judge whether or not rhetoric translates into action for a particular mining project may often be assessed only in retrospect. In 30 years, when the proposed mine is due to close, will the reflections on its contribution to Fiji's development be garlanded with the image of new found economic wealth and stability, or with the tears of Namosi and an eyesore where the dragon once bared its teeth?

Acknowledgements

Roger Moody of Minewatch, London, kindly provided various pieces of information. I am grateful to Professor Eric Waddell, Dr Paddy Nunn, Dr Bill Aalbersberg, Andrew Crosby and Heather McShane for comments and advice.

Chapter 13

Dynamics of the Coastal Zone in the High Islands of Oceania: Management Implications and Options

Gilbert David

Introduction

The years 1991 and 1992 saw the emergence of a worldwide preoccupation with the themes of environment and sustainable development as humanity prepared for the Earth Summit, which took place in June 1992 in Rio de Janeiro within the framework of the United Nations Conference on Environment and Development (UNCED) (Strong, 1992). Within the island Pacific, 13 states and territories[1] became deeply involved with this subject, first at the national scale--each nation preparing a detailed state-of-the-environment report--then at the regional scale through two workshops sponsored by the South Pacific Regional Environment Programme (SPREP).

The result of these reflections, presented as a synoptic document entitled "Environment and Development: a Pacific Island Perspective" and representing the island Pacific's contribution to the Earth Summit, underlines not only the fundamental importance of the coastal zone in the island environment and its potential for sustainable development, but also its vulnerability and the changes which it is currently undergoing. It is encouraging to note the concern with which the island nations view their foreshore zones. This concern stems, to a great extent, from the facts that the majority of the people of Oceania live in coastal areas and that they are aware of the dangers presented by global warming and the resulting risk of sea-level rise.

This emerging concern for the welfare of the foreshore is clearly demonstrated by the direction taken by the South Pacific Applied Geoscience Commission (SOPAC) over the last few years, where research into coastal and nearshore environments has gradually gained importance at the expense of deep-water research, the original raison d'être of the organization. It is also evident in the importance given by SPREP to coastal areas in its

1991-1995 Action Plan (SPREP, 1991). This organization is making a particular effort to generate and encourage an awareness of integrated coastal zone management among Pacific Islands governments (Holthus, 1992).

This article focuses on the relationships between the human and the physical parameters of the coastal zone. The first part is concerned with defining the boundaries, terrestrial and maritime, of the coastal zone. The second part deals with its dynamics. It first discusses the overall dynamics of the relationships between the foreshore and both the land and marine environments adjacent to it. It then proceeds to explain the internal dynamics of the coastal environment itself, distinguishing between the land component, the marine component, and the interface between the two. The third and final part concerns the preservation of the coastal zone and its place in the sustainable development of high islands. Following a brief overview of the dangers that threaten this fragile environment, it stresses its economic and human potential, and discusses problems raised by the pricing of the coastal zone.

The Boundaries of the Coastal Zone

Definitions

It is essential, but not easy, to begin by defining the boundaries of what we mean by 'coastal zone'. As Coutts (1989: 320) points out: "the coastal zone does not exist as a measurable or even clearly definable entity but as an idea, a concept of an area where land and sea meet and merge." Any setting of boundaries for a phenomenon is closely linked to the definition that we accept for the phenomenon. Unfortunately, the various definitions of the coastal zone are far from consistent.

For marine ecologists, the coastal zone includes the whole of the sea bed (the benthic region) of the continental shelf, from the highest level where will be found species of marine life that can survive on sea-spray and very occasional immersion, to depths beyond which even the most resistant multicellular algae cannot survive for lack of sunlight (Péres, 1990: 918).

For marine geomorphologists, the coastline is the interface of sea, land and air, and it includes the whole area where "morphogenetic processes are substantially altered by the proximity of the convergence of interfaces" (Pinot, 1990: 667). Thus, the coastal zone is defined as "between that part of the sea bed which is not subject to the direct action of the land and that part of the land which is not subject to the direct action of the sea" (Coutts, 1989: 320).

Although precise, all definitions formulated by naturalists overlook the human aspect of coastal zones. People make use of the coastal zone, manage it, develop it, and sometimes change it irreversibly. One of the few definitions that takes this essential aspect into account is that of Cornforth (1984), for whom the coastal zone is an interface of land, sea, air, wind, tides and administrative authorities. Yet this definition is also unsatisfactory.

This definition lumps together two very different kinds of factors: on one hand, four parameters whose boundaries are clearly defined and constant, namely air, land, ocean and administrative jurisdiction (this latter made up mostly of the Exclusive Economic Zone and territorial waters, to which are added some administered zones subject to specific fishing, navigation, underwater quarrying and aquaculture regulations); on the other hand, two parameters with highly changeable profiles, namely winds and tides, whose spatial impact varies in time.

Furthermore, this definition acknowledges the human factor only through the presence of authority, ignoring the users of the coastal zone and more particularly those inhabitants who, because of their occupation and their culture, are true creators of space. Through their physical activity, they affect the coastal biological habitats around them and the species which inhabit them. Through their culture, people have made the space their own, they have defined it, fixed its boundaries with their own particular geosymbols[2] and lore. Thus, having made it their territory, they imbue the coastal zone with a cultural dimension.

Thus, we arrive at another definition of the coastal zone: the interface of five kinds of space with fixed boundaries--air, ocean, land, administrative jurisdiction, cultural space of the foreshore dwellers--and of three kinds of energy flow, two of natural origin with fluctuating space/time boundaries--winds and tides--and one of human origin. Although more comprehensive than the previous ones, this definition is still insufficient to allow us to pinpoint the boundaries of the coastal zone. The difficulty lies in the fact that this zone does not correspond to any one specific ecosystem; rather it is at the interface of several different systems, each with its own spatial dimensions. It is therefore necessary to define these boundaries, to seaward and to landward, in the specific case of the high islands of Oceania.

Seaward boundaries

Geomorphologists agree that the deposition of terrigenous sediments differentiates the coastal zone from the adjacent marine environment (Pinot,

1990). This parameter can be very different along the coastline, with sedimentation off beaches or mangroves being totally unlike that off rocky or reef-fringed shores. This is difficult to assess unless one can combine it with a bathymetric criterion, as has been done in New Zealand where the 15-metre (m) depth contour, which includes all embayments in the shoreline, was chosen as the boundary of the coastal zone (Healy, 1980).

The sedimentological parameter is poorly adapted to coral waters where biotic factors play an essential role in zone differentiation (Guilcher, 1987). Battistini et al. (1975) differentiate coral coasts into five categories that are consistent from the point of view of morphology, bionomy, hydrodynamics and sedimentology. In order of increasing depth, they are:

- the foreshore made up of the non-reefal shoreline, particularly sedimentary deposits like beaches and beachrock;
- the intra-reef system made up of the boat channels separating a fringing reef from the foreshore or of the lagoon within a barrier reef;
- the reef flat of both fringing and barrier reefs;
- the frontal reef which includes the spurs and grooves of the outer reef slope in its upper part, and the fore-reef slope in its lower part;
- the extra-reef system, the non-reef covered slopes of the continental or insular shelf (Figure 13.1).

According to this classification, the boundary of the coastal zone falls at the limit between the foreshore and extra-reef systems.

The growth of coral reefs is the result of a symbiosis between coral polyps and endozoic algae which live within the coral's calcareous skeleton. Thus, the availability of sunlight determines the difference between the frontal reef and the extra-reef systems, and so the extent of the coastal zone. This boundary definition does not consider the human factor; as such it is unsatisfactory. It is preferable to consider a shallower boundary, that of the limit between the outer slope spurs and grooves and the fore-reef slope, or, in the case of a deep lagoon, the limit between the inner edge of the spur-and-groove system and the lagoon floor.

Setting the boundary in this way has the merit of introducing a human factor: in many parts of the Pacific, this corresponds to the seaward boundary of fishing territories (Ruddle, 1989). Fishermen recognize the boundary between the fishing grounds, areas of sea bed with which they are familiar, and the open ocean, which may be fished occasionally but is not part of

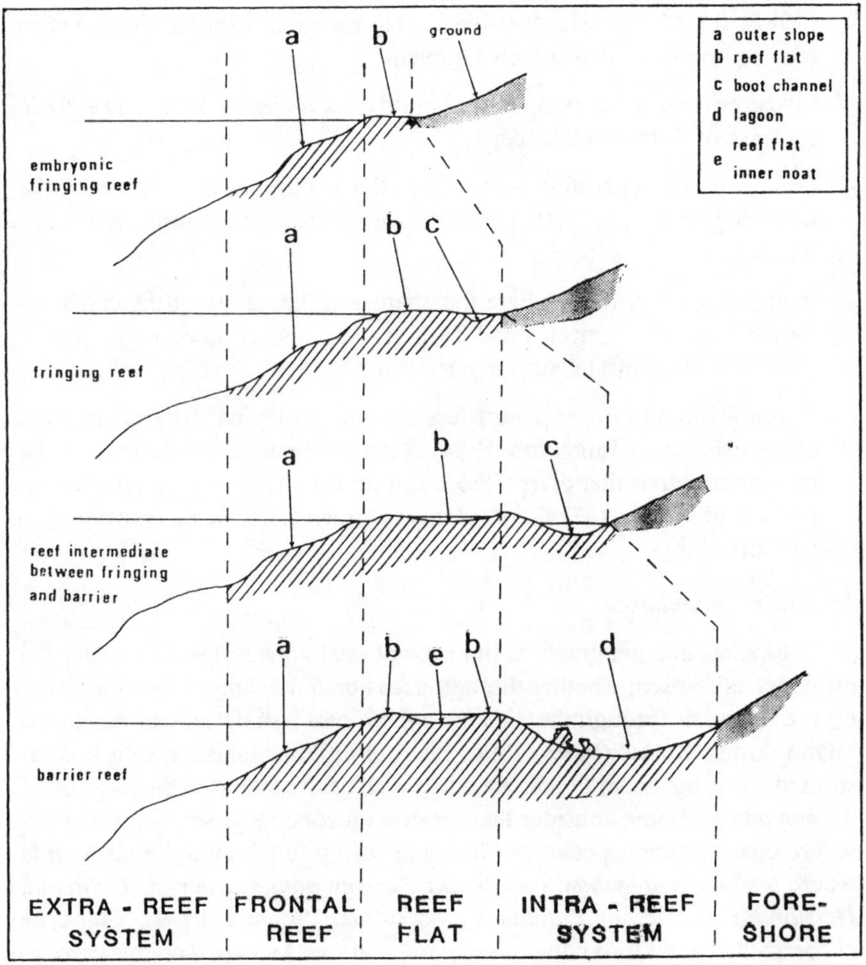

Figure 13.1. Zonation of Pacific Island reefs (after Battistini et al., 1975).

their traditional fishing area. Thus, Ni-Vanuatu have a rich and complex taxonomy concerning shallow-water fish but a considerably poorer one for deep-sea species.[3]

This delimitation of fishing areas can take several forms. It can materialize or be explained by:

- a change of place name between one zone and another, without any explicit reason for the change. Many examples of this are given by Sudo (1984) for Micronesia; Carrier (1981) mentions similar situations in Manus Province, Papua New Guinea;
- visual criteria, such as bottom visibility, as noted by Baines (1989) in the case of Solomon Islands;
- criteria based on fishing techniques; the maximum distance from the outer edge of the reef flats where the most usual fishing implements can be used;
- ichthyological criteria, where the change in the nature of the catch occurs between reef species and deep-sea species, as noted by Akimichi (1986) in the central Caroline Islands; or
- a combination of depth parameters and ichthyological criteria, as is the case in Vanuatu (Taurakoto, 1984) where the boundary is defined by the maximum depth that divers can reach in search of their target species, particularly trochus *(Trochus niloticus)*, greensnail (*Turbo marmoratus*) and lobster.

Landward boundaries

Ecologists and geographers limit the coastal zone to the area under the influence of the sea, whether through occasional dousing of the vegetation by sea spray, or through the distance which beach material can be moved inland during storms (Péres, 1990; Pinot, 1990). Botanists take a less restricted view, but generally do not agree with each other as to the location of the boundary. Some consider that the coastal zone includes all those areas where coastal forest species are found, a strip a few hundred metres wide where *Intsia, Calophyllum, Terminalia, Barringtonia, Casuarina, Ochrosia, Hernandia, Acasia and Pandanus* predominate (Schmid, 1979). This type of forest thrives on low-lying raised coral platforms where it enjoys particular drainage and soil conditions (rapid rain-water infiltration, poor soils). Thus, most botanists define 'coastal' through two ecological factors and through flora. The coastal forest is distinct from that of the adjacent alluvial terraces and swamps which are environments characterized by greater soil water retention and greater fertility owing to ground-water inputs. Other botanists consider that topography, particularly elevation, and proximity to the sea, give the whole coastal plain and lower reaches of the valleys a geographical unity, making it distinct from the foothills (Marten, 1985).

Here we shall use the limit, indicated by a change in gradient, between the coastal plain and the foothills as the landward boundary of the coastal zone.[4] Although seemingly purely physical in nature, this definition has human significance: villages which fish regularly are usually located within the coastal plain or at the lower end of valleys. At the same time, and because of lack of space, their food gardens and fallow fields frequently extend upslope.

Dynamics of the Coastal Zone

The coastal zone can be seen as a 'black box' containing the relationships between it and its land and marine peripheries.

System dynamics

The coastal zone is constantly subjected to the effects of energy flows and receives inputs of organic and mineral matter issued from the land and marine ecosystems around it. Through streams and rain-water runoff, terrestrial ecosystems export various materials resulting from the soil erosion to the coastal zone through the river system, organic matter, both living (adult and juvenile fish, larvae) and dead (particulate matter, plant detritus) finds its way there. For its part, the ocean contributes mineral salts and planktonic material.

Five types of energy flow affect the coastal zone: tides, waves and swells, wind, solar radiation and rivers. Of these, the first two come from the ocean, the last from the land; as for the wind and solar radiation, their origin is atmospheric, one acting parallel to the surface, the other perpendicular to it. The diversity of these energy flows, and of the area of the affected surface, is what makes the coastal zone the richest environment for bio-energetic exchanges within the biosphere, and accounts for the fact that it is one of the most biologically productive. Odum (1971) estimates the gross primary productivity of reef/estuarine systems at 20,000 kilocalories per square metre per year (kcal/m^2/year), which is similar to the productivity of broad-leafed evergreen forests, and is well in excess of that of contemporary agricultural land (12,000 kcal/m^2/year) in spite of the latter's heavy reliance on artificially-added nutrients. Thus, the coastal zone may be considered as a bio-energetically open system, constantly exchanging energy and nutrients with the ocean, land and atmosphere.

This representation of the inter–relationships between the coastal zone and its adjacent land and marine environments is incomplete without the human factor. Indeed, people are the major influence in the dynamics of the coastal zone today, through the information and energy flows that they generate through work and population pressure. From the human point of view, the place that the coastal zone occupies in the islands has evolved considerably over the last two centuries--marginal, especially in Melanesia before the coming of the Europeans, it has now become essential to human well-being.

Compared to the land, the ocean played a very minor role in the traditional societies of the high islands of Melanesia. Wherever ecological conditions allowed,[5] the interior of these islands was settled, the population density being higher than that of the coast. In the whole of Melanesia (Bonnemaison, 1986a) and in some of the high islands of Polynesia, such as Wallis and Futuna (Di Piazza, 1993), we observe a cultural, agricultural and territorial split between the people of the coast and the people of the interior. The former catch fish, grow yams and coconuts, and raise pigs which feed on coconut; the latter grow taro, sometimes kava, and raise pigs with difficulty because coconuts are scarce and they must feed on surplus root-crops. Where interior people lack a traditional ('custom') means of access to the foreshore, they have created for themselves a mental island-space which is limited to their highlands. There exists a system of exchange for taro, kava, pigs, yams and products of marine origin, but this barter is seldom direct; rather, it relies on networks of alliances. Bonnemaison (1987) gives a good example of this in the sharing cycle of turtles on the island of Tanna in Vanuatu.

The arrival of Europeans considerably upset the ancestral balance between coastal and inland dwellers. Coastal populations, psychologically vulnerable and defenceless against viral and sexually transmitted European-borne diseases, first targets of the blackbirders, paid the heaviest toll. In places coastline that was practically depopulated was left open for settlement by missionaries and other colonists. A new kind of authority ruled over the coastal areas, that of the church and of the trading post. This would eventually shift to the governments of the emerging colonial nations. The new masters could rely on a solid, Pacific-wide, economic and political support network, and they were determined to extend their authority over the whole native population. To this end, the easiest and cheapest way was to lure or force the inhabitants of the interior to the coast. This was undertaken on a grand scale through the second half of the last century and the first half of the present one, with each mission (invariably established near the coast) as the focus of a new Christian settlement. There, apart from religious indoctrination, the new convert discovered education, health care, and the novel joys of a consumer society. European settlement of the coastal zone of the islands turned it into a centre of outward-oriented economy, linked to the international marketplace through the sale of copra, sugarcane, coffee, and occasionally cocoa (Panoff, 1986).

Within this framework the coastal zone received inputs of population from the interior, which constituted a future workforce and a receptacle for the information flow delivered by the missionaries, at the same time receiving from seaward a flow of goods, money, and information, plus a trickle of population input in the form of clergy and native lay preachers (Doumenge, 1966).

The increasing involvement of the island nations within the world system has contributed powerfully to the alienation of the hinterland in favour of the coastal areas.[6] This has also brought about the appearance of a new phenomenon, this time within the coastal human environment itself, involving the alienation of the rural areas in favour of urban and suburban centres. This observation leads us now to consider the internal dynamics of the coastal zone itself.

Internal Dynamics of the Coastal Zone

The coastal zone can be seen as an 'open system'. Similarly, we can picture it as a system of nested sub-systems that are open, made of adjoining spaces, each one affected by the passage of energy flows, of flows of organic and/or inorganic matter, of information flows, and each one affecting the direction, velocity and amplitude of these flows. Some of these sub-systems can themselves be the origin or the final destination of the flows (Figures 13.2 and 13.3).

Schematically, the coastal zone is made of three parts: a marine component, a land component, and an interface component between land, salt water, fresh water, and the atmosphere. The whole takes the shape of three parallel bands, each containing several types of space, themselves arranged in either parallel bands or mosaics.

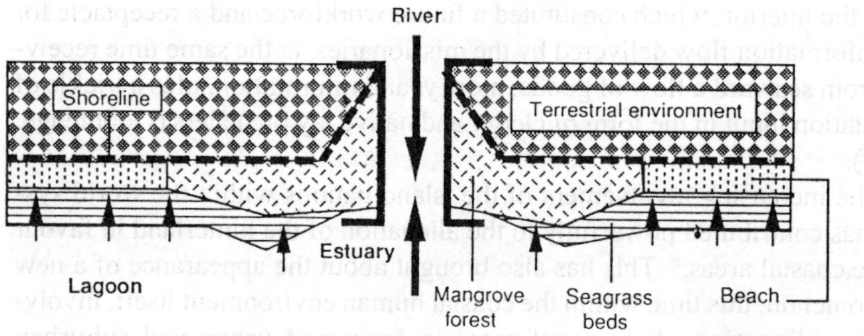

Figure 13.2. Structure and functions of the coast in terms of energy flows.

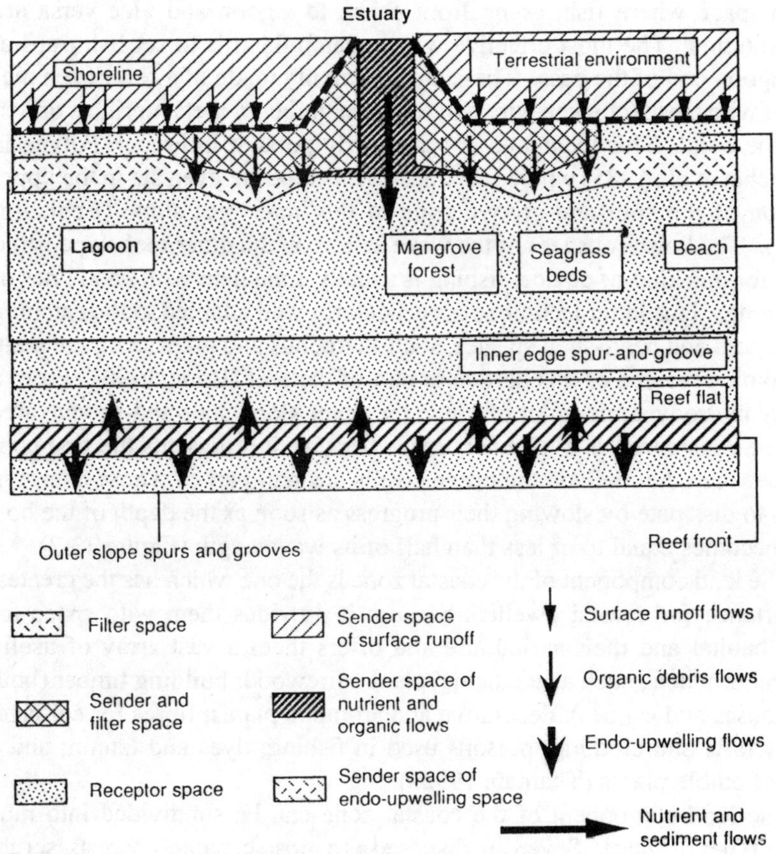

Figure 13.3. Structure and functions of the coast in terms of nutrient and sediment flows.

The marine component of the coastal zone is made of three major types of space: the outer reef slope spurs and grooves, the inner edge spurs and grooves, and the passes. The first two areas are parallel to the shoreline, the third is perpendicular to it, so lies across the first two and connects them. Thus, the pass may be seen as a 'corridor' space, allowing exchanges through the flow of the tides between a 'sender' space and a 'receptor' space. This relationship of sender and receiver will reverse according to the direction of the tidal flow.

From the point of view of fishing potential, the passes constitute a privileged space where fish, going from ocean to lagoon and vice versa are concentrated. The most effective way to catch them is to set fish traps at the lagoon end of the pass. These are commonly made of a few dozen metres of wire mesh (chicken wire) stretched on timber or metal uprights driven into the coral. This technique is particularly popular in French Polynesia (Blanchet et al., 1985) where fish traps of this type are even set in the upper portion of the spur-and-groove zone of the inner reef slope (Echinard, 1972). The boisterousness of the wave action on the outer reef slope is too great for this kind of device; fishing is usually done here with hand lines or by diving. This latter technique is particularly well adapted to the catching of lobsters and pearl-shell species, such as trochus and greensnail, the main economic resource of this particular part of the reef (Bour, 1990). From a purely hydrodynamic point of view, the outer slope spur-and-groove area may be considered as a 'damper' space because it represents the first contact between the reef and the ocean swells, a small part of whose energy it tends to dissipate by slowing their progress as soon as the depth of the bottom becomes equal to or less than half of its wavelength (Figure 13.2).

The land component of the coastal zone is the one which has the greatest importance for coastal dwellers because it provides them with space for their habitat and their agriculture and offers them a vast array of useful natural products, such as medicinal plants; firewood; building timber (both for houses and canoes); decorative and aromatic plants; fibres for cordage; handicrafts and clothing; poisons used in fishing, dyes and tannin; and a host of edible plants (Thaman, 1992a).

The land component of the coastal zone can be subdivided into nine major types of space. Seven are disposed as a mosaic, namely forests, scrubland and fallows, grasslands, commercial fields and plantations, villages and urban centres, subsistence farming gardens, and fresh water swamps and wetlands. An eighth type of space lies parallel to the shoreline, consisting of the upper portion of beaches or of rocky or coral coastlines beyond the intertidal zone. The ninth type of space consists of the lower reaches of rivers and is usually roughly perpendicular to the shore.

To a varying degree, these spaces have been – and frequently still are – subject to traditional management or development by humans. This is most obvious in the case of cultivated gardens, habitat and grasslands, usually cleared by the use of fire, but less so in the case of natural – or seemingly natural – environments, such as forests, thickets, upper reaches of beaches, swamps and rivers. Although subtle, human management of such areas is nonetheless real and is based on an in-depth understanding of coastal flora and fauna. As pointed out by Walter (forthcoming), in the case of forests and thickets, it can be considered as a very scattered type of gardening, characterized by the small number of work hours per unit area. It can take the form of a crude weeding of wooded areas aimed at encouraging the growth of certain desirable species, to which might be added the occasional transplanting of young shoots or, more rarely, the topping of young trees in order to slow down their growth and make the gathering of their fruit or nuts easier. In the case of swamps and marshes, human activity is more in the nature of land development than of plant management: it typically consists of the creation of small artificial islands on which taro is grown. The area where the material making up the island is taken from becomes its drainage ditch. Such artificial ecosystems are often far more productive than the natural environment.

A similar approach is seen in the construction of earth mounds for the planting of yams in New Caledonia's flood-plains (Doumenge, 1984) or the creation of irrigated taro gardens in the low-lying areas of the coastal plain on Futuna (Di Piazza, 1993). Such approaches aim at limiting the natural constraints and the hazards imposed on cultivation by the environment while keeping the energy output (i.e., the number of work hours required) to a minimum. The concern with minimizing the risks to the crops stems from a general philosophy of trying to improve the chances of survival of the village community, which has led the people of Oceania to seek the greatest possible diversity in their agriculture, in terms of the number of cultivated species and of the number of varieties within each species. So we see root-crops, vegetables and fruit systematically cultivated side by side, selected because they mature in different seasons.

The respective dimensions of the nine spaces are unchangeable. The population dynamics of the coastal people of the high islands of Oceania also cause change. Everywhere forests, thickets and wooded fallow areas are being replaced by cultivated fields. In certain districts, the forest is cleared for the creation of grasslands, but there the motive for extension is quite different: the primary cause is not demographic pressure, but the economics of land speculation. As Ward (1993: 14) points out under customary practices in many areas, if one clears land from forest it remains under one's control as long as it continues to be used. If abandoned to fallow, it would gradually revert to the common pool, perhaps to be reused by the same kin group in the future--or perhaps by another group. In the new context, simply by keeping the land in use, for example by fencing it for extensive grazing, one could retain authority over it, and have what might be almost permanent tenure. Traditional mechanisms were being used for non–traditional purposes.Thus in Western Samoa 7% of the whole country has been cleared from forest within the last three years, and 20% since the end of 1950 (WSDEC, 1991).

Generally speaking, spaces used by people tend gradually to encroach on natural spaces, even taking them over completely as is the case in the vicinity of urban centres. These urban spaces are the most dynamic of the nine types of space defined for the land component of the coastal zone. They generate population flows, both by natural increase and by being the final receptor space for the migration from the rural areas.[7] Just as we can establish a progression in dynamics from habitat in general to urban centres, a similar progression can be observed from urban centres in general to capital cities. In a region where international aid per capita reaches a level unparalleled anywhere else in the world (Antheaume & Bonnemaison, 1988; Gibson, this volume), the bulk of this aid ends up concentrated in the capital cities, little of it finding its way to rural areas. The capital city is frequently the only port of sufficient size to allow unloading of container and roll-on-roll-off ships, thus tending to monopolize most of the industrial, service, and even agricultural drive of the island nation.

As noted by Bayliss-Smith et al. (1988) and Ward (1993: 5), "despite government subsidies for freight services, a copra producer on an outer island in Fiji must produce 50 percent more copra than one located on the main island in order to buy the same basket of goods". The same comments can be applied to artisanal fishing in Vanuatu (David, 1991), where commercial fishing is economically viable only on the islands of Efate and Espiritu Santo, where the country's two main urban centres are located. This process of concentration of island nations' economies around their capital cities/major ports can only lead to depopulation of outlying islands, as their inhabitants tend to migrate toward the city, the only place where paid employment may be found.

The area of interfaces supports the bioenergetic system of the coastal zone and is responsible for both its high level of biological productivity and its fisheries-based economy. Acting as a buffer between land and ocean, it protects the former from the energy flows of the latter, while protecting the ocean from the flow of land matter and from the pressure of overfishing by redirecting this pressure onto its own space (Figures 13.2 and 13.3).

A total of six main types of space can be identified within this area: the reef front (formed of an algal ridge or an outer biogenic ridge), the reef flat, the beaches, the seagrass beds, the mangrove swamps and the estuaries. The first five are included in the intertidal zone and constitute an interface between sea, land and atmosphere, and their location varies to some extent with the rhythm of the tides. The estuaries, on the other hand, represent a complex interface that can be broken down into two elements existing side by side:

- a main interface bringing into contact fresh water and sea water and
- a secondary interface, part of the intertidal zone, which at low tide brings into contact the shallowest parts of the bottom of the estuary with the atmosphere.

The reef front plays an essential role in dissipating wave energy, so in protecting the shoreline from erosion, particularly when this shoreline is of a sedimentary nature. Thus, the reef front can be seen as a 'barrier' space. It is also extremely biologically rich on account of the intensity of the energy exchanges that take place, both through the breaking of the waves and the diffusion of endo-upwelled water. This upwelled water originates in the deeper layers of the ocean – it is in fact Antarctic water – and is extremely rich in nutrient salts, such as phosphates, nitrates and silicates. Once it penetrates the porous lower portion of the reef base or the permeable underlying volcanic formations, it is raised by thermal convection to the upper layers of the reef. This interstitial reef water then drains toward the ocean at the level of the reef front, where zooxanthellae living in the coral and the algae of the algal ridge consume its nutrients. As pointed out by Rougerie and Wauthy (1993), this dynamic process induces a permanent release of blooming zooxanthellae from coral and can be viewed as a starting point of the specific reef food chain.

So, the reef front is a barrier space which provides protection, nutrition and fertilization, functions which give it a major role in the economy of the coastal zone, particularly as it also provides a spatially limited but important environment for fishing activities. The reef front is used by line fishermen as a platform, and it serves as anchoring point for gill nets during low-tide calm-weather fishing operations on the reef slope.

The reef flat, although far larger than the reef front, is considerably poorer from the biological point of view. Large portions of it consist of dead coral, and life only really abounds in the pools and hollows. From the energy point of view, the reef flats impede the propagation of the wavelets resulting from the breaking of the ocean waves against the reef front and dissipate their energy. The reef flats can thus be described as a 'filter' space. Yet, from the point of view of fishing, the reef flats are essential. It is the space most frequented by the coastal inhabitants for this purpose. A wide range of fishing devices and techniques are used there: hand lines, gill nets, casting nets, hand spears, spear guns, bows and arrows, bush knives, holding pens, fish traps and vegetable poisons, among others. (David, forthcoming). The whole coastal population, including women and children, fish here, the latter concentrating on collecting shells, crustaceans and octopus.

Mangrove swamps, located along the line of contact of land and sea, are the only example of a marine forest on the planet. Providing the triple function of protection, nutrition and fertilization for the coastal environment, mangrove swamps are as economically important as the reef front for the high islands of Oceania.

Placed as a buffer between the destructive force of the ocean that of the land and the threatened coastal space, mangrove swamps act as a filter and reduce the potential for harm. This filter space is made of two superimposed sub-spaces: one aerial, the crowns of the trees, and the other semi-aquatic, the part of the their aerial root system that is submerged at high tide, made of both buttress roots and pneumatophores. The main effect of this aerial root system is to protect the sedimentary base on which it grows from erosion by wave action. In estuaries, by encouraging settling of suspended sediment, mangroves also contribute to reducing muddiness of the water, which otherwise would be destructive for coral growing near the river mouths. The aerial root system of the mangroves also creates a sanctuary where herbivorous fish such as *Clupeidae* and juveniles of other species may take refuge from the predators of both ocean and river mouth. The tree crowns act purely as filter: if the mangrove swamp is sufficiently large, it will absorb some of the force of ocean-born onshore storm winds, thus protecting dwellings and gardens lying inland.

Generally speaking, mangrove swamps are environments which are rich in nutrients for the species that shelter there. Decaying organic matter is abundant, and the part of the aerial root system submerged at high tide supports a number of small and microscopic marine algae. For this reason, a large population of coprophagous species, macrophagous herbivores, and species which feed on matter in suspension is found in mangrove swamps. In turn, the presence of these organisms attracts numerous predators. Thus, the mangrove swamps act as an 'biological magnet' for marine species particularly the following:

- shells and crustaceans which spend their entire existence there;
- species which come there to feed at each rising tide;
- species that feed there occasionally;
- fish species whose presence in the mangrove is linked to their reproductive cycle; and
- species that are born and live in deep water and migrate to the shore only for the duration of their juvenile stage; mangrove swamps provide them with optimum conditions for growth and survival.

The influence of mangrove swamps on the marine environment extends well beyond the adjacent waters. Exportations of leaf material can be assessed at an average value of eight to ten tonnes (t) per hectare (Lugo & Snedaker, 1974), and productivity, defined as the amount of biomass produced during a set time over a set area, has been estimated at approximately 30t per hectare per year where the mangrove trees are 15-20m tall (Chapman, 1977). The decay of this material provides a large quantity of nutrients to the marine environment and constitutes the basis of the food chain of the detritus consumer species which recycle organic matter directly without going through phases of mineralization and primary production (David, 1985).

Beaches constitute a final 'receptor' space where the energy flows generated by waves and tides terminate (Figure 13.2). Beaches are found mostly in bays and other locations protected from prevailing ocean swells. Surf action can nevertheless generate littoral drift which constitutes a powerful erosion factor. From the biological point of view, beaches provide a suitable environment for turtles to lay eggs.

Seagrass beds are found in a variety of locations. They occur most frequently seaward of mangrove swamps, on reef flats, and in the lower portion of well-sheltered beaches. From the energy point of view, their action is twofold: on one hand, the slowing down of the wavelets arriving at the shoreline and that of longshore currents--in this, the seagrass bed can be considered as a 'filter' space much as for the reef flats. On the other hand, they trap sediments carried by longshore drift (Figure 13.3).

Thus, seagrass beds play a substantial role in protecting the coastal zone from erosion. Their biological role is also important. Beyond the fact that they constitute the staple diet of dugongs and green turtles (*Chelonia mydas*), they fulfil a dual function of nutrition and protection for a number of invertebrate and fish species who either permanently inhabit the seagrass beds, or, more frequently, reef or mangrove species which occasionally wander there. Chambers et al. (1990: 98) note that seagrass beds provide protection and shelter to animals in a number of ways: by providing attachment surfaces for epibiota; by reducing current velocity; by reducing environmental extremes of temperature, salinity and light, particularly in intertidal and shallow water situations. For this reason seagrass beds constitute an attractive spawning zone for adults and a safe nursery for young fish. From the economic point of view, it is the bêche-de-mer found in seagrass beds that constitutes their main attraction (Conand, 1986).

The Coastal Zone and Sustainable Development

The dangers for the coastal zone

Being a buffer between ocean and land environments, the coastal zone is subject to attack by both. Although well adapted to withstand attack from natural causes, the coastal zone is particularly vulnerable to depredations caused by people. This situation is steadily worsening as island economies modernize and demographic pressures increase.

Among the factors tending to escalate the aggression on the coastal zone, the first one, which affects mostly coral reefs, is the increase in the volume of terrigenous sediment commonly attributed to intensification of human activity upstream. The quantity of this sediment has substantially increased over the last two decades owing to a shortening of the time the land is left to lie fallow (when the practice of fallow has not been altogether abandoned), the cultivation of sloping sites, the adoption of new agricultural techniques, the deforestation of steep catchment basins, and the changing climate (Nunn,

1990). This increase in soil erosion, particularly when compounded by damage to the mangrove swamps, may lead to a lasting increase in the suspended sediment content of coastal waters, severely disrupting coral ecosystems and affecting the economy of coastal village communities.

Another factor contributing to increased the pressure on the coastal zone is the discharge of waste products resulting from human activities. This can be domestic sewage, linked to increasing urbanization, soil and heavy-metal contaminated tailings entering the river system as a result of mining activity, pesticides from agricultural activity, and accidental spilling of petroleum products or industrial chemicals. All this contamination is particularly hard on mangrove swamps and coral reefs and can lead to their complete destruction (see McShane, this volume).

A third type of attack on the coastal environment is the destruction of natural spaces to make way for human activity. Here again, mangrove swamps and reefs are prime targets. In island nations where, on account of increasing demographic pressure, residential and public works projects are multiplying, the coastal zone often represents the only source of building materials. Reefs and underwater sand deposits are intensively dredged, often without any prior assessment of the possible sedimentological and biological repercussions of this disruption (Salvat, 1987). As for mangrove swamps, when they are not used for rubbish disposal, they are often filled to create new land for residential development or roads. In rural districts, mangrove swamps are also sometimes turned over to aquaculture projects[8] or simply to agricultural land.

Over-harvesting of resources also affects the coastal zone. Over-harvesting is commonly a function of population growth and the resulting increased demand for fisheries products. It can also be attributed to the introduction and spreading of more effective fishing devices, such as nets and spear guns. Yet, provided seriously damaging techniques, such as the use of dynamite, are avoided, this type of aggression on the coastal environment is less dangerous than the previous three. Indeed, while it endangers the sustainability of fishing activities, it does not seriously threaten the survival of most marine species; reef fish populations have demonstrated a great ability to recover their densities once fishing has significantly decreased, either through internal demographic dynamics or through migration from adjacent reef habitats. On the other hand, destruction of live coral on the reef flats by trampling and damage to submerged coral heads by boat chains and anchors in areas heavily frequented by pleasure boaters, constitute a far more serious danger. There, the very habitat of the marine species is threatened, and this is much slower to recover from damage than the species themselves.

Social and Economic Value of the Coastal Zone: the Example of Urban and Suburban Areas

Under attack from the four types of human aggression described above, the shorelines of urban and suburban areas are today the most threatened coastal zones in the high islands of Oceania. This is undesirable for ecological reasons and for social and economic reasons, which are seldom taken into account by the authorities. For Islanders living in towns and cities, the waterfront represents an important source of foodstuffs and a place for recreation. Mangrove swamps and reefs provide ways of varying the daily fare without financial outlay and offer the townfolk, who are often former country dwellers, a break from urban routine and the opportunity to spend a healthy day outdoors. For many of these people, urban living is often difficult from a material point of view, and culturally upsetting; fishing outings offer an ecological and cultural link with their former way of life. The more underprivileged these populations are, the more the role played by the waterfront in their perception of the world becomes important. These aspects have been but little discussed in the literature.

The majority of Pacific Islanders living in towns and cities were not born there. They are rural people who were lured to urban spaces in search of employment and a more modern life-style. Even though the rural migrant arriving in the city is often received by relatives or friends which helps lessen the shock of uprooting, the shift can nevertheless still be socially and culturally traumatic. The new migrant is confronted with an alien landscape and has to learn the ways of a new type of space.

The urban life-style, made of wage earning and a market economy, requires new habits and new rules of conduct. The migrant will have to become integrated into a new territory, a portion of which he will possibly have to claim as his own. Unlike his original territory, this new space is bare and devoid of familiar geosymbols, except for the site of his dwelling where he can bask in the warmth of his family, a small island of identity in the emotional vacuum that is the city. To fill this vacuum is no easy matter. Although in the rural setting every child is taught the ways of the village territory by the community, making the urban territory one's own can be achieved only by individual effort.

The kind of 5- to 10-storey residential buildings that are common in certain 'Islander' districts of Noumea and where hundreds of families live cheek by jowl in the heat and the din cannot possibly offer any shelter or protection against culture shock to the new rural migrants. Such an urban environment can only be culturally devastating for its inhabitants if they do not have the possibility occasionally to 'return to the source' through access to the reef flats and mangroves which have so far been spared by urbanization and which frequently constitute for them the last ecological and cultural link with their rural past.

Destruction of the foreshore means the loss of this last link leading, for the whole population, to a destructuring of perceived space,[9] a general feeling of dissatisfaction, and, for the youth, an escalation of a potentially dangerous kind of idleness which fishing activities could otherwise alleviate. Here, we uncover an essential aspect of the management of the coastal zone: the value that we can place on it.

Economic Planning and the Price of Nature

Far from being simply a physical space whose only economic interest resides in the part of its area that has potential for development, the coastal zone's real economic value derives from its ability to provide protection, nutrition and fertilization to marine animal communities used by people. The coastal zone can thus be considered as a piece of capital that returns a dividend every year, the amount of this corresponding to what the services it has performed are worth. By looking at it this way, once we have assessed the value of the dividend, we should be able to estimate the value of the entire capital.

Unlike human constructions, biological capital does not depreciate with time, provided it is managed in a rational manner and following the principles of maximum sustainable yield. The span of a generation (25-30 years) would seem to me sufficiently long to correspond to the resource management objective of maintaining a balance, which is the basis of sustainable development. It also corresponds to the most usual time frame chosen by the authorities for the granting of leases for harvesting of marine resources (Munro-Faure, 1992). Based on this assumption, the price of a mangrove swamp or a coral reef would correspond to the accrued interest generated by these assets over 25-30 years.

Another method for calculating the value of the coastal zone consists of calculating the cost of the technological equipment and constructions required to carry out the same functions as the natural heritage in the event of the latter being destroyed. In the case of mangrove swamps, two types of installations would have to be considered: first, the building of erosion protection installations in order to take over the function of protection of the land component of the coastal zone normally provided by mangrove swamps and, second, the creation of aquaculture ponds able to produce yearly a quantity of fish equivalent to that which would be lost, in their juvenile or adult stages, for lack of the protection and the feeding and spawning grounds afforded by the mangrove swamp.

Both of the above replacement measures require as precise knowledge as possible of the actual productivity of the threatened environment. This can be acquired by carrying out an extensive ecological inventory, which, because of the need for a large staff and for specialized craft, would be quite expensive. The high cost of such a survey can be considerably lowered by the use of high-resolution satellite remote sensing systems.

Given the difficulty of distinguishing sea-bed features below a depth of 5m, inventories can be taken only for species living in shallow waters. In places where the fringing reef is very narrow, the ground resolution of satellites is often inadequate to properly identify the sea-bed features (David, 1989). The solution is to use satellite data and aerial photographs in conjunction with each other, these latter having first been digitized and geometrically normalized prior to image processing analysis.

The ability to attribute a price to the coastal zone constitutes a valuable tool for decision makers (INSEE, 1986). So often in the past, coastal environments, such as mangroves or coral reefs, were sacrificed for the purpose of urban development and expansion of agricultural projects. The lack of pricing used to be associated with a lack of inherent value, whereby natural resources could not be expressed in monetary terms. The public authorities did not hesitate to replace natural space that they deemed of no value with an anthropic space that cost money to set up and was intended to be a source of eventual profits.

From now on, through a simple cost-benefit analysis, the planner and the politician will be able to assess the respective advantages of preserving the natural environment versus replacing it with an artificial environment. This should greatly facilitate the task of managing the coastal zone.

Conclusion

In view of the increasing concentration of population and economic activities around coastal cities prevalent in island nations, there can be no doubt that management of the coastal zone, still seen by most island governments as an esoteric discipline, will become central to planning.

Four objectives are as follows:

1. to make use of the potential of the natural environment with care to preserve the ecological balance;
2. to fulfil the current requirements of village communities and plan for their future needs;
3. to fulfil the requirements of the public authorities and of the developers; and
4. to minimize conflicts between the needs of the various current or potential users of the space.

It is essential to respect this last objective in order to avoid contradictions in the application of objectives 2 and 3, and the risks that this could mean for objective 1. The diversity of the interfaces found in the coastal zone and the diversity of the associated flows of energy and matter give the coastal zone potential for productivity of which human communities must be able to take full advantage. The long-term preservation of this productivity at its highest possible level for the least possible cost must be the golden rule on which to base any future management policy for the coastal zone. This rule will be adhered to only if development planners and public leaders, in whose power rests the decision to either destroy or preserve this unique environment, are fully aware of its value to the community.

The ability to assess the price of the various components of the coastal zone is invaluable in developing this awareness. In urban areas, because of their population density, their limited area, and the intensity of the use to which they are put, the coastal zone is the most threatened. The preparation of integrated coastal zone management plans for these urban areas should be one of the first priorities in the formulation of any coastal zone management policy. Such management plans must take into account the cultural and social role played by mangroves and reef flats in the lives of low-income urban families. The importance of the foreshore in the perceived space of these populations, therefore the consequences of its total or partial disappearance, is a subject which has not been sufficiently analysed.

In this particular field, as in the technical aspects of coastal development and management, geographers can play an essential role in the future. Geography's main concern is with the study of the interaction between the physical and human environment; it represents the meeting of physical sciences and human studies, and makes use of increasingly sophisticated tools, such as satellite high-resolution remote sensing, statistical cartography applied to data analysis, and geographical information systems.

Notes

1. Cook Islands, Federated States of Micronesia, Fiji, Kiribati, Republic of the Marshall Islands, Niue, Papua New Guinea, Solomon Islands, Tokelau, Kingdom of Tonga, Tuvalu, Vanuatu and Western Samoa.
2. By "geosymbol" we mean a place, an itinerary or an area which, for religious, political or cultural reasons is considered by certain people or ethnic groups to possess a symbolic dimension in which they find comfort and which helps them define their own identity (Bonnemaison, 1981).
3. This was noted for the Banks Islands by Vienne (1984) and confirmed by my own observations in Pentecost and Malakula. I believe it can be extrapolated to the whole country, when one considers the fishing techniques used at village level, where 70% of fishing outings consist of either wading in shallows or underwater diving (David & Cillaurren, 1989).
4. In her study of subsistence horticulture in the islands of Wallis and Futuna, Di Piazza takes this boundary even further because she considers that "coastal vegetation occupies the coastal plains and the lower slopes of the islands between elevations 0 m and 20 m" (1993: 18).
5. Elevation is the major limitation to human settlement in high islands. Apart from Papua New Guinea, where populated areas exist even above 2000m, human settlement is usually below 800m. In large, mineral-rich islands, such as New Caledonia, soil saturation in metallic salts constitutes an important limitation to agricultural expansion, thus to human settlement. For this reason, people have never permanently occupied the interior of the extreme south of New Caledonia.
6. Today, throughout much of the island Pacific, the population shift from the interior to the foreshore can be considered as complete. Yet Bonnemaison (1986) has noted one instance, in the interior of Pentecost Island, Vanuatu, of migration in the opposite direction, where people

settled on the coast were moving back to the empty interior. Yet, in most of the larger Melanesian islands, where only a few years ago one could still find isolated pockets of highland people which had had but few contacts with the outside world, migration is proceeding apace. In western Espiritu Santo, Vanuatu, the 1979 and 1989 census showed that many hill dwellers had left their mountains to resettle on the west and south coasts of the island, in search of a more modern way of life.

7. In the case of Western Samoa, Tonga and the Cook Islands, the urban space has also become a "sender" space, origin of a migratory population flow toward foreign countries, particularly New Zealand and the United States.

8. Aquaculture in these areas does not necessarily have to mean the destruction of mangrove swamps, as evidenced in New Caledonia where salt-water prawn farms have been established in the salt-saturated mud flats lying at the back of mangroves. This example, however, represents something of an exception. Most everywhere else in the Asia-Pacific region, where salt-water pond aquaculture has become an economic priority, mangrove swamps have been destroyed. Parish (1989) estimates that 70% of all Philippines mangrove swamps have disappeared to make way for aquaculture.

9. The role played by the disappearance of the natural foreshore in the destructuring of perceived space, followed by its restructuring on a different basis offers the geographer a wide field for investigation. Logically, it would seem that two scenarios are possible. Either one places the greatest value on the nature of the landmarks which structure one's perceived space, thus one is prepared to enlarge one's familiar territory in order that it may include, for instance, a new piece of shoreline, or one prefers to place greater value on maintaining the boundaries of one's territory, thus will seek a new landmark, of a different nature, to take the place of the vanished foreshore. If such a landmark does not exist, one will demand one of the authorities, such as a community recreation centre, a stadium, etc.

Chapter 14

Geographers at Sea: An Old Approach to Integrated Ocean Resources Management

Joeli Veitayaki

Introduction

Someone once asked me why geographers seemed prominent authorities in ocean resources management. I do not recollect the explanation I gave, but the question was conveniently forgotten until I was recently asked why a geographer, such as myself, currently holds a lectureship in ocean resources management. Apparently, it is perfectly normal if a lawyer, geologist, economist or a biologist is in my position, but, with a geographer, an explanation is needed. It is not clear why many people ignore the obvious connections between geography and ocean resources management. Whether born of ignorance or misconception, I am uncertain, but there is an obvious need to explain. For this reason, I write this chapter.

My aim in this chapter is to explain the reasons why geographers are perhaps the most suited specialists to be involved in ocean resources management. In attempting to explain and clarify the relationship between geography and ocean resources management, I reiterate Taylor's point that, as geographers, we "do not need any further 'proof' of the innate worthiness of geography but we do need self-conscious analyses and evaluations of our collective role in the society that supports and distorts us" (1985: 92). The relationship between geography and ocean resources management should be considered in the light of this predicament because the two subject areas are closely linked. Current academic biases have prevented people from understanding the close ties between the two subject areas.

Geography and ocean resources management both focus on human utilization of ocean resources and related issues. In both areas of study, the human relation with ocean resources is paramount as attempts are made to understand the nature of the resources and their use by humans. Geography, according to the late, well-known Fijian geographer, Isireli Lasaqa, is charged with the task of analysing the spatial realities of the real world based on the study of themes and problems that would ultimately "contribute to the understanding of the world and man's place inside it" (1973: 299).

Ocean covers 71% of the earth's surface which justifies a geographer's interest in this predominant feature of the human home. Ocean resources management focuses on the spatial realities of the ocean as the home of humankind and endeavours to enhance the understanding of people's use of, and relationship to, the ocean environment. Through studies in both geography and ocean resources management, humans strive to better understand their aquatic environment to ensure their continued survival.

I remember vividly the counselling which determined my career in geography and ocean resources management. Supervised by W.C. Clarke and R.R. Thaman, two distinguished Pacific geographers with keen interests in ocean resources, I was encouraged to carve a niche in the sea. Initially, I was hesitant because I was not too sure the move was a correct one. Fortunately, it did not take long before I was convinced that for my academic survival and distinction I had to renew and redefine the linkage between the two areas of study. It was not easy at first as books were not in familiar places, information was not to be found in the normal source areas, and authorities other than geographers had to be consulted, but my personal interest had already been sufficiently nurtured and was flourishing.

My fascination with the vastly important and little understood area of ocean resources management was enhanced by my involvement at an early age in rural village fishing and my interest in the unique and dynamic qualities of small-scale artisanal fisherfolk. I had experienced the demanding nature of fishing, the frustrating lack of equipment, and the depleting resources of the commonly worked fishing areas. I was also familiar with the disabling feeling of failure, the seemingly endless periods of hunger, the insatiable urge for fish, and the fishing techniques that I now know to be very destructive.

In undertaking my study, I was convinced that I was to make a contribution with small-scale fisheries utilization. The qualities of the skilful men and women who reside in villages, who invest the barest minimum in their fishing, who pursue fish in their realm as if there were no tomorrow and use equipment, which is an eclectic combination of old and new, intrigued me. I presumed all the time that fisherfolk at this level were misconstrued and their contribution was underestimated. Being a Pacific Islander, I wanted to describe the nature of these fisherfolk as they really are, to reinforce the understanding of the role of small-scale commercial fishing in villages and in the national economy and to contribute to our knowledge of the world of which we are a part.

The importance of the ocean to humans is clearly evident in the life of Pacific Islanders. The sea is their food basket and hunting ground, their recreational arena, theatre and art gallery, and the highway that links them to the surrounding world. Yet, in spite of the ocean's invaluable nature and the Pacific Ocean's coverage of 32% of the surface of the globe, Pacific geographers have not been quick to apply their expertise to issues and themes that focus on ocean affairs.

I am alarmed to note that in spite of a land to sea ratio of 1:100 in the Pacific, scholarly work is overwhelmingly concentrated on terrestrial issues, exemplifying the global human disregard for ocean resources. Even at the University of the South Pacific (USP), a university serving a region where the dominant feature of the environment is the ocean, there is no specific geography course on ocean resources and management. The Geography Department at the USP, fully aware of this deficiency in its programme, allows some students the option of taking the courses available within the Ocean Resources Management Programme. This situation is lamentable because most of our graduates, particularly those from smaller nations, will be working in the field of ocean affairs following graduation. The USP's recent establishment of the Marine Studies Programme is indicative of the desire to rectify this situation and highlight the importance of the sea to this region.

The Last Frontier

The ocean distinguishes the Earth from other planets in the solar system. The presence of water on the "blue planet" allows for life as humans know it. As an important domain in the home of mankind, the ocean has been influential in the development of the global system. The discovery and colonization of continents and islands were the result of humankind's ability to conquer the ocean. Great nations and empires were associated with powerful naval forces capable of transcending the seas and defending their interest anywhere in the world. For these extraordinary feats, geographical skills and knowledge of navigation, positioning and mapping, were used to enhance the movement from one place to the next.

Amongst the great ocean explorers were some of the founders of geography. These people had exceptional qualities to make observations and to identify patterns and processes. The early explorers, such as those that came to the Pacific in the 16th and 17th centuries, drew maps and diagrams and helped establish settlements in the 'new' world. Communication and shipping between nations linked the continents and created a globally interdependent system. Information on the location, climate, plant and animal life-forms, and the origin of islands was added to previously acquired knowledge as these pioneers extended human knowledge. The resultant scramble for offshore territories and colonization were the consequence of the new sources of supplies and markets that were secured in the new world across the sea.

The ocean is the last major frontier on earth for the exploration and development of resources to sustain humankind in the future. Despite the rapid exploration of ocean and coastal areas and the much slower penetration of inland regions in earlier times, the more demanding nature of the ocean has made our knowledge of it and its resources minimal. The exploration of the ocean is comparatively expensive and demands sophisticated technology. Storms, currents, ice, depth, its vast size and hidden state are characteristic features of the ocean environment which impede exploration and research work and presently hamper our understanding of ocean systems and environments. Compared to its potential, the sea has been little exploited.

The treatment of ocean resources as the solution to world problems has heightened our desire to understand ocean resources systems and the relationship between humans and the marine environment. Figure 14.1 summarizes some of these intricate interrelationships. The multiple uses of the ocean is well illustrated in the Pacific where, apart from all the common uses, the deployment of nuclear weapons and the disposal of dangerous waste are causes of great concern because of the associated threats of ocean pollution and degradation of coastal, littoral and pelagic habitats.

The increasing human interest in the ocean is the result of the perception that it is the most important future source of food, energy, minerals, chemicals and space. The current high population, its unprecedented growth rates and the expansion of human settlements are of great concern. Humans are intruding on the best agricultural land which is continually being replaced by less suitable and marginal areas. The ensuing crop failures, advances of desert margins, and the subsequent food scarcity and protein deficiency in many parts of the world have compelled humans to direct their attention to the ocean. Aquaculture and mariculture are becoming increasingly significant as human knowledge extends to more species, better breeding and cultivation techniques. Yet, recent discoveries have shown that, unless

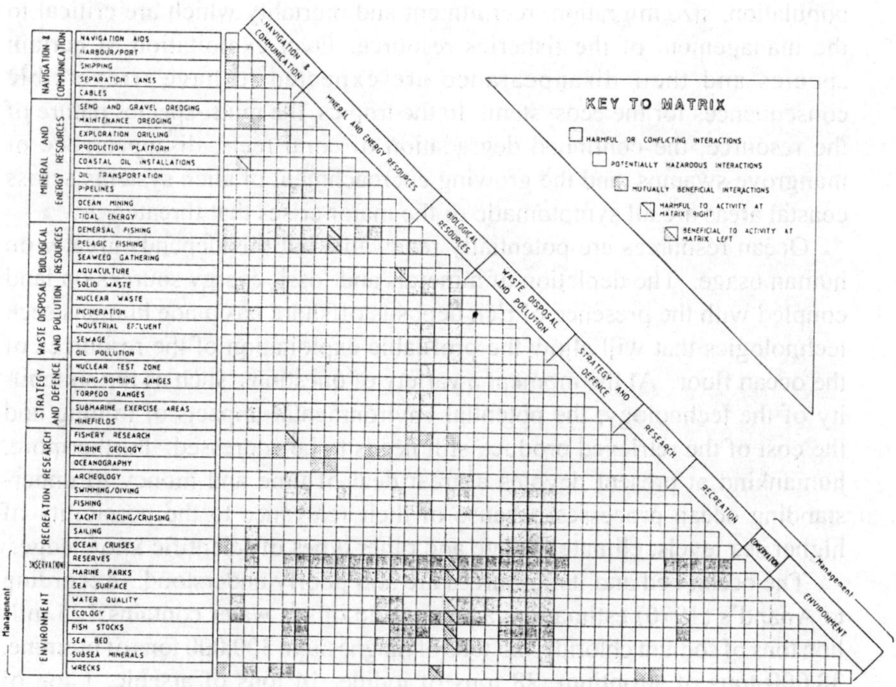

Figure 14.1 The global marine interaction model representing the main relationships between sea uses and a range of environmental implications (Vallega, 1990: 48; reprinted with permission of the author).

humans exercise more caution in their utilization of the ocean, this whole scenario may be problematic because the ocean, like the land, is becoming degraded.

Boundless Wealth

Present global fisheries production is around 100 million metric tonnes which is far in excess of what was once considered the carrying capacity of the world's ocean. The production figure is greater if the by-catch discarded at sea and the catch used for fishmeal production are included. Reliance as at present on the maximum sustainable yield (MSY), although theoretically sensible, is pragmatically illogical, particularly given the difficulties in determining the figure. Other considerations involve issues of fish population, size migration, recruitment and mortality which are critical to the management of the fisheries resource. Over-exploitation of certain species and their disappearance are expected to have irreversible consequences for the ecosystem. In the tropics, the multi-species nature of the resource, the continued degradation of coral reefs, disappearance of mangrove swamps, and the growing encroachment of alien systems across coastal areas are all symptomatic of the major crises that threaten us.

Ocean resources are potentially renewable but this depends greatly on human usage. The depletion of minerals and fossil energy sources on land coupled with the presence of rich deposits offshore has made humans seek technologies that will allow the profitable exploitation of the resources of the ocean floor. At the moment a variety of questions, such as the suitability of the technology, the potential environmental impacts of mining and the cost of the retrieved product, still needs to be addressed. Furthermore, humankind at present devotes a great deal of time and money to understanding ocean processes because of their relevance to the possibility of higher sea levels, climate change and other types of scientific knowledge.

The ocean bed and its resources are still poorly understood. According to Anand's (1976) estimation, a cubic mile of sea water contains 125 million tons of sodium chloride, 6.5 tons of magnesium, 300,000 tons of bromine, 38,000 tons of strontium, 28 tons of iodine, 14 tons of arsenic, 1 ton of silver, 0.02 tons of gold and 14 tons of uranium. The resources are staggering when we consider that there are 324 million cubic miles of sea water in the ocean. The red clay that covers half the Pacific Ocean floor and a fourth of that in the Atlantic and Indian oceans contains 920 trillion tons of aluminium, 650 trillion tons of iron, 73 trillion tons of titanium and more than

1.5 trillion tons of vanadium, cobalt, nickel copper, lead and zirconium. Although the figures appear overwhelming, human knowledge of the sea is so negligible that many may be excessively imprecise. For the time being, in most Pacific nations, common salt, sand and gravel remain the most commonly exploited non-living resources of the sea.

The sea unites and divides human settlements. Movements across the ocean allow humans to extend their horizons and acquire a global perspective. The need for safe and reliable transport necessitates the study of wind systems, stars, circulation, waves, tides and other phenomena such as the El Niño-Southern Oscillation. The earliest coastal dwellers, such as those in the Pacific, demonstrated uncanny ability to sail from one location to another using such knowledge. Unfortunately these skills, which were taught through experience and by word of mouth, have nearly all been lost with modernization.

Global dependence on sea transport is important in spite of the use of other forms of transportation. In a world so dependent on the heavy transfer of commodity goods, boat and port design and size, equipment and other back-up facilities have been improved as attempts have been made to make shipping faster, safer and capable of meeting the increasing demand.

Ocean transportation was the first mode of communication developed to support the global system. Even today, all nations including the superpowers and landlocked states are dependent on ocean transportation. The concentration of population and urban centres in coastal areas reflects the importance of an association with ocean transport. The trade relations and the dependence of nations on external producers, which replace the independent traditional systems, make it fundamental that ocean transport be reliable and of high standard.

International cartels were formed amongst the operators to enhance efficiency on particular routes. Through time, flags of convenience emerged under which vessels are registered in countries which do not care about enforcing regulations regarding taxation, registration, safety standards and crew qualification. Consequently, concern has been voiced for the health of the oceans because of shipping accidents, discharge of waste, criminal conduct in relation to international shipping regulations, and conflict among countries over access and ownership of maritime areas. To address these concerns, international conventions and regulations have been adopted to ensure the safety and lawful conduct of maritime transport operators.

New technology is now employed to enhance control over shipping as problems costing millions of dollars are faced through piracy or fraudulent maritime activities. Meanwhile the use of containers has revolutionized the shipping industry. This illustrates the demanding nature of the trade which continues to evolve at such a fast rate that those who do not adapt quickly enough to the changing trends lose their business.

The use of ultra-big vessels, wharves and machinery is a burden to coastal nations which also have to attract vessels to their ports by the trading in which they partake. Although bigger vessels are more efficient in meeting the demands of bigger nations, they may be excessive for small nations. These small nations, therefore, must decide whether to have bigger vessels and be part of the global shipping circle, or to use smaller, more appropriate ships which serve their purpose yet effectively exclude them from the rest of the world. Mechanization of ports has to be weighed against the need to provide employment to the local labour force; the size of the port should be based on the ability of the nations to pay for, and sustain, either modern ports capable of handling ultra-big vessels, or smaller more appropriate ones that can never be used by the world's major shipping companies. The expensive nature of such investments makes such decisions critical.

Contemporary Challenges

Humankind today faces two challenges which are critical to the management of ocean resources and the survival of human civilization. The first is the ecological problem associated with the environment humankind has created. Human use of natural resources and disposal of waste have upset the ecosphere's state of natural equilibrium so much that it seriously threatens the habitability of the earth.

The second challenge is the political one associated with the decision of nations either to compete with each other for power and wealth or to co-operate and combine their purposes, ingenuity and resources in an international order that considers human interest globally. Ocean resources transcend national boundaries while the effects of events in some parts may be transported to other areas around them. In such cases, international co-operation is necessary to unravel quickly the mysteries of the ocean, to exploit its resources in a sustainable manner to provide food, and to secure the exploitation of energy and minerals to replace rapidly depleting terrestrial resources.

The multiple uses of the ocean are often a cause of conflict creating conservational and ecological problems. Fisherfolk, tourist operators, national developers, civic authorities and local villagers often have conflicting interests. In the meantime, while humans are turning to the sea to provide resources that supplement those that were once abundant on land, they are using the ocean as the convenient portion of the earth in which to hide and store waste. As shown in the case of the Mediterranean Sea, which is one of the world's most heavily used seas, the situation can easily become overwhelming (Figure 14.2).

Now threatened by the world they have created, humans are using scientific technological knowledge to correct the wrong they have lived with since the beginning of industrialization. Polluted coastal areas are now being cleaned, rejuvenated and monitored while a better understanding of the world system is being used to guide human activity. Natural reserves and marine parks are being set up to stimulate the recovery of fishing areas while environmental impact assessments are routinely conducted as part of proposed new development projects.

The increasing importance of the ocean has caused marked changes over the question of its ownership. The oceans of the world are being subdivided and subjected to more exclusive national controls as nations are convinced of the opportunities associated with their ocean resources. The concept of *res communis* which means that the sea was under common ownership and open for common use at all times is now replaced by *res nullius* which denotes that the sea is not common to all, but that, in its original state, it belongs to no one and is available for national appropriation.

The United Nations Convention on the Law of the Sea (UNCLOS) III was thus created to "avoid another era of modern colonialism resulting in a dangerous race between nations for the choice areas of the ocean and ocean floor" (Evensen, 1984: 5). The resulting international agreement, designed to protect and preserve the marine environment, conserve its living resources, properly manage its non-renewable resources, facilitate international communications, promote efficient and peaceful uses of the sea, and advance the interests and needs of humankind, is the most comprehensive political and legislative multilateral work accomplished by the United Nations.

It is most fitting that the first comprehensive international agreement undertaken by the nations of the world is a guideline on the use of the sea. Given the attractions of UNCLOS III and the determination of developing countries to realize the full benefit of its provisions, there is a possibility that it will initiate a new world order. The nations of the Pacific

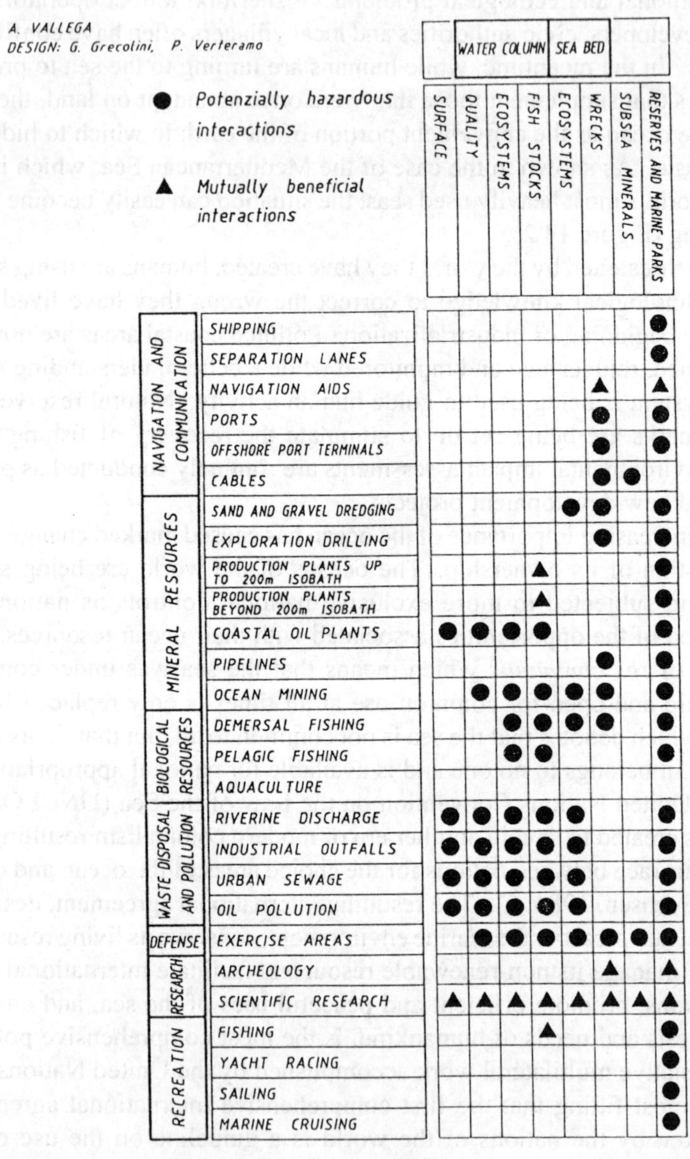

Figure 14.2. The web of uses in the Mediterranean Sea. The methodological approach reflects the "global marine interactions" model (Vallega, 1990: 52; reprinted with permission of the author).

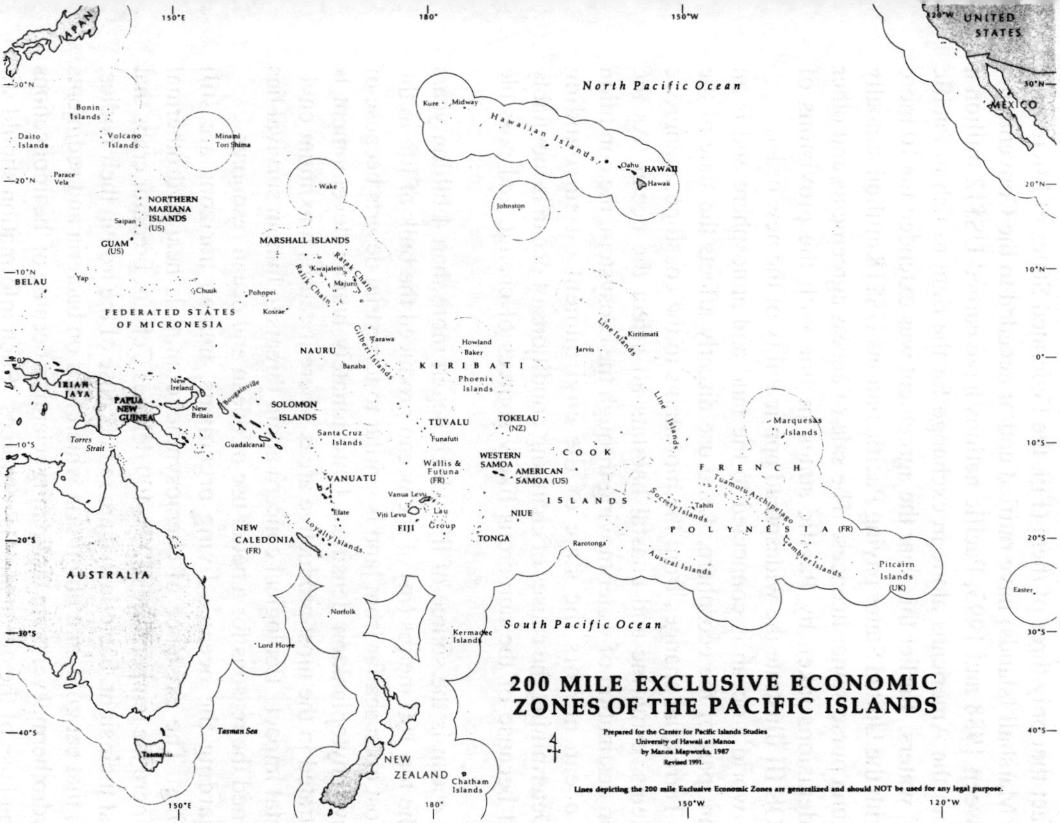

Figure 14.3. The vast area constituted by the Exclusive Economic Zones of the Pacific Island countries. (Reprinted with permission from the Center for Pacific Islands Studies, University of Hawai'i at Manoa.)

are now responsible for managing a significant portion of the Pacific Ocean (Figure 14.3). These nations are now managing their collective zone the way they want it, earning money and having their claims observed in spite of the fact that only three of them (Fiji, the Federated States of Micronesia and the Marshall Islands) have ratified and/or acceded to the Convention.

Between 1988 and 1993, Pacific nations have earned US$12 million a year from the Americans alone in exchange for the right to fish in Pacific nations' waters. Earlier this year the agreement was extended for 10 more years with the United States paying Pacific nations US$18 million annually for 55 tuna purse-seiner licences. The sale of access agreements and other major decisions taken by Pacific states in line with the provisions of UNCLOS III illustrate the widespread applicability of the new order.

The world's ocean is connected to the land and atmosphere and is an important part of the ecosphere. Land use directly affects the state of the ocean. Terrestrial changes from the mountains to the coastline, mangrove ecosystems, estuarine and coastal habitats all affect the ocean. As the common destination of water moving through the ecosystem, the condition of the ocean mirrors the state of the environment on surrounding land. Determining the causes of changing conditions of ocean is inevitably difficult because of the numerous likely sources of change and possible causes.

The ocean is the source of life which began more than 4 billion years ago. The top 100 metres (m) of the ocean produced the bulk of life in the sea. Most open sea far from land is similar to terrestrial deserts because of their low phytoplankton densities. Unfortunately human development is concentrated in the most productive areas where it causes maximum environmental impact. Ecological concern about threats to human survival has heightened the reasons for a better use of ocean and ocean resources.

Regarding the ocean's living organisms, human horizons are still expanding. The existence of chemosynthetic animals near hydrothermal vents where the temperature is 295-400 degrees Celsius, predator crabs that have lost their sight, bacteria that are red because of the iron in their bodies, bacteria that eat gold, and holothuria which feed on bacteria and sediments from hydrothermal vents are fascinating scientists because of the implications for human use of the ocean and its resources. Such information should stir interest into a wide range of possible new uses of ocean resources.

Our knowledge of the ocean has increased greatly since Magellan sailed around the globe and proved that the world was round, not flat as previously believed, or when Wegener first proposed the idea of continental drift, but there is still a lot to be learned. With the advent of sophisticated scientific technology, more information is becoming available on volcanism, earthquakes, tsunami, El Niño, marine organisms and the mineral resources of the sea bed. Yet, with the depth of the oceans averaging 4,000m, the task of understanding the ocean to levels comparable to our knowledge of terrestrial features presents awesome challenges.

Anthropogenic Influences

Fishing technology and skills have evolved through time as people attempted to understand their ocean resources to allow their more effective use. From early times when it was a matter of the prey being outmanoeuvered by the hunter, sophisticated fishing technology and equipment have made fishing very efficient compared with many other forms of hunting. Such efficiency has led to the depletion of fish in some areas and now threatens the fish population throughout the world. Purse seiners, draggers and drift nets are so efficient that fish stand little chance of escape. With the use of fish finders, helicopters and other sophisticated devices, the odds are stacked heavily against the fish. Modern industrial fishing is so wasteful that millions of tons of non-targeted species or by-catch are discarded or used for fishmeal production yearly. The failure of fisheries around the world, such as the one that resulted in the 2-year moratorium on cod fishing off Newfoundland, Canada, is a continuous reminder of the delicate balance that humans are upsetting.

Amongst rural coastal dwellers, the intensive utilization of fish resources is continuing under the banner of economic development. Villagers are abandoning subsistence fishing methods and are taking up artisanal fishing whereby they fish to cater for their needs and those of their buyers residing further away. The use of modern technology, such as fishing equipment, storage facilities and outboard motors, has made fishing in remote areas accessible to major urban markets.

It is ironic that governments provide assistance for fisherfolk to be more efficient and productive but, as soon as they are hooked on making money, the government tries to convince them to reduce their catch and sustainably use the fish resources which by then are often under serious threat. Various regulations, including prohibition periods, gear bans and size limitation, often poorly enforced, have been devised to sustain a lower productivity.

Amongst coastal areas, the challenge is often the decision between the maximization of productivity and sustainable fisheries use. Although the idea of achieving sustainable fisheries development is noble, the act is debatable. Management practices have nearly always failed as fisherfolk are encouraged by market forces to disregard them. Unless the enforcement officers are checking closely, regulations are invariably ignored. Many fisherfolk are not attached to the resources or committed to their management because they do not regard them as their own.

Although we have some idea of what the resources are like out there, we are unaware of the resources in totality. Thus, although we may rely on maximum sustainable yields to protect the resources, such levels may well be in excess of the ecosystem's carrying capacity. Similarly, the concept of economic optimum yield is pointless unless there is total control over fishing activity. Under open access conditions, levels of fishing can easily exceed the maximum sustainable yield. The management task is staggering because of the existence of different fishing categories, resources, fishing areas and practices.

It seems that the mineral riches of the ocean are boundless. Yet, the excavation of sand, gravel and coral from coastal areas is associated with increasing coastal erosion and ecosystem change. The exploitation of deep sea minerals, such as manganese nodules using either the bucket or vacuum cleaner (suction) method, is expected to disturb the ocean floor. The suitability of the mining technology, the impact of the mining, the processing, and the storage of waste are the subject of much debate. Should ultra-big vessels be used for ore processing at sea or should the bulky product be shipped to land? How should the development be undertaken? Must those with the means and technology be given the blessing to exploit the resources or must those states within whose waters the development falls be encouraged to participate? Then, there is the question of, and arrangement for, technology transfer and access agreements. These are some issues which make this the most widely debated topic in ocean affairs today.

The ocean and coastal areas are prominent features of the picture postcard image of islands. Yet, the clean and healthy white sandy beaches, swinging palm trees, colourful coral reefs and fishes and dark blue sea are now confined to remote locations. Human use and abuse of the marine world is even catching up with them. The polluted rivers and coastlines, altered foreshore and estuarine areas, and the depletion of fisheries resources are examples of poorly managed coastal areas. In the Pacific, Suva harbour, Pagopago and other major urban centres all exemplify the extent of the problems in what many still term 'paradise'.

The ocean has long been regarded the appropriate part of the earth to place human wastes. Human preoccupations with economics and short-term safety have led to dangerous and life-threatening wastes being tucked away in parts of the ocean. Nerve gas and other toxic waste discarded by the United States are stored and burnt at Johnston Atoll because, according to the U.S. government, it is the safest and most appropriate site. Nuclear wastes sealed in containers that will eventually disintegrate and release their deadly contents to the sea, long before the waste decomposes, are stored beneath the sea. Supertankers use sea water for ballast and release this directly into the sea just before they enter ports. Such activity adds to the millions of tons of waste that find their way to the sea from countless land sources. For too long, humans have taken advantage of the ocean's capacity to cleanse itself and have turned it into a cheap and convenient dumping ground. In spite of its large size, the ocean today exhibits the impact of human activity.

Conclusion

My paper has shown the importance of geography to ocean resources management. Not only do geography and ocean resources management address compatible issues, their use of the integrated approach (that is now considered revolutionary by many others) has been far-sighted. In both subject areas, emphasis has been placed on the human uses of the ocean, in particular the sustainability and management of ocean resources. Geographical issues associated with the analysis of the spatial realities of the real world based on the study of themes and problems that contribute to understanding the world and humanity's place within it are connected to ocean resources management which covers any aspect of human utilization of the marine environment and its resources.

The geographer's way of handling issues as systems that influence, and are influenced by, a number of interrelated factors makes them suitable authorities on ocean resources management. A geographical analysis of fishing, for instance, is not restricted to just the act of catching an available species of fish; rather, it is the result of a variety of processes that include the ownership of fishing grounds, accessibility of fishing resources, technology sophistication, marketing schemes, fisheries resources management practices and training arrangements. It considers variations in fishing emphasis, fish products and fishing traditions. In contemporary societies, such an integrated approach means the success or otherwise of a fishing project. The imposition of commercial fishing projects by outsiders and the lack of appreciation of socio-economic situations are two factors now commonly associated with the widespread failure of village fishing projects. The imposition of supposedly workable management strategies have often failed because they did not consider the local way of doing things.

With its physical and cultural components, geography is perhaps the only single discipline that can cover the study of ocean and ocean resources in its totality. The issues are varied, but they are within the geographer's holistic sphere of interest. Competence in understanding the physical forces at work in the ocean on one hand, and the skill to relate these to the cultural and socio-economic implications of the physical events on the other, are perhaps the main reasons why geographers make such good ocean resource managers.

The multi-disciplinary approach suits the nature of both geography and ocean resources management because of the coverage of a wide range of topics and issues that indicate the broad nature of ocean studies and the wide usage of ocean resources. This situation requires knowledge of various concepts, such as is the case with geography and ocean resources management which are associated with both science and social science. While humans are social beings, they are part of an environment which is best understood scientifically. On the other hand, although the provisions of the Law of the Sea are based on extensive scientific knowledge and findings, the amicable effectiveness of the convention is based on the social notion that the enjoyment of rights and benefits of states simultaneously involves their undertaking of duties and obligations.

In the Pacific, geographers, like good cricket all-rounders, are prominent in the public and private sectors and in decision making. Now the onus is on contemporary geographers to become effective marine resource managers as well. There is no better time to do that than the 25th anniversary of existence of the principal University in this vast oceanic region.

I have never regretted my involvement in ocean resources management. My continued existence and association with ocean resources management is sufficient evidence of the close relation between the two areas of study. As with other geographers before me, my concerns are well founded and necessary for the management of ocean resources. Indeed, the niche is expanding as more and more people become convinced that geographers are providing appropriate advice on how the complex issues of ocean resources management can be best addressed.

Chapter 15

Afterword: Learning from Ngirapo: Indigenous Knowledge and Sustainable Agricultural Development

William C. Clarke

Even in today's world of computer-based Geographic Information Systems, the fundamental part of a geographer's research into the rural tropics remains field-work. As professional academics, we geographers prepare ourselves for going into the field by reading the literature on the area, acquiring maps and aerial photos, gathering together the brute statistical facts, and planning the physical and intellectual aspects of our field campaign. Then, in our stout boots, running shoes, or plastic thongs, we venture forth, armed with pencil, paper, maps, and other tools of our trade, in the hope that we can capture worthwhile geographical knowledge about some particular part of the earth. We make our own observations, but we almost always also seek informants from among the people of the area we study. We strive to learn from them more about the relationships between rural folk and their earth. We carry out formal or informal interviews, getting to know individuals who become our local mentors, instructing us about their lives, their place, their geography.

When the time comes for us to return to our desks – to move from "Being There" to "Being Here", to use Clifford Geertz's (1989) apt and arresting terms – we carry back with us a world of feeling and fact gained from our field-work. We remember our informants as individuals, often as persons we liked. We are grateful to them for what they taught us, and, usually, we offer them distant thanks in our Acknowledgements. In our written texts, however, we invariably generalize what we have learned from them. The individuals we talked with in the field are veiled behind the forms of academic discourse. The local knowledge we haltingly acquired from real people during rainy or dusty days on a hillside or river bank is smoothed into a cohesive report directed to another world. That world – if I may extend to geography what Geertz (1988) says about our sister science anthropology – is the world that produces geographers, that licenses us to do the kind of work we do, and within which the kind of work we do must find a place if it is to be worth attention. Of itself, Being There is an exotic postcard experience. It is Being Here, a scholar among scholars, that gets our geography read, published, reviewed, cited, taught, and trickled into textbooks, aid projects and consultancy reports.

Not so many decades ago such self-conscious, reflexive concern – when it existed at all – found this dissociation acceptable, for it helped keep the scientists sufficiently detached or objective in their work. It was good scientific method for the scientist to be estranged from the Other – the diversity of researched peoples of a culture or, at least, of a socio-economic class different from the scientist's. Now the concern focuses more on whether or not scientists are sufficiently engaged with the people they study (Geertz, 1988; Marcus, 1986). Our present worry is less about objectivity and more about the proper form of engagement or the propriety of scientists Being There at all in a post-colonial world, amid the tatters of Western self-confidence, the inequalities of wealth, the remnants of ineffective aid projects, and an ebbing belief both in the salvational powers of science and in the possibilities of development, whether sustainable or not.

In many ways, worry about insufficient engagement or about the ethics of a dichotomy (or a bridge) between Being There and Being Here is beside the point. Geographers and anthropologists are no longer able, even if they so desired, to separate There from Here. They can no longer write about the rural folk of X or Y as though X or Y were in a world remote from that of the scientists. Particularly in universities, such as the University of the South Pacific, researchers find students from X or Y reading their books and papers or attending and responding to their lectures. Beyond that, all peoples now live in a world of global pollution, media permeation, and economic connection, where There, Here, and Everywhere are inseparable, where the imperative of development leads the academic geographer, as well as other scientists, working in less developed regions to feel a requirement to turn research towards applied purposes on the ground, rather than using it solely for academic purposes and career advancement.

It is within the context of the foregoing thoughts and the world they make reference to that I take the opportunity offered by this volume, first, to pay a kind of homage to a Papua New Guinean man called Ngirapo, from whom I learned so much of value early in my career as a geographer working in the Pacific Islands. He will most likely never know what I write; more than likely he is dead; but I mean my homage to him also to be a general tribute to all the Pacific men and women who over many years have taught me and my colleagues about their agriculture, their use of plants, their ecological concepts, their geography, and much more. I have chosen Ngirapo to represent them all, partly because he had a rare charisma that I can never forget and partly because he spent his youth in the veritable Stone Age, so once stood firmly in an archetypal There, now of an almost vanished remoteness from the modern world.

Second, and bearing directly on the process of learning from indigenous informants in the field, I will discuss the quite remarkable increase of interest over the past few years in 'indigenous knowledge', a term now so widely popular that it has its own acronym (IK). By indigenous knowledge is usually meant knowledge held about, and techniques used in, resource management and utilization by local, indigenous peoples within their own territories. Recent researchers into indigenous knowledge often praise IK in comparison with modern information and inputs, asserting that it offers a path to sustainable agricultural development and resource conservation. Although much of my research work has focused on the indigenous knowledge of Pacific Islanders in relation to agriculture and plants, and I have often argued for the value of such knowledge in today's world (*e.g.*, Clarke, 1971, 1977, 1978; Clarke & Thaman, 1993), I will make the perhaps paradoxical point in this paper that too much is now being made of it. Geertz's There is too often being seen as a magical treasure trove of knowledge, technique, and wisdom that will save the village, if not the world, from environmental degradation. My view now is that indigenous knowledge has much to offer but it is not a miracle fix. The belief that it is turns our attention away from its other, perhaps more valuable, attributes and diverts us from broader, more difficult tasks than the application of another technology.

Meeting Ngirapo

I met Ngirapo in 1964 when I first visited his home territory in the Bismarck Mountains in what was then the Australian administered Territory of New Guinea. From the outside world, to reach his homeland, which I called the Ndwimba Basin, I had flown from the coastal town of Madang into the mountains fringing the great highland basins in the centre of the island of New Guinea to land on the short, grass covered airstrip at the

Simbai Patrol Post, the small and unimportant administrative centre for the Simbai Valley and several neighbouring valleys. From the airstrip, near the headwaters of the Simbai Valley, I walked down the valley for two days along earthen tracks cut into the steep slopes of the valley's southern side. A notable feature of the walk was the change in vegetation along the way, from the extensive grasslands of the upper Simbai Valley, manifesting much human activity, through the mosaic of forest, garden, and grass in the middle valley, to the region of the Ndwimba Basin, which had almost no grassland and beyond which along the north side of the Bismarck Range lay a great stretch of almost uninhabited forest. The Ndwimba Basin's location at the edge of the empty forest and far from the Simbai Patrol Post led people in less remote locations – remote in the modern context – to say that Ngirapo and his fellow clan members were a particularly rustic band, who lived "at the tail of the snake" (Clarke, 1980).

During my first hours in the Ndwimba Basin, Ngirapo was one of the few local men to emerge in my consciousness as an individual. With the flamboyance of many New Guinean men, he stepped forward from the curious crowd of welcoming onlookers, hugged and lifted me from the ground, then stood back and broadcast a welcoming oration, expressing gladness that a European had come to stay with his people. Altogether, I spent many months in the Ndwimba Basin during 1964, 1965, and more briefly in 1970 and 1977. During these stays, I came to know Ngirapo and his family well and passed many days walking with him in the forest and in his gardens and orchards, questioning him and learning from him.

Because Ngirapo was a few kilos heavier and slightly shorter than was average for the men of the Basin, he looked particularly robust, an attribute that was heightened by his vigorous style of speech and movement. In early 1965, when I took a census in the basin, I estimated him to be 40 years old. Certainly strong, he appeared to be in excellent health. Even his teeth still looked sound, although he suffered from the common condition among the local people of tooth enamel receding from the gums.

In 1965 he had two wives, each of whom had come from a clan outside the basin. He also had eight living children, six with Ant'wen, his long-standing wife (Plate 15.2), and two with Kuka, a younger, more recent acquisition. The children, five boys and three girls, ranged in age from a nursing infant to a son about 18 years old. Ngirapo lived with his older sons in a man's house, which, as was customary, was often used as sleeping quarters by other men. For each wife, he had built a separate woman's house

Plate 15.1. Ngirapo, at ease, with the forested wall of the Ndwimba Basin behind him.

Plate 15.2. Ant'wen, Ngirapo's older wife, in a *Pandanus-Gnetum* orchard, admiring the *Pandanus* fruits developing on a mature tree.

at some distance from each other in different hamlets, for Ant'wen was a "strong woman" who had beaten Kuka with a stick, not wanting to share Ngirapo's gardens or pigs with the younger wife. Despite this trouble, which was common between co-wives in highland New Guinea (Read, 1954), Ngirapo explained to me that "a man wants two wives because he wants many pigs and also many children, who will grow up, marry, and work in the gardens." A factor in this calculation was that his children would take care of him and his wives in their old age, but I believe, on the basis of many talks with him, that beyond this practical concern he experienced an almost metaphysical sense of continuity flowing from past generations to the present one and to those of the future, all comprising people strongly linked with the same land, living and working there. Although when his father died, Ngirapo was an adolescent only old enough to have begun to make gardens and to build his own fences, he had kept in mind many locally named sites where his father had planted gardens. This knowledge, shared with other older men in the clan, not only entitled him and his sons to use the sites again for their own gardens but also, I judged, made him feel a chain of connection between each patch of land and its successive occupants over a long time, a feeling that endowed his whole landscape with points of high significance.

I have described elsewhere in detail the agriculture practised by Ngirapo and his fellow inhabitants of the Ndwimba Basin (Clarke, 1971). Here, I will note only that it was a classic form of long-fallow, polycultural shifting cultivation, or swidden, carried out in a forested region with a population density of about 26 persons per square km (approximately 68 persons per square mile), a figure that falls below the carrying capacity for swidden in similar environments as estimated or calculated by several anthropologists and geographers working in tropical areas (Clarke, 1971). The virtual absence in the basin of retrogression of forest to grassland together with the complexity and full maturation of the secondary forest gave evidence on the ground that the carrying capacity was not exceeded. Elsewhere, not far away in the Simbai Valley and the neighbouring Jimi and Kaironk Valleys where population densities were higher, there was more grassland, and the secondary forest was more degraded (Clarke, 1966).

As a consequence of the low population density and abundant forest, there was no necessity in the basin for any of the many forms of agricultural intensification that occurred elsewhere on the island of New Guinea where land degradation had set in because of pressure on the agricultural base

Plate 15.3. Nakemba, a cohort of Ngirapo's, standing in a small patch of temporary grassland in an old garden, looking out over Ndwimba Basin's landscape, a mixture of spontaneous forest, gardens of various ages, and orchards.

(Brookfield, 1962; Brown, 1978; Clarke, 1966; Waddell, 1972). The agriculture practised by Ngirapo and his fellows had not suffered the simplification of product usually associated with intensification and degradation because there was little necessity for human input of labour to maintain soil fertility – the forest did that work – and because the system produced, without much drudgery, an adequacy of food while causing little if any land degradation. Thus I saw his agriculture to be energy efficient (with regard to labour) and to possess a resilient permanence, unlike industrial agriculture. I argued (Clarke, 1977) that the underlying principles that allowed or supported the permanence were:

- very low or absent technometabolism, to use Stephen Boyden's (1992) term, meaning resource and energy use and technological waste production;
- no input or outflow of toxic materials;
- strongly positive net energy yields from the agricultural system, that is, the return for each unit of work energy invested by the gardeners was around 18 units of food energy (but this net return does not include the energy consumed when patches of forest were burned to clear gardens, a consideration that some authorities argue lessens the seemingly high energy efficiency of swidden agriculture);
- the use of the forest (largely a free good) as a potent tool for maintaining soil fertility, suppressing weeds, and helping to increase slope stability, at the same time providing many useful products (more abstractly, this is the modest use of a product of a short period of past time, quite unlike the pollution-producing use of fossil fuels, which is the indigestible consumption of past time on a geological scale);
- autarky, local control of resource use, and a largely egalitarian society with an equitable distribution of goods;
- garden management that saw secondary arboreal regrowth as a "garden mother", that is, something from which would issue later sustenance, an understanding that led gardeners to practise selective weeding in order to give useful tree species a head start in plant succession; and
- a subsistence system based on polycultural diversity, with gardens and hamlet plantings containing over three dozen species of food-producing plants, with several species containing dozens of named

cultivars, each with individual characteristics and different seasonal patterns of production.

I will return to these principles of permanence, for they and similar abstractions may be a more significant lesson to be learned from indigenous agriculture than the sets of specific agronomic techniques that make up much of the reporting of IK in the literature. First, however, I will tell a little more about Ngirapo, how he had passed in his lifetime from using stone axes to using steel axes and bush knives, and how he begot orchards on sites of old gardens. My tales bear morals, to which I will return later.

From Stone to Steel

The people of the Ndwimba Basin first received steel axe blades sometime in the 1940s, when the new tools passed along trade routes over the Bismarck Range from the Jimi Valley to the south, whence they had moved from the Central Highlands, which had by that time been penetrated by Europeans. Initially the steel blades were hard to come by, and few men had them. By 1958, when a government patrol reached the basin for the first time, steel axes were becoming increasingly available. By 1964, when I lived in the basin, all men had one or more steel axes apiece, used for wealth and for bride payments as well as for chopping. Before steel, two kinds of stone axes were in use, both imported through indigenous trade connections from a quarry of suitable stone in the Jimi Valley. One kind was the thin-bladed, large, highly polished ceremonial axe, valued for use in ritual and war, for display, and for bride wealth. The other kind was the thick-bladed, small, less highly polished work axe, the essential garden tool for men. With the coming of steel, the men abandoned stone work axes almost immediately in favour of the superior steel tool.

Because I was curious about the effect of the introduction of steel axes on labour input and patterns of forest clearance, I had one of the scrapped stone work axes, still lying about in men's houses, hafted in the traditional style. When I asked Ngirapo, who had possessed only stone axes until well into his young manhood, to show me how stone axes had been used, he regarded the request as ludicrous. Why chop down a tree with a stone axe when the far more effective steel tool was available? Finally, after much cajolery and explanation, I succeeded in getting him and some of the other older men to demonstrate. On the average, work with a stone axe took four times as long as the same job with a steel axe, a relationship similar to that recorded by Salisbury (1962) for the Siane of the Central Highlands. From

Plate 15.4. Ngirapo, posturing with a stone work axe in his right hand and a steel axe in his left hand. He considered the stone axe, which he had used solely in his youth, a quite inferior tool to the steel axe.

the men's point of view, the major effect of the introduction of steel was to shorten the time needed to clear and fence gardens. As Ngirapo said, "Once I had to work all day every day; now I work a little before midday, and then I have time to sit and talk with you." Similarly, the introduction of the bush knife speeded the clearing of grasses and other weeds. With a stone axe, these could be cut laboriously only by laying a sapling on the ground, bending grasses and weeds over the sapling, and chopping them against that solid base. The bush knife also proved a very effective tool for rapidly clearing young arboreal growth. The ecological effect of the new tools was to increase the area cut for gardens, whereas previously only the exact area needed was cleared and there was more of a tendency to use small plots opened by the windfall of large, dead trees. Moreover, within the garden site, more trees were felled, rather than girdled as previously. These changes would of themselves have acted to slow secondary succession and gradually to decrease the area of mature forest, even without an increase in population or an expansion of cultivated land for cash cropping. Only a most zealous and foolish conservationist, however, would have suggested to Ngirapo that, in order to preserve the forest, he revert from steel back to stone.

Ngirapo's Orchards

When I first went to the Ndwimba Basin, I knew that a diversity of trees – most notably breadfruit, coconut, and a coastal species of *Pandanus* – were of great importance as subsistence foods in coastal villages across the Pacific and dominated the entire food production systems of some islands, especially atolls. I did not expect to find orchards to be of great significance in a forested, mid-elevation site far from the coast in New Guinea. Once I was there, it took me a while even to recognize that many aggregations of trees were orchards rather than part of the spontaneous regeneration of secondary trees following gardening. As this became clear to me, I began to learn from Ngirapo that the orchards were far more than incidental to the agricultural system. As I have recently reiterated in a general work on agroforestry in the Pacific Islands, orchards like Ngirapo's, in combination with the gardens, made up an integrated, sophisticated agroforestry system that merged easily and productively into the basin ecosystem (Clarke & Thaman, 1993; Thaman, this volume).

Most orchards originate when a man decides that he will use a particular garden site to plant any or all of four tree species as well as the usual variety

Plate 15.5. In a *Pandanus-Gnetum* orchard, with a man holding a *Pandanus* cutting that will soon be planted.

of shorter-term crops. As the harvest of the shorter-term crops (such as yams, sweet potato, taro, various greens, sugar-cane, and bananas) comes to an end, the site of the expiring garden gradually transmutes into an orchard. The most important orchard tree is the spiny-leafed, palm-like *Pandanus conoideus,* known widely as *marita* in Papua New Guinea. The massive fruit of this tree contains an oil-rich mesocarp that is a very important supplementary food. Cooked by steaming in the earth oven and made into a bright red, tasty sauce, it is eaten with various edible leaves and provides the largest amount of vegetable oil in the diet and is probably the major source of vitamin-A precursors. The strong, long leaves of this domesticated *Pandanus* make a good roofing material, as do the leaves of several wild *Pandanus* species. The other major orchard tree is the graceful *Gnetum gnemon,* which bears edible leaves, inflorescence, and fruit, and the underbark of which provides an excellent fibre, used for making string bags and pubic aprons. The two minor trees in the orchards are the breadfruit (*Artocarpus altilis*), important in this region for its edible seeds rather than the flesh of its fruit, and a small fig tree (*Ficus wassa*), which provides material for bark cloth and bears edible leaves and fruit.

Once established, the orchards do not require much labour, only weeding of competitive secondary growth when the orchard trees are young and occasional slashing of the shade-tolerant undergrowth as the trees mature so that harvesting is easier – though even these "weeds", such as the undergrowth ferns that bear edible leaves, may be useful. Not all garden sites are used as orchards, but most men have several orchards of different ages scattered throughout their territory. Some of their oldest orchards will have been planted by their fathers; other, younger orchards, which they have planted, will outlive them and pass to their sons. In area, orchards make up a significant part of the total domain of domesticated plants: about 41% according to my measurements in 1965 (Clarke, 1971), based on a figure of 0.065 ha of orchard for each person in the basin compared with 0.093 ha of active garden area for each person.

The orchards thus come to be scattered widely throughout the forest area used for agriculture and provide a valuable supply of materials and foods throughout the year. As they age over several decades, the orchards merge back into secondary forest. Their sites again become available for swidden clearing so that the orchards extend production from garden lands for several decades. At the same time the land is receiving benefits similar to those gained from fallow under spontaneous secondary forest.

Plate 15.6. A man of Ngirapo's clan, his wife, and daughter, all with their characteristic implements: the man with an axe and his bow and arrows, the woman and daughter with dibbles. All are wearing the traditional pubic aprons, made of fibre from *Gnetum* and other trees. The woman also wears her string bag, made of similar fibre, down her back; this utensil is of great importance in carrying planting material and harvested crops.

Ngirapo and his fellows also recognized unplanted secondary forest communities as a resource, one that is more valuable than primary forest. Because the secondary forest provides the reinvigorating functions of fallow vegetation that make shifting cultivation possible, it is referred to in the vernacular as the "garden mother". Beyond this important function, the whole secondary zone – which derives from clearing for gardens combined with the protection of tree seedlings during weeding – serves as a foraging zone for domestic pigs and as a hunting ground for the men who pass through it daily on their rounds. The secondary communities also serve as sources of plant foods and materials. The common *Alphitonia-Cyathea* woodlands provide easily cut wood for fencing and fuel. In addition, the *Cyathea* tree fern provides edible leaves, and the understory plants, growing in the light shade, provide cordage, edible leaves, and medicines. The secondary *Albizia falcataria* community is recognized as most valuable for increasing soil fertility for future gardens, presumably through the usual nitrogen-fixing processes of leguminous plants. *Albizia*'s wood is also valued for carving. Jungle regrowth provides edible leaves as well as wild *Musa* leaves for wrapping materials and for clean surfaces for food preparation. In other words, not only does the temporal alternation of forest fallow with gardens make the gardens productive, the successional stages of the forest are themselves valuable for other purposes (Clarke, 1971).

As my knowledge grew – thanks to the tutelage of Ngirapo and his cohorts – I began to realize how poorly the model of Western agriculture as something that farmers do with annual regularity on single, particular units of terrain fitted with the kaleidoscopic gardens, orchards, and secondary forest communities I was walking through in the Ndwimba Basin. Of course, Ngirapo and his wives were gardening particular plots at any particular time, but, more consequentially, he was managing a whole landscape wherein various forms of anthropogenic vegetation (including gardens and orchards) were continuously evolving and shifting. Or, perhaps, rather than 'managing' the landscape, Ngirapo was in a constant process of 'designing' a landscape, which was forever new in that its components kept moving about while continuously evolving but which also had the capacity to remain stable and productive for a long time.

This kind of swidden fallow management and secondary growth enrichment within systems of tropical forest agriculture is by no means unique to the Ndwimba Basin. It has now been described from all tropical-forest areas. Yen (1974), for instance, referred to it as arboriculture in Solomon Islands; Thaman & Clarke (1987) and Clarke & Thaman (1993) applied the

Plate 15.7. A view of a portion of the Ndwimba Basin. On the ridge in the left foreground are some new and older gardens. In the centre and right foreground is a mixture of types of secondary forest, including the spreading, soil-enriching *Albizia falcataria.*

Plate 15.8. A young *Pandanus* orchard developing beneath *Albizia falcataria* trees, which (as Ngirapo would say, thinking about the rich fat of his pigs) add grease to the soil. Garden clearings in the left background.

terms "agrosilviculture" and "agroforestry" to the variety of such systems across the Pacific Islands. Recently, it has been studied in Amazonia, as reported in at least three notable collections of papers (Anderson, 1990; Denevan & Padoch, 1988; Posey & Balée, 1989), many of which clearly demonstrate that areas classified as "abandoned gardens" by earlier research workers are actually highly managed agroforestry systems. Everywhere these systems seem to be eminently suited to their environment and to offer their indigenous practitioners long-term production combined with protection against land degradation. As Irvine (1989: 235) argues with regard to Amazonia, this form of resource management is a way whereby native people living in rain forests increase resource availability by exerting direct environmental control to enhance the habitat of desired resource species. Such environmental manipulation is achieved through succession management in tropical rainforest societies. In this biome, individuals of the same species are normally rare and dispersed. Succession management in traditional agroforestry enables people to concentrate scarce forest resources near to home by altering plant succession in previously cleared areas to favor useful plants and game animals. In this way they can increase both the abundance and distribution of targeted species.

Most writers on such systems also see merit in combining indigenous knowledge of agroforestry with modern science and technology in an effort to create some form of ecologically sound development. At the least, they argue that long-standing traditional fallow management systems should be examined before attempting to introduce modern systems, for the older systems have a role to play in economic development or sustainable survival (Clarke & Thaman, 1993; Padoch & Denevan, 1988; Raintree, 1983). As Padoch & Denevan (1988: 97) conclude following their study of the systems in Amazonia:

> The use of swidden fallows in the tropics is an ecologically and potentially economically viable means of both reducing the destruction of mature forests and providing a source of useful products and income to small farmers....Fallow management is a means of increasing the return per land unit for the shifting cultivator, and that return can range from very small to substantial.

Indigenous Knowledge: Its Recent 'Discovery'

Attitudes toward indigenous agricultural knowledge have greatly changed and studies by geographers and anthropologists of that knowledge have vastly expanded during the four decades since anthropologist Harold Conklin (1954: 133) wrote of shifting cultivation that it is often categorically condemned as primitive, wasteful, or illegal, with little or no regard for such pertinent local variables as population density, available land area, climate, or native agricultural knowledge. For most areas, detailed field reports against which such statements might be tested are totally lacking.

In the same vein, geographer Carl Sauer (1956: 68) wrote at about the same time, in speaking of the effects of the modern "ever dynamic economy" on "wise and durable native systems of living with the land":

> Our programs of agricultural aid pay little attention to native ways and products. Instead of going out to learn what their experiences and preferences are, we go forth to introduce our ways and consider backward what is not according to our pattern.

In contrast, during the preparations for the 1992 United Nations Conference on Environment and Development (or the Earth Summit, the largest international meeting ever held) its Secretary-General Maurice Strong (1991: 39) wrote:

> The vast experience of indigenous people, as custodians of some of the Earth's most precious and vulnerable ecosystems, was frequently referred to in the working group meetings. Indigenous people's organizations and delegations at the plenary session stressed the capacity of local communities to identify their own measures to stem environmental degradation and requested that the UNCED secretariat consider the relevance of traditional knowledge and practices on the UNCED agenda.

Strong's words indicate the contemporary importance given to indigenous knowledge. The proliferation of publications and the profusion of meetings and conferences on the topic give further evidence of the rapidly expanding attribution of significance and practical value to indigenous knowledge. For example – to begin only a very selective mention of some IK publications and meetings on indigenous knowledge – one of today's leading development theorists, Robert Chambers, includes a chapter on the wealth, depth, and usefulness of rural people's knowledge in his 1983 book *Rural Development: Putting the Last First*. On a similar theme, Paul Richards (1985) has written *Indigenous Agricultural Revolution: Ecology and Food Production in West Africa*. Many papers in *Tribal Peoples and Development Issues* (Bodley, 1988) explore ethnodevelopment (tribal development from within, based on autonomous control and management of resources). A focus on gathering traditional environmental knowledge and integrating it with Western science appeared in *Lore: Capturing Traditional Environmental Knowledge* (Johnson, 1993). Three other recent works on indigenous knowledge or 'traditional ecological knowledge' (TEK) are Inglis (1993), Freeman & Carbyn (1988) and Johannes (1989).

The latest of the Worldwatch Institute's renowned *State of the World* reports (Brown et al., 1993) contains a chapter entitled 'Supporting Indigenous Peoples' (Durning 1993), which stresses the traditional stewardship techniques of indigenous peoples. Much information on indigenous knowledge and its relationship to development policies and practice is gathered together in *Indigenous Knowledge Systems: The Cultural Dimension of Development* (Warren et al., 1993).

The World Health Organization (WHO) has a series of publications on traditional medicine. The World Wildlife Fund (WWF) supports the use of tradition to advance conservation (Stone, 1991). Even the World Bank is encouraging discussion of the use of indigenous knowledge (Warren, 1991). A new journal *Indigenous Knowledge and Development Monitor* was begun in 1993. Produced by the Centre for International Research and Advisory Networks (CIRAN) in the Netherlands, the journal is intended to provide a forum for the growing number of individuals and institutions "that are interested in the role that indigenous knowledge can play in truly participatory approaches to sustainable development". In 1992 the Canadian International Development Research Centre (IDRC) and the International Institute of Rural Reconstruction in the Philippines sponsored an "International Symposium on Indigenous Knowledge and Sustainable Development" at Silang in the Philippines. A special issue of *Indigenous Knowledge and Development Monitor* (vol. 1(2), 1993) provides a full report of the Philippines symposium and abstracts of the papers presented there. The International Center for Living Aquatic Resources Management (ICLARM), in co-operation with the Food and Agriculture Organization (FAO) of the United Nations, has developed FISHBASE, a computerized repository of ethno-ichthyology or indigenous knowledge about fishes. On the more popular side, the news magazine *Time* devoted a cover story to "Lost Tribes, Lost Knowledge" (*Time*, 23 September 1991) and the book *Wisdom of the Elders* by Knudtson and Suzuki (1992) has enjoyed wide publicity.

More specifically focused on the Pacific Islands was a major conference on "Science of Pacific Island Peoples" held at the University of the South Pacific in mid-1992 (the papers of which will be published by the Institute of Pacific Studies). Other works with a strong focus on indigenous knowledge and sustainable development in the Pacific include Ruddle & Johannes (1989), Morauta et al. (1982), a paper I wrote in *The Contemporary Pacific* on 'traditional knowledge and sustainable development' (Clarke, 1990), Lawrence & Cansfield-Smith (1991), Williams & Baines (in press), and an entire issue of *Cultural Survival Quarterly* (vol 15(1), 1991) devoted to 'Western Oceania: Caring for the Ancestral Domain'. Finally, at the level of international environmentalist agencies in the Pacific, one goal of the South Pacific's regional *Action Strategy for Nature Conservation in the South Pacific Region* (SPREP/IUCN, 1991) is to promote the integration of traditional knowledge and customs into contemporary practices aimed at the conservation of sustainable resources and the management of conservation areas.

The complex set of reasons for the present celebration of indigenous knowledge by Western academics, development planners, sustainable-development activists, and indigenous peoples themselves cannot be fully examined here. Indigenous knowledge has many different meanings. For some people, it is a specific technique that seems to work well in a particular environment. For others, it is a rich empirical science, generations old, that can augment western science with details about the habits of fish or the different edibilities of various wild plants. For others, it is a political weapon to authenticate tribal rights over portions of land or sea. For still others, it is an ideology – a wisdom from an earlier and better time – that provides a moral basis for the crusade against deleterious development.

The local and global contexts for these views are multifarious. There is the disillusionment that comes with the realization that in tropical regions the initiation of thousands of agricultural aid projects (overseas development assistance) over the past several decades has "not delivered the promised results" or, more bluntly, shows us "a past replete with distressing failures" (Gliessman, 1990: 33; Porter et al., 1991: xv). The imported modern technologies and the 'efficient' scale of operations have failed outright, or have brought environmental degradation, or have become bogged down in a morass of unpaid debts, low enthusiasm, sinking yields, and rising inequalities. Why not turn to local ways, which at least have a past record of moderate success over a considerable time? Perhaps the indigenous techniques can be incrementally improved rather than supplanted. On a broader canvas, the environmental and economic deterioration sensed everywhere is often seen to be a result of the penetration of indigenous economies by the modern world system (Wallerstein, 1974). That deterioration and the associated loss of self-reliance can be resisted, at least rhetorically, through respect for indigenous knowledge, which is local, which is something possessed by the small worlds. The growth of Fourth World consciousness linked with the disintegration or morbidity of larger nation-states encourages belief in local, indigenous ways, which validate and enhance cultural identity. In today's world, certainly in the Pacific, cultural identity is a means of structuring political relations (Keesing, 1982a,b; Linnekin, 1990).

In Western consciousness, there is guilt over destruction of indigenous peoples, their ways of life, their traditional habitats. Ruth Benedict's metaphor of the cup of life haunts us ever more. Every people have a cup from which they drink their life. "They all dipped in the water, but their cups were different" (1934: 21-22). Now the cups of most indigenous peoples are broken. In atonement, Western science can at least try to sponge up some indigenous knowledge even if it cannot save indigenous lives. Preserving indigenous knowledge becomes an ethical undertaking as well as a nostalgic concern for things we think are of value that have been left behind as the pace of modernization has accelerated.

Indigenous Knowledge and Sustainable Agricultural Development: Weaknesses

Whatever the practical or ideological motives, there is currently much praise of indigenous knowledge and much work being carried out to collect it. In this context, to express uncertainty about its value may seem contradictory if not downright perverse. Along with some other students of indigenous knowledge, I do feel ambiguity. Saving indigenous knowledge is clearly worthwhile; it is something to be celebrated, as I am trying here to celebrate Ngirapo's life, knowledge, and skills. Indigenous knowledge, like all knowledge, however, has limits as to what it can reveal to us, as well as limits to the extent to which it can be successfully applied. The conviction sometimes put forward that indigenous knowledge offers salvation, that it is wisdom from another world that can save the modern world, rouses enough disquiet to compel discussion of the weaknesses inherent in IK.

One weakness of indigenous knowledge is its otherworldliness. In some senses, all peoples of the world are now indigenes, all denizens of a single

Earth. Indigenous knowledge, extracted from other contexts, is now to be applied to save that Earth, but all the bits and pieces of indigenous knowledge from various localities are shorn of the social, cultural, and ecological context that gave the knowledge or skills their fullest meaning and potential. The rolling sequence of Ngirapo's gardens, orchards, anthropogenic secondary forest communities, and gardens again is an exquisite design *in the context of Ngirapo's world.* Can that design, which depends not only on the use of land but also on the use of decades, survive in the world of Ngirapo's sons and grandsons – a world where population is growing; a world where groves of coffee trees are being established as a cash crop; where men and whole families drift away to towns, perhaps never to return, so that rights to portions of land fade; where secondary succession of vegetation regresses from forest and woodland to grass; where the oil-rich *Pandanus* sauce can be replaced by imported grease?

This is another way of saying that Ngirapo's knowledge and agricultural activities were embedded in his society, his culture, his place, his sense of time. It is wholly in keeping with modernity, that modern science should lift out that sort of indigenous knowledge and make it a part of Western science (Giddens, 1990). Specific aspects of the knowledge can be extremely useful, as, for example, the recent successful dispersal to the African Sahel of a drought-resistant Australian *Acacia* species that bears nutritious seeds, which now supplement African diets in a degraded environment. The development agents dispersing the tree initially learned of the nutritional value of its seeds directly from the indigenous knowledge of Australian Aborigines. Some species of Ngirapo's trees might well become useful components in modern agroforestry systems, currently very popular in development circles (Clarke & Thaman, 1993). There is nothing mystical about the knowledge that a certain *Acacia* has edible seeds or that *Pandanus* and *Gnetum* trees growing together make a good orchard. Ngirapo is no wiser than a modern ecological agronomist. Indigenous knowledge may seem extraordinary because, when it is observed and discovered by Western science, it is so tangibly connected with a people's activities, and because it so often cuts across the sectoral boundaries of modern economics and the disciplinary boundaries of Western science – which makes it seem 'holistic'.

More true is that all indigenous knowledge collected is fragmentary, which does not lessen its value but does mean that it is not imbued with special qualities of harmony or oneness. In tribal and peasant societies, the whole population is directly engaged in subsistence pursuits, but the 'people's knowledge' is not uniform. Men, women, the old, the young, the shaman, the people ignorant of mystic powers all do things differently, know different things, and have different levels of skill in natural-resource management. While researching indigenous fodder tree management in a community in Nepal, Gold & Rusten (1993) noted the strong preference of women for one particular species of tree for use as livestock fodder whereas the men said they preferred another species. Wondering why, the researchers uncovered a set of reasons having to do with location, accessibility, ease of harvest, and product sought from the livestock. Both trees are useful, but concepts about them vary considerably between men and women. In anthropological literature on Papua New Guinea, the existence of specialist biologists and agronomists within the tribe has been much discussed. Malinowski (1935) described for the Trobriands the "garden masters" or "garden magicians", who were so specially proficient in gardening and in growing the "great yam" (*Dioscorea alata*) that they received special titles and social prestige. More recently, there has been concern with "great men", who – unlike the "big men", who were social and political manipulators – possessed special levels of skill in hunting or agriculture or other activities and so gained social prestige (Godelier, 1986; Godelier & Strathern, 1991). Essentially, the "great men" were highly skilled indigenous scientists. The knowledge that they possessed would have become available to modern science only if they, as individuals, had been questioned about it and if they had been willing to share it. Healey (1990: 105) recently wrote about specialist hunters among a Papua New Guinean group who live not far from, and speak the same language, as Ngirapo's clansmen.

> A hunter builds his blinds or searches for birds, display trees, and fruiting trees on the basis of the personal knowledge he has accumulated over a long period of intense association with a particular tract of land....he has acquired a richly textured understanding of the local environment – the conformation of the land and the particularities of the plant and animal communities it supports. The unique knowledge a man may build up over time of a particular locality is the product of his own physical and intellectual efforts, even if it is grounded on a more general, less-detailed collective knowledge of the environment....Detailed knowledge of natural history tends to be highly particular, rather than general: certain individuals are deeply knowledgeable about particular localities; some are acknowledged experts on high-forest birds, others on cassowaries, and yet others on phalangers and giant rats and so on. There is, in short, a tendency toward specialist areas of expertise.

Another weakness of indigenous knowledge – rather, another conceptual weakness among some people who overpraise indigenous knowledge – is that indigenous peoples sometimes practised unsound environmental management; they had a dynamic, but not always a benign, effect on their environment (Blaikie et al., 1987; Clarke, 1990). Although traditional land use and agriculture were dynamic, they were not 'in harmony' with the environment. What Kirch (1984) has written about Polynesia is true for all the Pacific Islands, as well as the rest of the world. The early inhabitants did not avidly practise a conservationist ethic that preserved their habitat as an unchanged paradise until the advent of Europeans brought major disturbance and degradation. Instead, the Islanders did what all peoples, especially pioneers, do: in their efforts to make a living, they manipulated, modified, and, at times, degraded the ecosystems in which they lived, producing environmental changes that in turn required ecological adaptations and social adjustments. It has been acknowledged for decades in the Pacific that the pre-European moa hunters and Maori of New Zealand exercised massive effects on the forests and bird life of the southernmost islands of Polynesia, playing the primary role in the extinction of a unique group of birds and greatly reducing forest cover by clearing and, particularly, by fire (Cumberland, 1963). It is now recognized that the early human occupants of all Pacific Islands similarly affected plant and animal life (terrestrial, avian, and near shore marine), caused soil erosion and degradation, and in some cases significantly modified even the topography of their islands. The rapid extinctions of some bird species and the over-exploitation of shellfish that were contemporaneous with earliest human settlement were in part the by-product of the necessity to depend heavily on those resources for food before the agricultural system was firmly established and adequately productive. Increasing alteration of habitats, especially forest clearance, continued the pressures on the bird populations, as has been recently discussed by Steadman (1991) for the southern Cook Islands.

Anthropologist Ralph Bulmer (1982:63), who probably wrote and knew more about indigenous knowledge in the Pacific and contributed more to the development of its study than any other scientist, noted in a paper on traditional conservation practices in Papua New Guinea that:

> the record of the past suggests that traditional Papua New Guinean societies scored more points for adaptation, innovation and development of new resources than they did for conservation. There is little evidence that Papua New Guineans were or are very different from the majority of humanity who have not been greatly concerned with

> the long-term conservation of their natural environment. What they were and still are concerned with, very directly and very profoundly, are the present and immediately foreseeable yields of their crops and catches and the amount of time, effort and care required to produce them....Many activities of pre-contact man were conservationally sound; but they were incidental to maximizing immediate yields for little labour. It was good conservational practice for shifting cultivators to let the land lie fallow for fifteen or twenty-five years or forty years – whatever the optimum period to ensure both an undiminished crop and less effort in hacking down additional primary forest or rooting out *pitpit* [a giant, strong, weedy grass]. But conservation was not the object of the exercise. The object was to get that next good crop for a reasonable minimum of labour. Erosion barriers constructed along the contours of hillside gardens were not primarily in the interests of long-term soil conservation, but to stop that year's sweet potato or taro crop from sliding down the hill. The barriers readily disappeared when the crops had been harvested and the pigs put in to forage; erosion then took place.

Related to the misconception that indigenous knowledge always brought harmonious relations between people and place is the misconception that indigenous knowledge is static, that it can be plucked like some unchanging jewel off the shelf of indigenous life to be used in the modern world. Rather, as research on the Pacific's prehistory over the past several decades illustrates clearly, a dynamic agronomic and botanical indigenous science has long existed, in terms both of basic understanding and applied techniques. For millennia, plants have been taken into cultivation, experimented with, transported, and modified into a variety of distinct cultivars. Agriculture and land use have been subject to constant experimentation, innovation, adaptation, intensification, and disintensification (Clarke, forthcoming). Many ethnographic field-workers in Papua New Guinea have noted the tendency of gardeners to experiment with new plants. Ngirapo's people, both men and women, told me many stories of their discovery of, or experimentation with, new varieties or species of food-producing plants: a woman might see a variety of sweet potato previously unknown to her and take a piece of its vine to her garden to see how it grew; or a man coming upon an unknown, recently introduced crop such as American taro (*Xanthosoma*) or maize would observe it, plant it, assume it was poisonous (of itself or magically), but see analogies with more familiar crops and eventually take the leap of trying it, finding it edible and attractive, and bringing it into cultivation.

There still remains to mention one other source of possible conceptual difficulty in transferring indigenous agricultural knowledge from the traditions of the Pacific Islands (and probably of other places) across the boundary into today's attempts at sustainable agricultural development. This is the character of traditional agriculture in relation to the landscape. Unlike Western agriculture, which focuses on the field – a distinct plot of land – as the hub of production, Pacific Island agriculturalists fixed their attention more on scales both smaller and larger than the field. On one hand, they were concerned with individual plants (trees, *Cyrtosperma* taro, giant yams), and, on the other, with the diversified portfolio of production from the whole landscape. Figure 15.1 is an attempt, modified from Jacques Barrau's classic works on subsistence agriculture in the Pacific (Barrau, 1958, 1961), to represent archetypal Pacific Island land use, which generates a complex landscape, not natural but designed by local people using traditional science to create a rich "subsistence sector", which by means of its shifting components within a stable framework meets a very wide range of needs (Bulmer, 1982). Using the landscape in this way as a unit of management is wholly in accord with modern ideas of landscape ecology or human-ecosystem science (Naveh & Lieberman, 1984) or watershed management, but it still does not mesh particularly well with aid-project planning or sectorally determined extension services in agriculture or forestry. Extracting indigenous knowledge about one of the components of such a landscape misses the mark of the whole system.

Indigenous Knowledge and Sustainable Agricultural Development: Uses

The preceding discussion of the weaknesses of indigenous knowledge in relation to sustainable agricultural development in no way demeans indigenous knowledge. Rather, the point is that as technique, as particular agricultural expertise, indigenous knowledge has no more, and perhaps no less, to offer sustainable development than does modern high technology agronomy. The wonderfully sustainable, well adapted Pacific Island agricultural methods, such as irrigated taro terracing or the mulched pit cultivation of *Cyrtosperma* in harsh atoll environments (Barrau, 1958, 1961; Klee, 1980), are just that: agricultural methods. Within the agronomic context, they possessed sustainability because they were based on the same

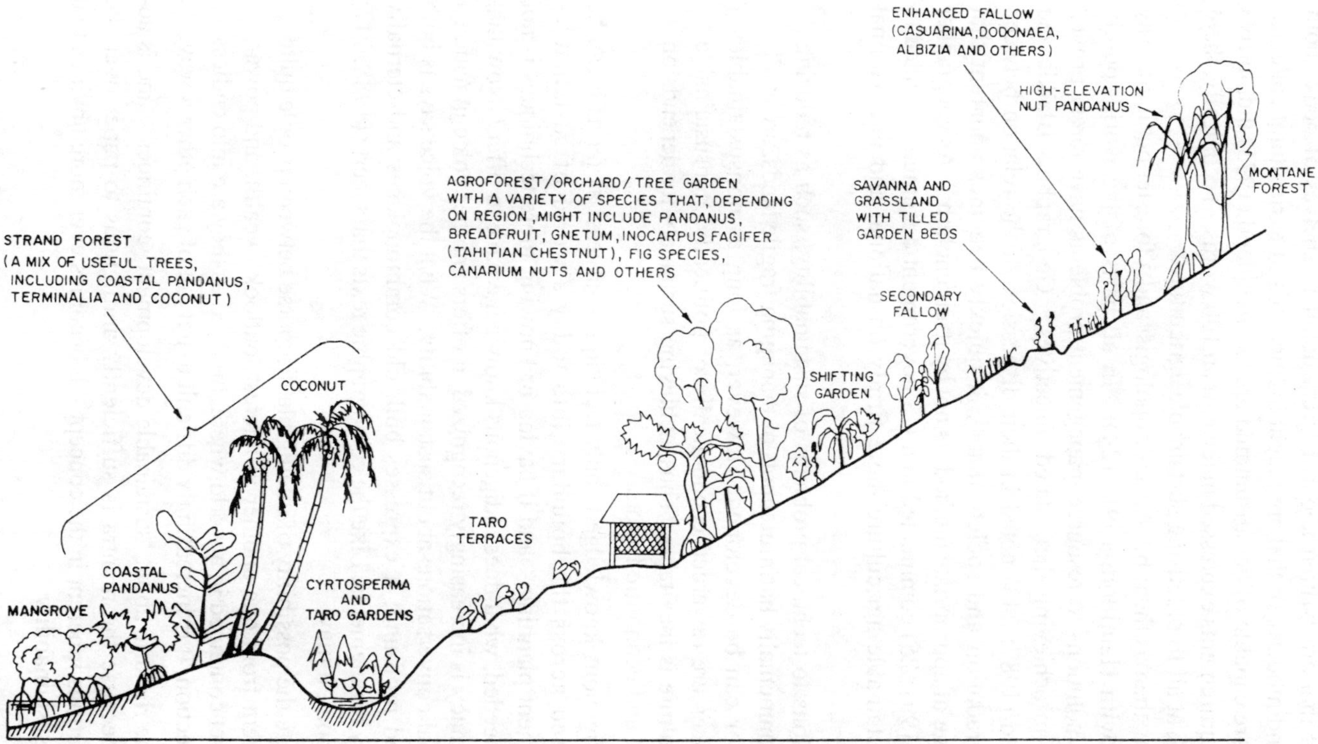

Source: Derived from Barrau (1958 and 1961)

Figure 15.1. Schematic representation of Pacific Island humanized landscapes.

principles that are written about in great detail in shelves of books both ancient and modern, or that are taught in hundreds of agricultural colleges, and that are capable of being summed up, as Greenland (1975) did, in five simple requirements expressed in fewer than 100 words. Technically, there is no trick at all to practising sustainable agriculture.

Where, then, is the rub? An anthropologist and a forester put it this way (Rambo with Hamilton, 1991: 124): "In all parts of the world, purely technical solutions to resource management problems have rarely proved effective in achieving their stated objectives." Geographers Blaikie and Brookfield (1987: 243) noted in their discussion of the relation between land degradation and society that "...it quickly becomes apparent that knowledge of appropriate methods is not by itself enough." As geographer Wilken (1991: 25) commented in a US government document intended to place sustainable agriculture more firmly on national and international agendas:

> Solutions to technical problems of sustainability, such as reducing environmentally harmful inputs or managing fragile lands, are available or can be developed. However, as long as nonsustainable practices are rewarded economically or politically, nonsustainable agriculture is inevitable. Thus, achieving sustainability depends on social and economic factors.

If indigenous knowledge is only technique – at least as far as it can be transferred across the boundary into today's world of sustainable-development planning – and if having or knowing more techniques is not what is needed, what does indigenous knowledge have to offer? Now that its legitimacy is increasingly recognized, it offers another voice in national and global conversations about sustainability. What the voice says is both banal and profound; it expresses both old commonplaces and eternally necessary restatements. Like the ethnographic texts that Geertz (1988: 147) writes about, it may

> enlarge the possibility of intelligible discourse between people quite different from one another in interest, outlook, wealth, and power, and yet contained in a world where, tumbled as they are into endless connection, it is increasingly difficult to get out of each other's way.

As the rhetoric about 'sustainable development' continues – and is accepted because the mantra is sufficiently ambiguous to paper over the contradictions inherent in the concept – it becomes ever more obvious that for true sustainability to become implanted in the political culture, the character of developmental and resource management institutions will require reform and remodelling. Opposition to such reforms is ideological and structural. Sustainability is not regarded seriously by those who really count, namely those at the top of political structures and those who control the flows of national and international capital (O'Riordan 1988: 39).

Although it is becoming policy, here and there, to collect indigenous knowledge, it remains largely true that indigenous knowledge does little to affect policy; nonetheless, the ideology intrinsic to IK provides a countervailing voice to the mainsteam ideology described above by O'Riordan. As much of IK's testimony has already been discussed, only a few brief reiterations, additions, and sources of further information follow.

Indigenous knowledge immediately suggests a 'bottom-up', local approach to land and coastal management, for the knowledge is local, and possessing it can serve as a source of local empowerment. As already argued, it cannot be claimed that local control as such ensures sustainable management, but proper state interventions and adequate institutional reforms (Blaikie & Brookfield, 1987) can enhance the possibility of conservationist actions by the local land managers as they put their spades or digging sticks into the ground, which is when and where the immediate relation between agriculturalists and environment takes place. Baines (1991) and Cordell (1991) provide examples from the Pacific of ways in which local knowledge, local control of resources or of access to resources, and local desires can be used to strengthen community conservation.

Indigenous knowledge suggests plurality. The vast range of indigenous knowledge demonstrates that there are many ways of doing agriculture. Intellectually, this brings IK well into post-modernism (Giddens, 1990); more directly relevant to sustainable agriculture is that a "pluralist-oriented" approach to development is more likely to be successful than a "control-oriented" rationally determined approach, as is cogently argued by Porter et al. (1991) in their study of a failed rural development project in Africa. That plurality offers such benefits arises at least in part because plurality is the raw material of natural selection and evolution. The prehistory of Pacific agriculture increasingly shows the ever changing adaptations, many remarkably successful, that arose from the plurality of the inhabitants' experiences on the wide variety of Pacific Islands. Conserving that plurality might now make evolution toward sustainable agriculture easier, while avoiding the dead end adaptations of an intrinsically unstable and restless modern economy dominated by the goal of increasing rewards to capital and to labour productivity while splurging resource productivity (Daly, 1991: 37).

Further to the earlier discussion of managing a landscape rather than fields as a characteristic of Pacific Island agriculture, it could be argued that landscape is a naive, humane concept, intuitively understood by all people, in contrast to functionally related terms, such as 'ecosystem' or 'natural resources' or 'natural capital' or 'biodiversity', which are used more in sustainable development literature. Landscapes lend themselves to being beautiful, or not, whereas nobody expects an ecosystem to be beautiful, or ugly. If beauty leads to ecological health and diversity, then traditional Pacific Island agriculturalists are well on their way to those goals. Anyone who has walked about in a traditional Pacific landscape with one of its older inhabitants knows the enjoyment felt at the arrangement of productive diversity all around. Medicine here, perfume there, fibre in the hibiscus stem, fruit, timber, edible leaves, and so forth. There is strong aesthetic pleasure in these observations of utilitarian diversity. That productiveness is recognized to be not spontaneous but the result of human care and design. Nature needs attention, grooming, and beautification just as the human body does (Clarke, 1990). Colourful, decorative plants are planted throughout the landscape, with their arrangement in accord with ideas about beauty and attractiveness, and often to express something significant with regard to ritual or ceremony. As Malinowski (1935, v.1: 80-81) wrote about the Trobriand gardens he made so famous:

> The gardens are, in a way, a work of art. Exactly as a native will take an artist's delight in constructing a canoe or a house, perfect in shape, decoration and finish, and the whole community will glory in such an achievement, exactly thus will he go about the laying out and developing of his garden. He and his kinsmen and his fellow-villagers as well, will be proud of his labours....During all the successive stages of the work, visits are exchanged and mutual admiration and appreciation of the aesthetic qualities of the gardens are a constant feature of village life.

Schmid (1991: 277,280) has written much more recently of the Nokopo people in Papua New Guinea:

> Notions of Nokopo art are not easily recognized by westerners' eyes but they are present, tightly interwoven with daily life. Aesthetic

> concepts are realized and transformed by every man and every woman. The expression of Nokopo aesthetics, their material visualization, are easily overlooked. They are either ephemeral, lasting only a few hours or days (*e.g.*, body ornaments from vegetable matters) or they may be found unexpectedly (*e.g.*, with the arrangement of crops in a garden plot)....Women also operate with the same aesthetic principles as the men use for their body decoration, when they arrange different crop cultivars in their gardens to create pleasing patterns. They alternatingly plant sweet potato cultivars with reddish or red tinged leaves and cultivars with light green or dark green leaves....Tall crops are rhythmically interplanted with low crops, for example corn and sweet potatoes or bananas and taro, or a plot is fringed by double bands of high and low growing crops, for example corn and beans or sugar cane and squash. Such rhythmic repetition of formal elements, accentuating colour or shape contrasts, is a principle of aesthetic activities....

Aside from their aesthetic concerns, traditional agriculturalists in the Pacific had other feelings and perceptions that also belong in the discourse on sustainability. One of these is a deep affection for their territories, perhaps associated with the feelings of integration and interdependence among an individual, his or her lineal group, and the land and sea with which that group is traditionally associated (Baines, 1991; Ravuvu, 1983). Although affection, in all its meanings, underlies economics, affection for place or land rarely surfaces in economic analysis. As economist Kenneth Boulding (1991: 30-31) holds, it is an important component of what he calls "integrative power", a third form of power together with threat power and economic power. Integrative power is "the power of legitimacy, loyalty, respect, affection, love, truth, and so on. In many ways this is the most fundamental form of power, as neither threat power nor economic power is very effective in the absence of legitimacy." Of course, as Boulding further points out, legitimacy is much subject to change and can, to some extent, be undermined by threat power and economic power; but it can also be created through a learning process.

In part, deep ecology moralizing about 'the respect we must feel for the land' may help in this process. As important is the extension of an eco-morality, which, though it needs to be pragmatic (O'Riordan, 1988), also needs the strength of metaphor. The medium of indigenous knowledge can teach in this regard. For instance, there is much power in the image of "enchanted gardens" (*jardins magiques*) on the island of Tanna in Vanuatu, as described by the French geographer Joël Bonnemaison (1984; 1986b). In these gardens, traditional horticultural practice unfolds as a ritual, and the intensity with which the garden tasks are carried out makes the yield abundant and the gardens beautiful. In large measure, the earth of these gardens is fecund because for the traditional gardeners "l'horticulture est un geste rituel" (Bonnemaison, 1984: 481).

Whether this sort of relation between people and land can somehow be regained or operationalized today is much open to question. The intensity of work required is no longer seen as worth the effort – just as Ngirapo had no intention of giving up his steel axe in favour of the more benign stone tool, traditional though it was to him. The high yields per unit of land that were once characteristic of intensive forms of Pacific Island subsistence agriculture have fallen. Indeed, there is evidence to support the view that the recent performance of agriculture – and smallholder agriculture in particular – has been disappointing over the past several decades in the Pacific, although some of the statistics are questionable (Fleming et al., 1991). Less questionable is that few Pacific Islanders will want to become or long remain peasants even though Pacific Islands will not support more than a peasant outcome, given their own resources, location, or economic potential (Ward 1993: 19).

The production capacity of the islands is itself degenerating. Catches of fish from reef and coastal waters are declining; pollution of all sorts is increasing; deforestation and erosion are serious issues in many places; biodiversity is diminishing; and, on many islands, human population is growing more rapidly than the economic or physical capacity to manage (Thaman, 1988; Thistlethwaite & Votaw, 1992; Bryant, this volume; David, this volume). All this is happening so quickly that thresholds are being crossed irreparably, as exemplified in changes in the rural economy of a village in North Malaita, Solomon Islands, between 1971 and 1985. Frazer (1987: ii) sums up the changes:

> A notable change over the period has been the growth in cash cropping. The area of tree crops doubled between 1971 and 1985, production of cocoa increased threefold and copra production increased four times. While this expansion has increased cash incomes, the increased area of tree crops, combined with population growth, have caused a growing shortage of land. Land for food cropping is scarce and much of that available is far away, imposing additional

work burdens on women who do most food crop gardening. One response to the land shortage has been to reduce bush fallow periods, causing declines in crop yields and some land degradation. Land scarcity is also a cause of the growing number of land disputes.

The environmental issues potent in the Pacific can stand in as a microcosm for the whole dreary roster of global issues, which were tersely summed up in a recent joint statement by the US National Academy of Sciences and the UK Royal Society (cited in Norse, 1992: 6):

> If current predictions of population growth prove accurate and patterns of human activity on the planet remain unchanged, science and technology may not be able to prevent either irreversible degradation of the environment or continued poverty for much of the world.

Despite such warnings, it proved fruitless for Maurice Strong (1991: 41) to have called for "a deep and profound stirring of the human spirit" among the delegates at the huge UNCED held at Rio de Janeiro in 1992. Certainly, nothing occurred at the meeting that approached anywhere near the "unique and united act of statesmanship" that Strong said would be necessary if the world's future were to be secured. To turn to Australia, where I am writing this paper, there was recently a hard fought national election campaign, during which employment and economic advance were the central issues, with the leading candidates of the two major political parties scarcely mentioning environmental matters and seeming literally never to speak of the country's official policy of "ecologically sustainable development".

Nevertheless, when I am most downcast with pessimism about our environment's future, I remember Ngirapo and recall how much I learned from him during our walks together through the landscapes of his homeland. I think again of his orchards, of how he and his wives established and then tended them, of how their close attention to these tasks brought a graceful transition from forest to garden to orchard and back to secondary forest until the soil was fertile enough to garden productively again. I think of how three decades after I first saw those orchards, at least some of the trees that Ngirapo planted then still bear fruit.

Like Ngirapo, our modern world has the knowledge to design sustainable agricultural systems; however, our political, economic, and ethical structures often do not allow or encourage us to do so. In frustration, we turn to indigenous knowledge as a miracle cure, as an untainted way to achieve the goal of sustainability, which at least rhetorically has to some extent replaced the goal of progress as the major purpose of human endeavour. The way to sustainability is not external to us; it is not to be found in the sets of facts, however serviceable they may be, that indigenous knowledge becomes when we collect it. Still, that knowledge seen in the context of indigenous lives and landscapes may help in our construction of a paradigm of sustainability modelled in part on the real sustainability that has existed now and then, here and there, in indigenous pasts. Our most vital task seems to be to pause long enough to avoid the fate that T.S. Eliot depicted in 'The Dry Salvages': "We had the experience but missed the meaning."

Notes on contributors

John Bigay was Lecturer in Geography at the USP from 1977-1983, joining initially as a United States Peace Corps volunteer. He is currently an environmental impact specialist for the United States Navy, based in Hawaii.

Jennifer J. Bryant-Tokalau is Reader in Geography at the USP. She joined the department in 1983 having previously taught at Monash University in Australia and the University of Papua New Guinea. Her key research interests are urban poverty and housing, and urban environmental degradation. She has just published a monograph on the subject: *Urban Poverty and the Environment in the South Pacific* (1993).

Rajesh Chandra has been working at the USP since 1976 and was Director of Planning and Development prior to his appointment, in January 1994, as Professor of Geography and Head of Department. His research interests include industrialization, urbanization and small island development. His most recent book is *Industrialization and Development in the Third World* (1993).

William C. Clarke was Professor of Geography at the USP for most of his time there from 1981-1989. With an undergraduate degree in anthropology and post-graduate studies in the 'Berkeley School' of geography at the University of California, he first carried out research in the Pacific in 1964-1965. The results of this—a cultural-ecological study of a Papua New Guinean community—were reported in his 1971 book *Place and People*. He has since written on development issues, conservation, indigenous ecological knowledge and agroforestry in the region.

Gilbert David is a *chargé de recherche* with ORSTOM in Nouméa, New Caledonia specializing in marine and insular geography. He was trained at the University of Brest and has worked in West Africa, Brazil as well as the Pacific. While conducting research on village-based subsistence fisheries in Vanuatu from 1983-1985 and 1989-1991, he taught human geography and human ecology at the USP Centre in Port Vila.

Lionel Gibson is Lecturer in Geography at the USP and a Fiji citizen. He has a BA (Hons.) in geography from the Victoria University of Wellington and is presently working on a PhD at the USP in the field of international aid and development.

Frank McShane has been Lecturer in Geography at the USP since 1992 before which he worked in the United Kingdom as a geologist and resource manager. His current research interests include geomorphology, environmental change and the impacts of mining.

Harley I. Manner is Professor of Geography and Chair of the Division of Social/Behavioral Sciences and Social Work at the University of Guam. He taught at the USP from 1979 to 1985. Born in Hawaii, he received his degrees from the University of Hawai'i (Manoa). His research interests centre on human-environment interactions, particularly subsistence agricultural systems, atoll environments and cultural ecology.

Patrick D. Nunn received his PhD from the University of London in 1983 and has been on the staff of the USP since 1985. A Fiji citizen, he is currently Reader in Geography. His interests span much of physical geography and related subjects, including geology and geophysics, and he has published widely on these topics as the result of his research in the south and west Pacific. His 1994 book *Oceanic Islands* testifies to the breadth of his interests.

John Overton is Lecturer in Geography at the University of Canterbury in New Zealand. His interests are in rural change in the developing world and he has conducted research in Kenya, Fiji and Malaysia. He taught at the USP in 1985 and has returned on several occasions to continue his fieldwork, particularly in Fijian villages.

Edward Simpson was the first Professor of Geography at the USP from 1970-1972. He is currently Professor Emeritus at the University of Newcastle-upon-Tyne in the United Kingdom.

Konai Helu Thaman is presently Pro-Vice Chancellor at the USP. A Tongan citizen and one of the Pacific Islands' foremost poets, her qualifications include a Bachelor's degree in geography from Auckland University and a PhD in education from the USP. Dr. Thaman lectured in geography and sociology from 1974 to 1976, prior to moving to the Department of Education.

Randolph R. Thaman has taught at the USP for 20 years and is currently Professor of Pacific Islands Biogeography. He is the founder and past chairman of the South Pacific Action Committee for Human Ecology and the Environment (SPACHEE) and has chaired the Fiji National Food and Nutrition Committee. In addition to biogeography, he is interested in ethnobotany, food and agricultural systems, and sustainable development.

Joeli Veitayaki was Lecturer in Geography from 1990-1992 and is now Co-ordinator of the Ocean Resources Management Programme at the USP. He is interested in human ecology, in particular the wider issues relating to human use of ocean resources.

Eric Waddell was Professor of Geography and Head of Department at the USP from January 1991 to January 1994 and has since returned to Université Laval (Québec). A Canadian citizen, he has been living and working in the Pacific on and off since 1963 in association with the Australian National University, the University of Hawai'i and ORSTOM. His research interests span the broad field of culture, ranging from adaptive strategies to the emergence of new collective identities and to geopoetics.

A. Crosbie Walsh is Director of the Institute of Development Studies at Massey University in New Zealand. From 1974 to 1976 he was Head of Geography and Population Studies at the USP. He has done research principally in Tonga, Niue, Fiji, Papua New Guinea and Solomon Islands, focusing on equity issues in development, as expressed in studies of urbanization, squatting, the informal sector, migration and regional social and ethnic differentiation.

References

Akimichi, T. 1986. Conservation of the sea: Satawal, Micronesia. In Anderson, A. (ed.). *Traditional Fishing in the Pacific*. Honolulu: Bernice P. Bishop Museum, Pacific Anthropological Records 37, 42-49.

Ali, I. 1988a. The dissociation of crop and livestock production on small-holder sugarcane farms in Fiji. In Overton, J. (ed.). *Rural Fiji*. Suva: Institute of Pacific Studies, The University of the South Pacific, 165-177.

Ali, I. 1988b. Specialization leading to increasing vulnerability on sugar cane farms in Fiji. In Hirst, J., Overton, J., Byron, Y., and Allen, B.J. (eds.). *Small-Scale Agriculture*. Canberra: Commonwealth Geographical Bureau and Department of Human Geography, Research School of Pacific Studies, Australian National University, 111-125.

Ambrose, W.R. 1978. The loneliness of the long distance trader in Melanesia. *Mankind*, 11, 326-333.

Anand, R.P. 1976. *Legal Regime of the Sea-Bed and Developing Countries*. New Delhi: Thompson Press.

Anderson, A., and McGlone, M. 1992. Living on the edge - prehistoric land and people in New Zealand. In Dodson, J. (ed). *The Naive Lands*. Melbourne: Longman Cheshire, 199-241.

Anderson, A.B. (ed.) 1990. *Alternatives to Deforestation: Steps Toward Sustainable Use of the Amazon Rain Forest.* New York: Columbia University Press.

Anderson, A.G. 1974. *Indo-Fijian Smallfarming: Profiles of a Peasantry*. Auckland: Auckland University Press.

Anon. 1989a. Placer Dome sets targets. *Mining Journal*, 313, p 471.

Anon. 1989b. There is evidence of damage to Porgera environment. *Times of Papua New Guinea*, 30 March-6 April.

Anon. 1989c. Placer told to clear up. *Pacific Islands Monthly*, 59, p 39.

Anon. 1989d. A massive national investment. *Times of Papua New Guinea*, 18-24 May.

Anon. 1991a. Promising signs from PNG mines: Three big players in the mining game are optimistic about the future. *Pacific Islands Monthly*, 61, p 41.

Anon. 1991b. Porgera stoppage. *Mining Journal*, 310, p 426.

Anon. 1991c. *The Far East and Australasia, 1992.* 23rd edition. London: Europa.

Anon. 1992. Want it right? Do it yourself. *Energy and Mining Journal*, December, p 11.

Anon. 1993a. Classified Advertisement. *The Fiji Times*, 4 April.

Anon. 1993b. Placer Dome returns to profit. *Metal Bulletin*, 8 March, p 13.

Antheaume, B., and Bonnemaison, J. 1988. Aide au développement. In *Atlas du Pacifique Sud*. Montpeiller: GIP Reclus, 47-48.

REFERENCES

Arif, G.M. 1993. Vanuatu. In Cole, R. (ed.). *Pacific 2010: Challenging the Future*. Canberra: NCDS, Australian National University, 80-90.

Ashton, C. 1991. The new wild west in the north. *Golden Wing, Ansett Air Magazine*, 77, p 34.

Baines, G.B.K. 1979. Mangroves for national development. A report on the mangrove resources of Fiji. Unpub ms.

Baines, G.B.K. 1989. A traditional base for inshore fisheries development in the Solomon Islands. In Ruddle, K., and Johannes, R.E. (eds.). *Traditional Marine Resource Management in the Pacific Basin: an anthology*. Study 2, Jakarta: UNESCO/ROSTEA, 289-300.

Baines, G.B.K. 1991. Asserting traditional rights: community conservation in Solomon Islands. *Cultural Survival Quarterly*, 15, 49-52.

Bakker, M.L. 1990. *Populations of the South Pacific: An Overview of Demographic Levels, Patterns and Trends*. Suva: Population Studies Programme, The University of the South Pacific.

Bakker, M.L., and Walsh, A.C. 1976. *Urban Fiji: Boundaries used in the 1976 Census of Population: a report to the Census Commissioner*. Suva: Government Printer.

Bank of Hawaii. 1989. *An Economic Assessment of the Federated States of Micronesia (FSM)*. Honolulu: Bank of Hawaii, Economics Department.

Barr, K.J. 1990. *Poverty in Fiji*. Suva: Fiji Forum for Peace, Justice and the Integrity of Creation.

Barrau, J. 1958. *Subsistence agriculture in Melanesia*. Bulletin 219. Bernice P. Bishop Museum, Honolulu.

Barrau, J. 1961. *Subsistence agriculture in Polynesia and Micronesia*. Bulletin 223. Bernice P. Bishop Museum, Honolulu.

Battistini, R., Bourrouilh, F., Chevalier, J.P., Coudray, J., Denizot, M. Faure, G., Fisher, J.C., Guilcher, A., Harmelin-Vivien, M., Jaubert, J., Laborel, J., Montaggioni, L., Masse, J.P., Mauge, L.A., Peyrot-Clausade, M., Pichon, M., Plante, R., Plaziat, J.C., Plessis, Y.B., Richard, G., Salvat, B., Thomassin, B.A., Vasseur, P., and Weydert, P. 1975. Eléments de terminologie récifale indopacifique. *Thétys*, 7, 111p.

Bauer, P.T. 1976. *Dissent on Development*. Cambridge, Masschusetts: Yale University Press.

Bayliss-Smith, T.P. 1976. *Koro in the 1970s: Prosperity through Diversity?* Project Working Paper 7, UNESCO/UNFPA Population and Environment Project in the Eastern Islands of Fiji. Canberra: Development Studies Centre, Australian National University.

Bayliss-Smith, T.P. 1978. Batiki in the 1970s: satellite of Suva. In Brookfield, H.C. (ed.). *The Small Islands and the Reefs*. Canberra: UNESCO/UNFPA Population and Environment Project in the Eastern Islands of Fiji, Island Reports 4, 67-128.

REFERENCES

Bayliss-Smith, T.P., Bedford, R., Brookfield, H., and Latham, M. 1988. *Islands, Islanders and the World: the Colonial and Post-Colonial Experience of Eastern Fiji*. Cambridge: Cambridge University Press.

Bedford, R. 1987. *Pacific populations in the 1980s: an overview*. Paper presented to Expert Meeting on New Approaches to Development Cooperation with South Pacific Countries, Institute for International Relations, Bonn, 25-28 May.

Bedford, R.D., McLean, R.F., and MacPherson, J. 1978. Kabara in the 1970s: home in spite of hazards. In Brookfield, H.C. (ed.). *The Small Islands and the Reefs*. Canberra: UNESCO/UNFPA Population and Environment Project in the Eastern Islands of Fiji, Island Reports 4, 9-65.

Bellow, L. 1989a. Trois jours avec Tjibaou. *Jeune Afrique*, 1480, 38-39.

Bellow, L. 1989b. Tjibaou: sa dernière interview. *Jeune Afrique*, 1481, 28-29.

Belshaw, C.S. 1964. *Under the Ivi Tree: Society and Economic Growth in Rural Fiji*. London: Routledge and Kegan Paul.

Benedict, R. 1934. *Patterns of Culture*. Boston: Houghton Mifflin Company.

Bensa, A. 1990. *Nouvelle-Calédonie: un paradis dans le tourmente*. Paris: Découvertes Gallimard.

Berger, P.L. 1976. *Pyramids of Sacrifice*. London: Penguin.

Besset, J.-P. 1989. Tjibaou 'le' Kanak. *Politis, le Citoyen*, 61, 21-22.

Bienefeld, M. 1984. *Work and Income for the People of Fiji. A Strategy For More Than Just Survival. The Final Report of the Fiji Employment and Development Mission*. Suva, Parliament of Fiji, Parliamentary paper 66 of 1984.

Black-Metzner, B., and Hughes, H. 1982. Growth experience of small economies. In Jalan, B. (ed.). *Problems and Policies in Small Economies*. London: Croom Helm, 85-101.

Blaikie, P., and Brookfield, H.C. (eds.) 1987. *Land Degradation and Society*. London: Methuen.

Blaikie, P., Brookfield, H.C., and Clarke, W.C. 1987. Degradation and adaptive land management in the ancient Pacific. In Blaikie, P., and Brookfield, H.C. (eds.). *Land Degradation and Society*. London: Methuen, 143-145.

Blanchet, G., Caillaud, L., and Paoafaite, J. 1985. Un aspect de la pêche artisanale en Polynésie Française, les pièges à poissons de Tikehau. *Centre ORSTOM de Tahiti, Notes et Documents d'Océanographie* 25, 116p.

Bloomfield, G.T. 1967. *Boundaries of Towns and Urban Centres in Fiji 1966: a Report to the Census Commissioner*. Unpub ms, Geography Department, Auckland University.

Bodley, J. (ed.) 1988. *Tribal Peoples and Development Issues: A Global Overview*. Mountain View, California: Mayfield Publishing Company.

Bonnemaison, J. 1981. Voyage autour du territoire. *L'espace géographique*, 4, 249-262.

REFERENCES

Bonnemaison, J. 1984. Les jardins magiques. Le géosystème de l'horticulture vivrière dans une île mélanésienne du Pacifique Sud (Vanuatu). In Blanc-Pamard, C., Bonnemaison, J., Boutrais, J., Lassailly-Jacob, V., and Lericollais, A. (eds.), *Le Développement Rural en Questions: Paysages, Espaces Ruraux, Systèmes Agraires*. Collections Mémoires 106, ORSTOM, Paris.

Bonnemaison, J. 1985. The tree and the canoe: roots and mobility in Vanuatu societies. *Pacific Viewpoint*, 26, 30-62.

Bonnemaison, J. 1986a. *L'arbre et la pirogue. Les fondements d'une identité. territoire, histoire et société dans l'archipel de Vanuatu (Mélanésie)*. Volume 1. Noumea: ORSTOM, 540p.

Bonnemaison, J. 1986b. *La dernière île*. Paris: Arléa/ORSTOM.

Bonnemaison, J. 1987. *Tanna; les hommes lieux. Les fondements d'une identité. territoire, histoire et société dans l'archipel de Vanuatu (Mélanésie)*. Volume 2. Noumea: ORSTOM, 680 p.

Boulding, K. 1991. What do we want to sustain?: environmentalism and human evaluations. In Costanza, R. (ed.). *Ecological Economics: The Science and Management of Sustainability*. New York: Columbia University Press, 22-31.

Bour, W. 1990. Les ressources halieutiques des pays insulaires du Pacifique, troisième partie: les trocas. *FAO, Document technique sur les pêches*, 272.3, 89p.

Boyden, S. 1992. *Biohistory: The Interplay Between Human Society and the Biosphere*. Paris: UNESCO, and Casterton Hill, Carnforth, Lancs: Parthenon Publishing.

Britton, S.G. 1983. *Tourism and Underdevelopment in Fiji*. Canberra: Development Studies Centre, Australian National University.

Brodie, J.E. 1990. The State of the Marine Environment in the South Pacific. *United Nations Environment Programme, Regional Seas Report* 127.

Brookfield, H. C. 1962. Local study and comparative method: an example from central New Guinea. *Annals of the Association of American Geographers*, 52, 242-254.

Brookfield, H.C. 1979. *Lakeba, the Eastern Islands and the Work of the Project in Retrospect*. Canberra: UNESCO/UNFPA Population and Environment Project in the Eastern Islands of Fiji, Island Reports 5.

Brookfield, H.C. 1985. An historical and prospective analysis of the coconut economy and the coconut districts of Fiji. In Brookfield, H.C., Ellis, F., and Ward, R.G. (eds.). *Land, Cane and Coconuts*. Canberra: Department of Human Geography, Research School of Pacific Studies, Australian National University, 91-215.

Brookfield, H.C. 1988. Fijian farmers each on his own land: the triumph of experience over hope. *Journal of Pacific History*, 23, 15-35.

REFERENCES

Brown, L., Flavin, C., and Postel, S. (eds.) 1993. *State of the World 1993*. (A Worldwatch Institute Report on Progress Toward a Sustainable Society.) New York: W.W. Norton.

Brown, P. 1978. *Highland Peoples of New Guinea*. Cambridge: Cambridge University Press.

Bryant, J.J. 1992a. *Urban Poverty in the Pacific Region*. Report to "State of Urbanization in Asia and the Pacific" Project, ESCAP, Bangkok.

Bryant, J.J. 1992b. *Urban Environment in the Pacific Region*. Report to "State of Urbanization in Asia and the Pacific" Project, ESCAP, Bangkok.

Bryant, J.J. 1993. *Urban Poverty and the Environment in the South Pacific*. Armidale, Australia: Department of Geography and Planning, University of New England.

Bule, W. 1990. *The Country Profile of Vanuatu*. Discussion paper for ESCAP Consultative Meeting of National Experts in Human Settlements of Small Pacific Islands, Port Vila, 3-6 October.

Bulmer, R.N.H. 1982. Traditional conservation practices in Papua New Guinea. In Morauta, L., Pernetta, J., and Heaney, W. (eds.) *Traditional Conservation in Papua New Guinea: Implications for Today*. Monograph 16, Institute of Applied Social and Economic Research, Boroko, Papua New Guinea, 59-77.

Callick, R. 1993. Pacific 2010: a doomsday scenario? In Cole, R.V. (ed.). *Pacific 2010 - Challenging the Future*. Canberra: NCDS, Australian National University, 1-11.

Carew-Reid, J. 1989. *Environment, Aid and Regionalism in the South Pacific*. Pacific Research Monograph 22, Canberra: National Centre for Development Studies, Australian National University.

Carpenter, R., and Maragos, J.E. (eds.). 1989. *How to Assess Environmental Impacts on Tropical Islands and Coastal Areas*. Honolulu: Environment and Policy Institute, East-West Center.

Carrier, J.G. 1981. Ownership of productive resources on Ponam Island, Manus Province. *Journal de la Société des Océanistes*, 72-73, 205-217.

Chambers, M.R, Nguyen, F., and Navin, K.F. 1990. Seagrass communities. In Done T.J., and Navin, K.F. (eds.). *Vanuatu Marine Resources, report of a biological survey*. Townsville: Australian Institute of Marine Science, 92-103.

Chambers, R. 1983. *Rural Development: Putting the Last First*. Harlow, Essex, England: Longman Scientific & Technical.

Chandra, R. 1977. The retail structures of food outlets in Suva. *The Journal of Pacific Studies*, 3, 23-54.

Chandra, R. 1980. *Maro: Rural Indians of Fiji*. Suva: Institute of Pacific Studies, The University of the South Pacific.

Chandra, R. 1985. Industrialization in Fiji. Unpub PhD thesis, Department of Geography, University of British Columbia, Vancouver.

REFERENCES

Chandra, R. 1988. Industrialization in Fiji: industrial structure and organization, *GeoJournal*, 16, 169-178.

Chandra, R. 1990. *Fiji's Tax Free System*. Honolulu: Pacific Islands Development Program, East-West Center.

Chandra, R. 1992. Breaking out of import-substitution industrialization: the case of Fiji. In Lockhart, D., Drakakis-Smith, D., and Schmebri, J. (eds.). *The Development Process in Small Island States*. London: Routledge, 205-227.

Chape, S., and Watling, R. 1991. *Republic of Fiji National Report to the United Nations Conference on Environment and Development*. Suva: Environmental Management Unit, Government of Fiji.

Chapman, M. 1991. Pacific Island movement and socioeconomic change: metaphors of misunderstanding. *Population and Development Review*, 17, 263-292.

Chapman, V.J. 1977. Wet coastal ecosystems, an introduction. In Chapman, V.J. (ed.). *Ecosystems of the World*, Volume 1. Amsterdam: Elsevier, 1-30.

Chesneaux, J. 1989. Tjibaou le paysan. *Politis, le Citoyen*, 61, 24-25.

Chung, M. 1991. Politics, tradition and structural change: Fijian fertility in the twentieth century. Unpub PhD thesis, Australian National University.

Clarke, W.C. 1966. From Extensive to Intensive Shifting Cultivation: A Succession from New Guinea. *Ethnology*, 5, 347-359.

Clarke, W.C. 1971. *Place and People: An Ecology of a New Guinean Community*. Canberra: Australian National University Press, and Berkeley: University of California Press.

Clarke, W.C. 1976. The maintenance of agriculture and human habitats within the tropical forest ecosystem. *Human Ecology*, 4, 247-259.

Clarke, W.C. 1977. The structure of permanence. In Bayliss-Smith, T.P. and Feachem, R.G. (eds.), *Subsistence and Survival: Rural Ecology in the Pacific*. London: Academic Press, 363-384.

Clarke, W.C. 1978. Progressing with the past: environmentally sustainable modifications to traditional agricultural systems. In Fisk, E.K. (ed.) *The Adaptation of Traditional Agriculture: Socioeconomic Problems of Urbanization*. Monograph No. 11, Development Studies Centre, Australian National University, Canberra, 142-157.

Clarke, W.C. 1980. At the Tail of the Snake. In Jennings, J., and Linge, G.J.R. (eds.). *Of Time and Place: Essays in Honour of O.H.K. Spate*. Canberra: Australian National University Press, 173-192.

Clarke, W.C. 1990. Learning from the past: traditional knowledge and sustainable development. *The Contemporary Pacific*, 2, 233-253.

Clarke, W.C. (forthcoming). Traditional land use and agriculture in the Pacific Islands. In Geraghty, P., and Morrison, R.J. (eds.). *Science of Pacific Island Peoples*. Suva: Institute of Pacific Studies, The University of the South Pacific.

Clarke, W.C., and Morrison, J. 1987. Land mismanagement and the development imperative in Fiji. In Blaikie, P., and Brookfield, H.C. (eds.). *Land Degradation and Society*. London: Methuen, 176-185.

Clarke, W.C., and Thaman, R.R. (eds.). 1993. *Agroforestry in the Pacific Islands: Systems for Sustainability*. Tokyo: United Nations University Press.

Cole, R.V. (ed.). 1993. *Pacific 2010 - Challenging the Future*. Canberra: NCDS, Australian National University.

Conand, C. 1986. Les ressources halieutiques des pays insulaires du Pacifique, deuxième partie: les holoturies. *FAO, Document technique sur les pêches*, 272.2, 108p.

Conklin, H.C. 1954. An ethnoecological approach to shifting cultivation. *Transactions of the New York Academy of Sciences* (Series 2), 17, 133-142.

Connell, J. 1984. Islands under pressure - population growth and urbanization in the South Pacific. *Ambio*, 13, 306-312.

Connell, J., and Howitt, R. 1991. Mining dispossession and development. In Connell, J., and Howitt, R. (eds). *Mining and Indigenous Peoples in Australasia*. Sydney: Sydney University Press, 4-16.

Connell, J., and Lea, J. 1993. Cities of parts, cities apart? Urban life in contemporary Melanesia. Paper delivered to conference 'Postmodern Cities', Sydney University, 13-16 April 1993.

Cordell, J. 1991. Negotiating sea rights. *Cultural Survival Quarterly*, 15, 5-10.

Cornforth, R.C. 1984. Towards a national coastal policy. In *Proceedings of the 3rd biennial coastal zone management seminar*. Wellington: Department of Lands and Survey, New Zealand (Information series 15).

Couhe, O. 1989. Avec eux, c'est tout qui disparait. *Politis, le Citoyen*, 61, 17-18.

Coutts, B. 1989. Mean high water as a cadastral boundary. *Ocean and Shoreline Management*, 12, 309-330.

Coyne, T., Badcock, J., and Taylor, R. (eds.). 1984. *The Effect of Urbanisation and Western Diet on the Health of Pacific Island Populations*. Technical Paper 186. South Pacific Commission, Noumea.

Crocombe, R. 1971. Review article - R.F. Watters, Koro: Economic Development and Social Change in Fiji. *Journal of the Polynesian Society*, 80, 505-520.

Crocombe, R. 1992. *Pacific Neighbours: New Zealand's relations with other Pacific Islands*. Christchurch: Macmillan Brown Centre for Pacific Studies, University of Canterbury, and Suva: Institute of Pacific Studies, The University of the South Pacific.

Cumberland, K.B. 1962. 'Climatic change' or cultural interference? New Zealand in moa hunter times. In McCaskill, M. (ed). *Land and Livelihood*. New Zealand Geographical Society, 88-142.

Cumberland, K. 1963. Man's role in modifying island environments in the Southwest Pacific: with special reference to New Zealand. In Fosberg, F.R. (ed.). *Man's Place in the Island'Ecosystem*. Honolulu: Bishop Museum Press, 187-205.

Cushing, J., Wenner, A.M., Noble, E., and Daily, M. 1986. A groundwater hypothesis for the origin of 'fire areas' on the northern Channel Islands, California. *Quaternary Research*, 26, 207-17.

Dahl, A.L. 1980. *Regional Ecosystems Survey of the South Pacific Area*. Technical Paper 179. South Pacific Commission, Noumea.

Daly, H.E. 1991. Sustainable development: from concept to theory to operational principles. In Davis, K., and Bernstam, M.S. (eds.). *Resources, Environment, and Population: Present Knowledge, Future Options.* Oxford: Oxford University Press, 25-43.

David, G. 1985. Pêche de subsistance et milieu naturel: les mangroves de Vanuatu et leur intérêt halieutique. *Mission ORSTOM de Port-Vila, Notes et documents d'océanographie*, 13, 67p.

David, G. 1989. Thematic mapping of Vanuatu's coastline by means of Spot imagery. Preliminary findings. In *Remote Sensing for Land and Sea Resources*, report of the ESCAP/UNDP workshop on remote sensing for land and sea resource surveys and evaluation in the Pacific, Port-Vila, 7-11 August 1989, 28-39.

David, G. 1991. Pêche villageoise et alimentation au Vanuatu, exploration d'un système. Unpub thesis, Université de Bretagne Occidentale, 1050p.

David, G. (forthcoming). The modern value of traditional village fishing in fisheries development planning in the Island Pacific: some thoughts on the case of Vanuatu. In Geraghty, P., and Morrison, R.J., *Science of Pacific Island Peoples*. Suva: Institute of Pacific Studies, The University of the South Pacific.

David, G., and Cillaurren, E. 1989. A survey of village subsistence fishing in Vanuatu. *Mission ORSTOM de Port-Vila, Notes et documents d'océanographie*, 19, 11-25.

Deane, P. 1965. *The First Industrial Revolution*. Cambridge: Cambridge University Press.

Denevan, W.M., and Padoch, C. (eds.) 1988. Swidden-Fallow Agroforestry in the Peruvian Amazon. *Advances in Economic Botany*, volume 5.

Di Piazza, A. 1993. Coté jardin, horticulture vivrière des îles Wallis et Futuna. *ORSTOM, Col. A travers Champs* (in press).

Diamond, J. 1992. *The Third Chimpanzee*. New York: Harper Collins.

Dodson, J. (ed). 1992. *The Naive Lands*. Melbourne: Longman Cheshire, 254 pp.

Douglas, N., and Douglas, N. (eds.). 1987. *Pacific Islands Yearbook.* 16th edition. North Ryde, Australia: Angus and Robertson.

Doumenge, F. 1966. *L'Homme dans le Pacifique Sud*. Paris: Musée de l'Homme, Publication de la Société des Océanistes 19, 634p.

Doumenge, J.P. 1984. Du terroir à la ville, les mélanésiens et leurs espaces en Nouvelle-Calédonie. *CEGET-CNRS, travaux de géographie tropicale*, 46, 488p.

Durning, A.T. 1993. Supporting indigenous peoples. In Brown, L., Flavin, C., and Postel, S. (eds.). *State of the World 1993*. (A Worldwatch Institute Report on Progress Toward a Sustainable Society.) New York: W.W. Norton, 80-100.

Durr, B. 1990. Placer Dome puts a shine on its activities. *The Financial Times, London*, 13 October.

Eaton, C. 1988. Vakavanua land tenure. In Overton, J. (ed.). *Rural Fiji*. Suva: Institute of Pacific Studies, University of the South Pacific, 19-30.

Echinard, M. 1972. La pêche dans le lagon en Polynésie par le système des parcs à poissons. *Journal de la Société des Océanistes*, 37, 345-363.

Ellis, D. 1989. *Environments at Risk: case histories of environmental impact assessment*. Berlin: Springer Verlag.

Ellis, D., and Ellis, K. submitted. Very deep submarine tailings disposal. Manuscript submitted to *Marine Pollution Bulletin*.

Emberson-Bain, A. 1992. Sustaining the unsustainable? Assessing the impact of mining in the Pacific, with particular reference to women. Unpub ms, SSED, The University of the South Pacific.

Enga Provincial Government. 1989. An open letter to the Office of the Prime Minister from the Enga Provincial Government. *Times of Papua New Guinea*, 23-29 March.

Enright, N.J., and Gosden, C. 1992. Unstable archipelagoes - southwest Pacific environment and prehistory since 30 000 B.P. In Dodson, J. (ed). *The Naive Lands*. Melbourne: Longman Cheshire, 160-198.

Esteva, G. 1992. Development. In Sachs, W. (ed.). The Development Dictionary: A Guide to Knowledge as Power. London: Zed Books, 6-25.

Evensen, J. 1984. The United Nations Convention on the Law of the Sea of 10th December 1982: legal status, peace promoting effects, denuclearisation. Unpub paper for the Symposium on Denuclearisation of the Oceans, Oslo.

Fanon, F. 1961. *The Wretched of the Earth*. London: Penguin.

Fiji Bureau of Statistics. 1986. *Overseas Trade, 1985*. Parliamentary Paper No. 49 of 1986. Suva: Government Printer.

Fiji Bureau of Statistics. 1989. *Current Economic Statistics, July 1989*. Suva: Fiji Bureau of Statistics.

Fiji Bureau of Statistics. 1991. *Current Economic Statistics, April 1991*. Suva: Fiji Bureau of Statistics.

Fiji Bureau of Statistics. 1993. *Current Economic Statistics*. Suva: Fiji Government, Bureau of Statistics.

REFERENCES

Fiji Employment and Development Mission. 1984. *Final Report to the Government of Fiji*. Parliamentary Paper No. 66 of 1984. Suva: Government Printer.

Fiji Government. 1975. *Laws of Fiji 1974*. Suva: Government Printer.

Fiji Ministry of Finance and Economic Planning. 1991. *Review of Performance and Prospects: Fiji Economy*. Suva: Fiji Ministry of Finance and Economic Planning.

Fiji Trade and Investment Board. 1988. *Fiji Investment Guide*. Suva: Fiji Trade and Investment Board.

Filer, C. 1990. The Bougainville rebellion, the mining industry and the process of social disintegration in Papua New Guinea. *Canberra Anthropology*, 13, 1-39.

Finney, B.R., and Houston, J.D. 1966. *Surfing: The Sport of Hawaiian Kings*. Rutland: Tuttle.

Fisk, E.K. 1972. Motivation and modernization. *Pacific Perspective*, 1, 21-23.

Fleming, E., Hardaker, B., and Delforce, J. 1991. Smallholder agricultural economy at the crossroads: policy priorities for sustainable agricultural development in South Pacific island nations. *Journal de la Société des Océanistes*, 92, 119-126.

Flenley, J.R., and King, S.M. 1984. Late Quaternary pollen records from Easter Island. *Nature,* 307, 47-50.

Flenley, J., Parkes, A., and Teller, J.T. 1991. A 500-year climate change record from Tahiti. In Hay, J. (ed). *South Pacific Environments: Interactions with Weather and Climate*. University of Auckland, Environmental Science Occasional Publication 6, p 31.

Forster, J.J.H., Bryant, J.J., Manner, H.I., Clarke, W.C., and Thaman, R.R. 1983. "Geography...The next most important subject". *Journal of Pacific Studies*, 9, 133-171.

Frazer, I. 1987. *Growth and Change in Village Agriculture: Manakwai, North Malaita.* South Pacific Smallholder Project, Occasional Paper No. 11, University of New England, Armidale, Australia.

Frazer, R.M. 1961. Land use and population in Ra province, Fiji. Unpub PhD thesis, Australian National University.

Frazer, R.M. 1973. The Fijian village and the independent farmer. In Brookfield, H.C. (ed.). *The Pacific in Transition*. London: Edward Arnold, 75-96.

Freeman, M.N.R., and Carbyn, L.N. (eds.). 1988. *Traditional Knowledge and Renewable Resource Management in Northern Regions*. Edmonton: University of Alberta.

Geertz, C. 1988. *Works and Lives: The Anthropologist as Author*. Stanford: Stanford University Press.

Geertz, C. 1989. Being there, writing here. *Dialogue*, 2, 58-63.

Geraghty, P., and Morrison, R.J. (forthcoming). *Science of Pacific Island Peoples.* Suva: Institute of Pacific Studies, The University of the South Pacific.

Gibbons, J.R.H., and Clunie, F.G.A.U. 1986. Sea level changes and Pacific prehistory. *Journal of Pacific History*, 21, 58-82.

Giddens, A. 1990. *The Consequences of Modernity.* Stanford: Stanford University Press.

Gilbert, A. 1992. Third world cities: Housing, infrastructure and servicing. *Urban Studies*, 29, 435-460.

Gliessman, S.R. 1990. Applied ecology and agroecology: their role in the design of agricultural projects for the humid tropics. In Goodland, R. (ed.). *Race to Save the Tropics: Ecology and Economics for a Sustainable Future.* Washington D.C: Island Press, 33-47.

Godelier, M. 1986. *The Making of Great Men: Male Domination and Power Among the New Guinea Baruya*. Cambridge: Cambridge University Press.

Godelier, M., and Strathern, M. (eds.) 1991. *Big Men and Great Men: Personifications of Power in Melanesia.* Cambridge: Cambridge University Press.

Gold, M.A., and Rusten, E. 1993. Learning from the farmers of Nepal. *Agroforestry Today,* 5, 10-12.

Gourlay, R. 1992. Philippines orders mine closure because of pollution problem. *The Financial Times, London*, 22nd April.

Government of Fiji. 1945. An ordinance relating to prospecting and mining precious metals and other minerals. In *Laws of Fiji.* Government House, Suva, 1326, Cap. 127 and later amendments.

Government of Fiji. 1966. The Mining Act. In *Laws of Fiji*. Government House, Suva.

Greenland, D.J. 1975. Bringing the green revolution to the shifting cultivator. *Science*, 190, 841-844.

Griffen, V. 1978. Namosi: An area undergoing the impacts of change. Pacific Women's Resource Centre, Suva, Fiji. Unpub manuscript.

Grynberg, R., and Nouairi, J. 1988. The environmental costs of development in PNG: The case of Bougainville Copper. Unpub ms, Department of Economics, School of Social and Economic Development, The University of the South Pacific, Suva, Fiji.

Guilcher, A. 1987. *Coral Reef Geomorphology*. New York: Wiley.

Gunasekera, H.M. 1985. Fiji. In ESCAP. *Patterns and Impact of Foreign Investment in the ESCAP Region*. Bangkok: ESCAP, 27-41.

Hardoy, J.E., Mitlin, D., and Satterthwaite, D. 1992. *Environmental Problems in Third World Cities*. London: Earthscan.

Hau'ofa, E. 1993. Our sea of islands. Paper arising from lectures at University of Hawai'i at Hilo, and East-West Center, March/April.

Hayter, T., and Watson, C. 1985. *Aid Rhetoric and Reality*. London: Pluto Press.

Healey, C. 1990. *Maring Hunters and Traders: Production and Exchange in the Papua New Guinea Highlands*. Berkeley: University of California Press.

Healy, T.R. 1980. Conservation and management of coastal resources: the earth science basis. In Anderson, A.G. (ed.). *The Land Our Future: essays on land use and conservation in New Zealand.* Wellington: Longman Paul/New Zealand Geographical Society, 239-260.

Holloway, J.T. 1954. Forests and climates in the South Island of New Zealand. *Transactions of the Royal Society of New Zealand*, 82, 329-410.

Holthus, P. 1990. Impact of industrial development on coastal marine ecosystems of Pacific Islands. Paper presented to UNDP Regional Workshop on Environmental Management and Sustainable Development in the South Pacific Region, Suva, April.

Holthus, P. 1992. Integrated coastal zone management (ICZM) in the South Pacific region. *South Pacific Regional Environment Programme concept document*, 19p.

Hore-Lacy, I. 1992. *Mining and the Environment*. Canberra: The Australian Mining Industry Council.

Hughes, P.J. 1989. The effects of mining on the environment of high islands: A case study of gold mining on Misima Island, Papua New Guinea. *South Pacific Regional Environment Programme, Case Study* 5.

Hughes, P.J., and Sullivan, M. 1989. Environmental impact assessment in Papua New Guinea: lessons for the wider Pacific. *Pacific Viewpoint*, 30, 34-55.

Hughes, P.J., and Sullivan, M.E. 1992. The environmental effects of mining and petroleum production in Papua New Guinea. *Port Moresby: University of Papua New Guinea*, 29 p.

Hunger Project. 1985. *Ending Hunger: an idea whose time has come*. New York: Praeger.

Inglis, J.T. (ed.). 1993. *Traditional Ecological Knowledge: Concepts and Cases*. Ottawa: Canadian Museum of Nature/ International Development Research Centre.

INSEE. 1986. *Les Comptes du Patrimoine Naturel*. Institut National de la Statistique et des Etudes économiques: collections de l'INSEE, série compte et planification, 137-138, 552p.

Irvine, D. 1989. Succession management and resource distribution in an Amazonian rain forest. *Advances in Economic Botany*, 7, 223-237.

Jalan, B. (ed.). 1982. *Problems and Policies in Small Economies*. London: Croom Helm.

Jessop-Tuimaleali'ifano, L. 1990. Country Profile of Western Samoa. Discussion paper for ESCAP Consultative Meeting of National Experts in Human Settlements of Small Pacific Islands. Port Vila, 3-6 October.

Johannes, R.E. (ed.). 1989. *Traditional Ecological Knowledge: A Collection of Essays*. Gland, Switzerland: The World Conservation Union.

REFERENCES

Johnson, M. (ed.) 1993. *Lore: Capturing Traditional Environmental Knowledge*. Ottawa: IDRC Books.

Kamikamica, J.N. 1991. *Budget 1992*. Suva: Fiji Ministry of Finance and Economic Planning.

Kau, J. 1993. Hear the landowners: they are the solution. *SPACHEE Environment Watch*, 5, 17.

Keesing, R. 1982a. Kastom in Melanesia: An overview. *Mankind*, 13, 297-301.

Keesing, R. 1982b. Kastom and anticolonialism on Malaita: "Culture" as political symbol. *Mankind*, 13, 357-373.

Keith-Reid, R. 1993. Hope in the hills: Namosi and the minerals that would make it a rags to riches story. *Islands Business*, May, 36.

Keyfitz, N. 1982. Development and the elimination of poverty. *Economic Development and Cultural Change*, 29, 650-659.

Khoo, K.M. 1976. Optimal utilisation and management of fisheries resources. *Journal of the Malaysian Economics Association*, 13, 40-50.

King, D. 1992. The demise of small towns and outstations of Papua New Guinea: trends in urban census populations and growth from 1966-1990. *Yagl-Ambu*, 16, 17-33.

Kirch, P.V. 1982a. Ecology and adaptation of Polynesian agricultural systems. *Archaeology in Oceania*, 17, 1-6.

Kirch, P.V. 1982b. The impact of the prehistoric Polynesians on the Hawaiian ecosystem. *Pacific Science*, 36, 1-14.

Kirch, P.V. 1984. *The Evolution of the Polynesian Chiefdoms*. Cambridge: Cambridge University Press.

Kirch, P.V., and Kelly, M., 1975, Prehistory and human ecology in a windward Hawaiian valley: Halawa Valley, Molokai. *Pacific Anthropological Records* 24.

Kirch, P.V., and Yen, D.E., 1982, Tikopia - the prehistory and ecology of a Polynesian outlier. *Bernice P. Bishop Museum, Bulletin*, 238.

Klee, G.A. 1980. Oceania. In Klee, G.A. (ed.). *World Systems of Traditional Resource Management*. London: Edward Arnold, 245-281.

Knudtson, P. and Suzuki, D. 1992. *Wisdom of the Elders.* St. Leonards, Australia: Allen and Unwin.

Koch, G. (G. Slatter, translator). 1983. *The material culture of Tuvalu*. Suva: Institute of Pacific Studies, University of the South Pacific (originally published in German in 1961 by Museum fur Volkerkunde, Berlin).

Lal, P.N., Swamy, A., and Singh, P. 1983. Mangroves and secondary productivity: fishes associated with mangroves in Wairiki Creek, Fiji. *Technical report 5*. Suva: Fisheries Division, Ministry of Agriculture and Fisheries.

Lappe, F., Collins, J., and Kindley, D. 1980. *Aid as Obstacle: twenty questions about our foreign aid and the hungry*. San Francisco: IFDP.

Lasaqa, I. 1973. Geography and geographers in the changing Pacific: an islander's view. In Brookfield, H.C. (ed.). *The Pacific in Transition: Geographical Perspectives on Adaptation and Change*. London: Methuen, 299-311.

Lasaqa, I.Q. 1984. *The Fijian People: Before and After Independence*. Canberra: Australian National University Press.

Lawrence, D., and Cansfield-Smith, T. 1991. *Sustainable Development for Traditional Inhabitants of the Torres Strait Region*. Great Barrier Reef Marine Park Authority, Townsville, Australia.

Lewis, A.D., Adams, T.J.H., and Ledua, E. 1988. Fiji's giant clam stocks--A review of their distribution, abundance, exploitation and management. In Copland, J.W., and Lucas, J.S. (eds.), *Giant clams in Asia and the Pacific*. Canberra: Australian Centre for International Agricultural Research, 66-72.

Linnekin, J. 1990. The politics of culture in the Pacific. In Linnekin, J., and Poyer, L. (eds.). *Cultural Identity and Ethnicity in the Pacific*. Honolulu: University of Hawaii Press, 149-173.

Lugo, A.E., and Snedaker, C. 1974. The ecology of mangroves. *Annual Review of Ecology and Systematics*, 5, 39-64.

McCoy, P.C. 1979. Easter Island. In Jennings, J. (ed). *The Prehistory of Polynesia*. Cambridge, Massachusetts: Harvard University Press, 135-166.

McDonald, M.A. 1978. *Ka lei: The Leis of Hawaii*. Honolulu: Topgallant Publishing.

McGee, T.G. 1975. *Food Dependency in the Pacific: A Preliminary Statement*. Canberra: Australian National University Development Studies Centre Occasional Paper 2.

McMurray, C. 1993a. Papua New Guinea, In Cole, R. (ed.). *Pacific 2010: Challenging the Future*. Canberra: NCDS, Australian National University, 50-64.

McMurray, C. 1993b. Solomon Islands, In Cole, R. (ed.). *Pacific 2010: Challenging the Future*. Canberra: NCDS, Australian National University, 91-104.

Mailer, N. 1993. Norman Mailer: 'Je vis comme un espion vis-à-vis de moi-même'. *Magazine littéraire*, 307, 96-103.

Malinowski, B. 1935. *Coral Gardens and Their Magic*. 2 vols. London: George Allen and Unwin.

Manner, H.I., and Mallon, E. 1989. An annotated list of the vascular plants of Puluwat Atoll. *Micronesica*, 22, 23-63.

Manner, H.I., Thaman, R.R., and Hassall, D.H. 1984. Phosphate-mining induced vegetation changes on Nauru Island. *Ecology*, 65, 1454-1465.

Marcus, G.E. 1986. Contemporary problems of ethnography in the modern world system. In Clifford, J., and Marcus, G.E. (eds.). *Writing Culture: The Poetics and Politics of Ethnography*. Berkeley: University of California Press, 165-193.

REFERENCES

Marten, K.D. 1985. Tropical forestry in Melanesia and some Pacific Islands. *UNEP Regional Seas reports and studies*, 69, 115-128.

Meunier, J. 1993. *Le Monocle de Joseph Conrad.* Paris: Payot.

Mezger, D. 1980. *Copper in the World Economy.* London: Heinemann.

Morauta, L., Pernetta, J., and Heaney, W. (eds.) 1982. *Traditional Conservation in Papua New Guinea: Implications for Today.* Monograph 16, Institute of Applied Social and Economic Research, Boroko, Papua New Guinea.

Munro-Faure, P. 1992. The pricing of marine resources. *UNEP Regional Seas Reports and Studies*, 147, 149-157.

Musée national des arts africains et océaniens. 1990. *De jade et de nacre: patrimoine artistique Kanak.* Paris: Ministère des Dom-Tom.

Namosi Joint Venture. 1979. Environmental progress report, 1 January-31 December 1978, 60p. Unpub rpt, Suva, Fiji.

Narsey, W.L. 1989. The Performance of the Fiji Manufacturing Sector, 1973-1985. *School of Social and Economic Development, University of the South Pacific, Working Paper* 14.

Natural Systems Research (Environmental Consultants Pty. Ltd.). 1992. Namosi Draft Environmental Inception Report. Unpub rpt for Placer Pacific Ltd.

Naveh, Z., and Lieberman, A.S. 1984. *Landscape Ecology: Theory and Application.* New York: Springer-Verlag.

Nayacakalou, R. 1975. *Leadership in Fiji*: Melbourne, Oxford University Press.

Nayacakalou, R. 1978. *Tradition and Change in the Fijian Village*. Suva: Institute of Pacific Studies, The University of the South Pacific.

Neal, M.C. 1965. *In Gardens of Hawaii*. Honolulu: Bishop Museum Press.

Norse, D. 1992. A new strategy for feeding a crowded planet. *Environment*, 34, 6-11, 32-39.

Nunn, P.D. 1988. Recent environmental changes along south-west Pacific coasts and the prehistory of Oceania: developments of the work of the late John Gibbons. *Journal of Pacific Studies*, 14, 42-58.

Nunn, P.D. 1990. Recent environmental changes on Pacific islands. *The Geographical Journal*, 156, 125-140.

Nunn, P.D. 1992. *Keimami sa vakila na liga ni Kalou: human and nonhuman impacts on Pacific island environments*. Honolulu: East-West Center (Program on Environment, Occasional Paper 13), 2nd revised edition, 69 pp.

Nunn, P.D. 1994. *Oceanic Islands*. Oxford: Blackwell, 418 pp.

Nunn, P.D. submitted. *Pacific Island Landscapes*. Institute of Pacific Studies, University of the South Pacific. 382 pp.

Nye, P.H., and Greenland, D.J. 1960. *The Soil Under Shifting Cultivation.* Technical Communication 51. Commonwealth Bureau of Soils, Harpenden.

Odum, E.P. 1971. *Fundamentals of Ecology*. Philapdelphia: Saunders, 574p.

Office of Planning and Statistics. 1990. *National Population Policy*. Majuro: Office of Planning and Statistics, Republic of the Marshall Islands.

Ogawa, H. 1990. Assessment and management of environmental health impacts in Pacific Island countries. Paper to UNDP Regional Workshop on Environmental Management and Sustainable Development in the South Pacific Region, Suva, April.

O'Riordan, T. 1988. The politics of sustainability. In Turner, R.K. (ed.). *Sustainable Environmental Management: Principles and Practice*. London: Belhaven Press, 29-50.

Overton, J. 1987. Fijian land: pressing problems and possible tenure solutions. *Singapore Journal of Tropical Geography*, 8, 139-151.

Overton, J. 1988a. A Fijian peasantry: galala and villagers. *Oceania*, 58, 193-211.

Overton, J. 1988b. Resettlement re-examined: accumulation and differentiation in Waibau and Lomaivuna, Fiji. In Hirst, J., Overton, J., Byron, Y., and Allen, B.J. (eds.). *Small-Scale Agriculture*. Canberra: Commonwealth Geographical Bureau and Department of Human Geography, Research School of Pacific Studies, Australian National University, 67-81.

Overton, J. 1989. *Land and Differentiation in Rural Fiji*. Canberra: National Centre for Development Studies, Australian National University.

Overton, J. 1992a. The limits to accumulation: changing land tenure in Fiji. *Journal of Peasant Studies*, 19, 326-342.

Overton, J. 1992b. Coups and constitutions: describing the political geography of Fiji. *New Zealand Geographer,* 48, 50-58.

Overton, J. 1992c. Farms, suburbs, or retirement homes: the transformation of village Fiji. *The Contemporary Pacific*, 5, 45-74.

Overton, J. 1993. Pacific futures? Geography and change in the Pacific Islands. *New Zealand Geographer*, 49, (in press).

Overton, J., and Ward, R.G. 1989. The coups in retrospect: the new political geography of Fiji. *Pacific Viewpoint,* 30, 207-216.

Padoch, C., and Denevan, W.M. 1988. Conclusions and recommendations. *Advances in Economic Botany*, 5, 97-102.

Panoff, M. (ed.). 1986. Les plantations dans le Pacifique Sud. *Journal de la Société des Océanistes*, 82-83, 219p.

Parish, D. 1989. Impact of coastal aquaculture on wetlands in South East Asia. In *Proceedings of the Third International Wetlands Conference*, 19-23 September 1988, 265-266.

Péres, J.M. 1990. Littoral maritime. *Encyclopédie Universalis*, 12, 918-920.

Perry, L.M., and Metzger, J. 1980. *Medicinal plants of East and Southeast Asia: Attributed properties and uses*. Cambridge, Massachusetts: Massachusetts Institute of Technology Press.

Pilcher, S. 1990. Environmental problems associated with cyanide heap leaching. Unpub testimony to the Canadian Environmental Quality Council by Chief of the Montana Water Quality Bureau, 9 March 1990.

Pinot, J.P. 1990. Côtes (Géomorphologie). *Encyclopédie Universalis*, 5, 666-674.

Piperno, D.R. 1990. Aboriginal agriculture and land usage in the Amazon Basin, Ecuador. *Journal of Archaeological Science*, 17, 665-677.

Placer Pacific. 1993. Current status of the Namosi Project as of March 31st 1993. Unpub ms, Placer Pacific Namosi, Suva, Fiji.

Ponter, E. 1986. The growth of wage labour and its consequences for a Fijian village. In Griffen, C., and Davis, M.M. (eds.). *Fijians in Town*. Suva: Institute of Pacific Studies, The University of the South Pacific, 24-49.

Porter, D., Allen, B., and Thompson, G. 1991. *Development in Practice: Paved with Good Intentions.* London: Routledge.

Posey, D.A., and Balée, W. (eds.) 1989. Resource Management in Amazonia: Indigenous and Folk Strategies. *Advances in Economic Botany*, volume 7.

Powell, J.M. 1976. Ethnobotany. In Paijmans, K. (ed.). *New Guinea vegetation.* Amsterdam: Elsevier, 106-183.

Prasad, P. 1984. Fiji: sugar cane production and land tenure in Fiji. In Acquaye, B., and Crocombe, R. (eds.). *Land Tenure and Rural Productivity in the Pacific Islands*. Suva: Institute of Pacific Studies, The University of the South Pacific, 102-113.

Raintree, J.B. 1983. Strategies for enhancing the adoptability of agroforestry innovations. *Agroforestry Systems,* 1, 173-187.

Rambo, A.T., and Hamilton, L.S. 1991. Social trends affecting natural resources management in upland areas of Asia and the Pacific. In Naya, S., and Browne, S. (eds.). *Development Challenges in Asia and the Pacific in the 1990s.* Honolulu: United Nations Development Programme/East-West Center, 111-126.

Rappaport, R. 1967. *Pigs for the Ancestors: Ritual in the Ecology of a New Guinea People.* New Haven: Yale University Press.

Ravuvu, A. 1983. *Vaka i Taukei: The Fijian Way of Life*. Suva: Institute of Pacific Studies, The University of the South Pacific.

Read, K.E. 1954. Cultures of the Central Highlands, New Guinea. *Southwestern Journal of Anthropology*, 10, 1-43.

Republic of the Marshall Islands. 1990. *Situation Analysis of the Marshallese Child.* Majuro: Office of Planning and Statistics.

Reti, I. 1990. Environmental problems in the South Pacific region: an overview. Paper to UNDP Regional Workshop on Environmental Management and Sustainable Development in the South Pacific Region, Suva, April.

Richards, P. 1985. *Indigenous Agricultural Revolution: Ecology and Food Production in West Africa.* London: Hutchinson.

Richmond, R.N. 1980. Case history of mineral development in Fiji: the Namosi Copper Project. Unpub paper for Workshop on Mineral Policies to Achieve Development Objectives, East-West Center, Hawaii, 9-13 June 1980.

Rizer, J.P., Lin, J., Waqavonovono, M., Saumatua, S., and Majoram, A.G. 1982. *The Namosi Copper Mine: a study in assimilation planning*. Suva: Centre for Applied Studies in Development, The University of the South Pacific.

Robertson, A. 1988. Changing environment, changing roles - a health risk? In Va'a, R., and Teaiwa, J. (eds.). *Environment and Pacific Women: From the Globe to the Village*. Suva: Fiji Association of Women Graduates, 19-24.

Rollat, A. 1989. *Tjibaou le Kanak*. Lyon: La Manufacture.

Rougerie, F., and Wauthy, B. 1993. The endo-upwelling concept: from geothermal convection to reef construction. *Coral Reefs*, 12, 19-30.

Ruddle, K., and Johannes, R.E. (eds.) 1989. *Traditional Marine Resources in the Pacific Basin: An Anthology*. Jakarta: UNESCO/ROSTSEA.

Rutz, H.J. 1978. Fijian land tenure and agricultural growth. *Oceania*, 49, 20-34.

Sahlins, M.D. 1962. *Moala: Culture and Nature on a Fijian Island*. Ann Arbor: University of Michigan Press.

Saldarriaga, J.G., and West, D.C. 1986. Holocene fires in the northern Amazon Basin. *Quaternary Research*, 26, 358-366.

Salisbury, R.F. 1962. *From Stone to Steel: Economic Consequences of a Technological Change*. Melbourne: Melbourne University Press.

Salvat, B. 1987. Dredging in coral reefs. In Salvat, B. (ed.). *Human Impacts on Coral Reefs: facts and recommendations*. Paris: EPHE, 165-184.

Sanford, R.L., Saldarriaga, J.G., Clark, J., Uhl, K.E., and Herrera, R. 1985. Amazon rain-forest fires. *Science*, 227, 53-55.

Sauer, C.O. 1956. The agency of man on earth. In Thomas, W.L. (ed.). *Man's Role in Changing the Face of the Earth*. Chicago: University of Chicago Press, 49-69.

Schmid, C.K. 1991. *Of People and Plants: A Botanical Ethnography of Nokopo Village, Madang and Morobe Provinces, Papua New Guinea*. (Basler Beiträge zur Ethnologie, Band 33) Basel: Wepf & Co. AG Verlag.

Schmid, M. 1979. Les écosystèmes forestiers mélanésiens. In *Ecosystèmes Forestiers Tropicaux*. UNESCO-PNUE, col Recherches sur les ressources naturelle, 15, 709-740.

Selwyn, P. (ed.). 1985. *Development Policy in Small Countries*. London: Croom Helm.

Setchell, W.A. 1924. *American Samoa: Part I - Vegetation of Tutuila Island, Part II - Ethnobotany of the Samoans, Part III - Vegetation of Rose Atoll*. Washington D.C.: Department of Marine Biology, Carnegie Institution of Washington.

Shand, R.T. (ed.). 1980. *The Island States of the Pacific and Indian Oceans; Anatomy of Development*. Monograph 23, Development Studies Centre, Australian National University, Canberra.

Slatter, C. 1991. *Situation Analysis of Pacific Children: A Regional Perspective*. Suva: UNICEF.

Sofer, M. 1988. Core-periphery structure in Fiji. *Society and Space* 6, 55-74.

REFERENCES

South Pacific Commission. 1992. *South Pacific Economies: Pocket Statistical Summary*. Noumea: Statistics Section, South Pacific Commission.

South Pacific Commission. 1993. *South Pacific Economies: Pocket Statistical Summary*. Noumea: Statistics Section, South Pacific Commission.

South Pacific Regional Environment Programme/IUCN. 1989. *Action Strategy for Nature Conservation in the South Pacific Region.* Noumea: South Pacific Regional Environment Programme (SPREP)/International Union for the Conservation of Nature and Natural Resources (IUCN).

South Pacific Regional Environment Programme. 1991. *1991-1995 Action Plan for Managing the Environment of the South Pacific region.* Noumea: South Pacific Regional Environment Programme, 20p.

South Pacific Regional Environment Programme. 1992a. *Environment and Development: A Pacific Island Perspective*. Manila: Asian Development Bank.

South Pacific Regional Environment Programme. 1992b. *Republic of the Marshall Islands*. Country Report for UNCED. Apia: South Pacific Regional Environment Programme.

Southern, W. 1986. The late Quaternary climate of Fiji. Unpub PhD thesis, Australian National University, Canberra.

Spate, O.H.K. 1959. *The Fijian People: Economic Problems and Prospects*. Suva: Legislative Council of Fiji, Legislative Council Paper 13 of 1959.

Spennemann, D.H.R., 1989, 'ata 'a Tonga mo 'ata 'o Tonga: early and later prehistory of the Tongan islands. Unpub PhD thesis, Australian National University, Canberra.

Steadman, D.W. 1991. Extinct and extirpated birds from Aitutaki and Atiu, southern Cook Islands. *Pacific Science*, 45, 325-347.

Stoddart, D.R. 1992. Biogeography of the tropical Pacific. *Pacific Science,* 46, 276-293.

Stone, L. 1990. Waste generation and preventative opportunities in the South Pacific. Paper to UNDP Regional Workshop on Environmental Management and Sustainable Development in the South Pacific Region, Suva, April.

Stone, R.D. 1991. *Wildlands and Human Needs: Reports from the Field*. Geneva: World Wildlife Fund.

Strong, M.F. 1991. Preparing for the UN Conference on Environment and Development. *Environment*, 33, 5, 39-41.

Strong, M.F. 1992. The promises and challenges of UNCED '92. *Ocean and Coastal Management*, 18, 5-14.

Sudo, K.I. 1984. Social organization and types of sea tenure in Micronesia. In Ruddle K., and Akimichi, T. (eds.). *Maritime Institutions in the Western Pacific*. Osaka: National Museum of Ethnology, Senri Ethnological Studies 17, 203-230.

Sullivan, M., and Gibson, L. 1990. Environmental Planning, Climate Change and Potential Sea Level Rise: Report on mission to Kiribati. Noumea: *South Pacific Regional Environment Programme Reports and Studies*, 50.

Swadling, P., and Hope, G. 1992. Environmental change in New Guinea since human settlement. In Dodson, J. (ed). *The Naive Lands*. Melbourne: Longman Cheshire, 13-42.

Taurakoto, P. 1984. Customary rights to reefs and landings. In Lamour, P. (ed.). *Land Tenure in Vanuatu*. Suva: Institute of Pacific Studies, The University of the South Pacific, 14-16.

Taylor, J.P. 1985. The value of geographical perspective. In Johnston, R.J. (ed.). *The Future of Geography*. London: Methuen, 92-110.

The Open University. 1978. *The Law of the Sea.* Milton Keynes: The Open University Press.

Thaman, R.R. 1982. Deterioration of traditional food systems, increasing malnutrition and food dependency in the Pacific Islands. *Journal of Food and Nutrition*, 39, 109-121.

Thaman, R.R. 1988a. *Environmental Issues in the Pacific Islands: Constraints to Sustainable Island Development.* Canberra: Pacific Circle Consortium.

Thaman, R.R. 1988b. By the people and for the people: home gardening and national development in the Pacific Islands. In Hirst, J., Overton, J., Byron, Y., and Allen, B.J. (eds.). *Small-Scale Agriculture.* Canberra: Commonwealth Geographic Bureau and The Australian National University, 167-182.

Thaman, R.R. 1988c. Health and nutrition in the Pacific Islands: development or underdevelopment. *Geojournal*, 16, 211-227.

Thaman, R.R. 1992. Batiri kei Baravi: the ethnobotany of Pacific Island coastal plants. *Atoll Research Bulletin*, 361, 1-62.

Thaman, R.R. 1993. Land, Plants, animals and people: Community-based biodiversity conservation as a basis for ecological, cultural and economic survival in the Pacific islands. Unpublished paper presented at CORAIL conference, Nouméa, New Caledonia.

Thaman, R.R. (forthcoming). The ethnobotany of Pacific Island coastal plants. In Geraghty, P., and Morrison, R.J., *Science of Pacific Island Peoples*. Suva: Institute of Pacific Studies, The University of the South Pacific.

Thaman, R.R., and Clarke, W.C. (eds.). 1983. *Food and National Development in the South Pacific*. Suva, The University of the South Pacific.

Thaman, R.R., and Clarke, W.C. 1987. Pacific Island agrosilviculture: systems for cultural and ecological stability. *Canopy International*, 13(1), 6-7; 13(2): 8-10; 13(3): 6-9.

The National Planner. 1991. *The Second National Development Plan, 1992-1996.* Palikir, Pohnpei: Office of Planning and Statistics, Federated States of Micronesia.

Thirlwall, A.P. 1991. The performance and prospects of the Pacific Island economies in the world economy. *Pacific Islands Development Program, East-West Center, Honolulu, Research Report Series* 14.

REFERENCES

Thistlethwaite, R., and Votaw, G. 1992. Environment and Development: A Pacific Island Perspective. Supporting Technical Document for the Pacific Island Developing Countries' Report to the United Nations Conference on Environment and Development. Asian Development Bank, Manila.

Thom, B.G. 1992. Environmental change in the late Quaternary. In Dodson, J. (ed). *The Naive Lands*. Melbourne: Longman Cheshire, 9-12.

Thomas, P. 1987. Urban fringe development in Apia. In Mason, L., and Hereniko, P. (eds.). *In Search of a Home*. Suva: Institute of Pacific Studies, The University of the South Pacific, 241-244.

Tjibaou, J.-M. 1976. Recherche d'identité mélanésienne et société traditionnelle. *Journal de la Société des Océanistes*, 32, 281-292.

Tjibaou, J.-M. 1981. Etre Mélanésien aujourd'hui. *Esprit*, 57, 81-93.

Tjibaou, J.-M., and Missotte, P. 1975. *Kanaké: Mélanésien de Nouvelle Calédonie*. Nouméa: Les Éditions du Pacifique.

Todaro, M. 1989. *Economic Development in the Third World*. New York: Longman, 4th edition.

Togna, O. 1993. Editorial. *Mwà Véé*, 1, 4.

Tuan, Y. 1989. On the rewarding human life. In Norwine, J., and Gonzalez, A. (eds.). *The Third World: States of Mind and Being*. Boston: Unwin.

Tubuna, S. 1985. Patterns of Fijian return migration in the Wainibuka River valley: Viti Levu, Fiji. In Chapman, M., and Prothero, R.M. (eds.). *Circulation in Population Movement*. London: Routledge & Kegan Paul, 213-224.

Tukai, M. 1988. Modernization theory and a Fijian village. In Overton, J. (ed.). *Rural Fiji*. Suva: Institute of Pacific Studies, The University of the South Pacific, 13-17.

Tupouniua, M.U. 1956. *Kingdom of Tonga: Report on the Results of the 1956 Census*. Nuku'alofa: Government Printer.

UNCTAD. 1988. *Protectionism and Structural Adjustment. Problems of Protectionism and Structural Adjustment. Statistical and Information Annex*. New York: UNCTAD.

UNESCO/UNFPA. 1977. *Population, Resources and Development in the Eastern Islands of Fiji*. Paris: UNESCO/UNFPA and Canberra: Development Studies Centre, Australian National University.

UNICEF. 1991. *Situational Analysis of Children and Women in the Federated States of Micronesia*. Pohnpei: Department of Human Resources.

UNIDO. 1986. *Industrial Review Series: Pacific Island States, Selected Countries*. Vienna: UNIDO.

United Nations. 1990. *Overall Socio-Economic Perspective of the World Economy to the Year 2000*. New York: United Nations.

United Nations. 1991. *World Urbanization Prospects, 1990*. New York: Department of International Economic and Social Affairs.

REFERENCES

United Nations. 1992. *World Investment Report: Transnational Corporations as Engines of Growth*. New York: United Nations.

United Nations Development Programme. 1990. *Human Development Report 1990*. Oxford: Oxford University Press.

United Nations Development Programme. 1992. *Human Development Report 1992*. Oxford: Oxford University Press.

University of Guam. 1990. *Academic Master Plan: Academic Years 1990-91, 1991-92 and 1992-1993*. University of Guam, Mangilao, Guam.

University of the South Pacific. 1984. *Calendar, 1985*. Volume 1. The University of the South Pacific, Suva, Fiji.

Vallega, A. 1990. *Ocean Change in Global Change Introductory geographical analysis*. Genoa: Università Degli Studi Di Genova.

Vanuatu Government. 1991. *Vanuatu National Report for UNCED*. Port Vila: Ministry of Home Affairs.

Vienne, B. 1984. Gens de Motlav, idéologie et pratique sociale en Mélanésie. *Publication de la Société des Océanistes*, 42, 432p.

Violette, J. 1989. Le message de Jean-Marie", *Bwenando*, 121-122-123-124, 9-50.

Waddell, E. 1972. *The Mound Builders: Agricultural Practices, Environment, and Society in the Central Highlands of New Guinea*. Seattle: University of Washington Press.

Wallerstein, I. 1974. *The Modern World-System*. New York: Academic Press.

Walsh, A.C. 1964. Nuku'alofa, Tonga: a Preliminary Study of Urbanization and In-Migration. Unpub MA thesis in geography. Victoria University of Wellington.

Walsh, A.C. 1969. A Tongan urban peasantry: conjecture or reality? In Bassett, I.G. (ed.). *Pacific Peasantry*. Manawatu: New Zealand Geographical Society, 87-107.

Walsh, A.C. 1970. Population changes in Tonga: an historical overview and modern commentary. *Pacific Viewpoint*, 11, 27-46.

Walsh, A.C. 1971. *More and More Maoris: a simple statistical survey of the Maori today*. Christchurch: Whitcombe and Tombs.

Walsh, A.C. 1972a. "Aspects of Subsistence Agriculture in Niue". *Compass* 6(1): 1-7. Dept. of Geography, Massey University.

Walsh, A.C. 1972b. *Nuku'alofa: a Study of Urban Life in the Pacific Islands.* Wellington: Reed.

Walsh, A.C. 1975. R.G. Crocombe, "The New South Pacific". *New Zealand Geographer*, 31, 85-88.

Walsh, A.C. 1978. Population distribution and migration. In *Niue: 1976 Census of Population and Housing*. Alofi: Department of Justice, Volume 2, Analysis of Demographic Data, 44-66, 121-128.

Walsh, A.C. 1982. *Migration, Urbanization and Development in South Pacific Countries.* Comparative Study on Migration, Urbanization and Development in the ESCAP Region. Country Report VI. New York: United Nations.

Walsh, A.C., and Trlin, A.D. 1973. Niuean migration: Niuean socio-economic background, characteristics of migrants and settlement in Auckland. *Journal of the Polynesian Society*, 82, 47-85.

Walter, A. (forthcoming). Vanuatu's fruit tree arboriculture. In Geraghty, P., and Morrison, R.J., *Science of Pacific Island Peoples*. Suva: Institute of Pacific Studies, The University of the South Pacific.

Ward, R.G. 1965. *Land Use and Population in Fiji: A Geographical Study*. London: HMSO.

Ward, R.G. 1986. Change in land use and villages - Fiji: 1958-1983 *Travaux et Documents de Geographie Tropicale CEGET*, 55, 109-120.

Ward, R.G. 1987. Native Fijian villages: a questionable future? In Taylor, M.J. (ed.). *Fiji: Future Imperfect?* Sydney: Allen and Unwin, 33-45.

Ward, R.G. 1993. South Pacific Island futures: paradise, prosperity, or pauperism? *The Contemporary Pacific*, 5, 1-21.

Warren, D.M. 1991. *Using Indigenous Knowledge in Agricultural Development.* Discussion Paper 127. The World Bank, Washington, D.C.

Warren, D.M., Slikkerveer, L. Jan, and Brokensha, D. (eds.) 1993. *Indigenous Knowledge Systems: The Cultural Dimension of Development.* (Vol. 1, The International Library of Development and Indigenous Knowledge.), London: Kegan Paul.

Watling, D. 1985. *A Mangrove management plan for Fiji. Phase 1. Zonation requirements and a plan for the mangroves of the Ba, Labasa and Rewa Deltas.* Suva: Government Printer.

Watling, D., and Chape, S.P. (eds). 1992. *Environment Fiji - The National State of the Environment Report*. Gland, Switzerland: IUCN.

Watters, R.F. 1969. *Koro: Economic Development and Social Change in Fiji.* Oxford: Clarendon.

Weissman, S. 1974. *The Trojan Horse: a radical look at foreign aid.* London: Ramparts.

Wendt, A. 1976. Towards a new Oceania. *Mana Review*, 1, 49-60.

Western Samoan Government. 1991. *National Report for UNCED*. Apia: Division of Environment and Conservation, Department of Lands and Environment.

White, J. 1974. *The Politics of Foreign Aid*. London: Bodley Head.

White, P., and Flannery, T. 1992. The impact of people on the Pacific world. In Dodson, J. (ed). *The Naive Lands*. Melbourne: Longman Cheshire, 1-8.

Wickler, S., and Spriggs, M.E. 1988. Pleistocene human occupation of the Solomon Islands, Melanesia. *Antiquity*, 62, 703-706.

Wilken, G.C. 1991. *Sustainable Agriculture is the Solution, But What is the Problem?* Board for International Food and Agricultural Development and Economic Cooperation, Occasional Paper 14. Agency for International Development, Washington, D.C.

Williams, N., and Baines, G. (eds). 1993. *Traditional Ecological Knowledge: Wisdom for Sustainable Development*. Canberra: Centre for Resource and Environmental Studies, Australian National University.

World Bank. 1986. *Fiji: A Transition to Manufacturing*. Report 6372-FIJ. Washington: World Bank.

World Bank. 1987. *World Development Report, 1987*. New York: Oxford University Press for the World Bank.

World Bank. 1990. *Social Indicators of Development*. New York: World Bank.

World Bank. 1991. *Fiji: Incentive Policies for Growth*. Report 9516-FIJ. Washington: World Bank.

WSDEC (Western Samoa Division of Environment and Conservation). 1991. *National Report for United Nations Conference on Environment and Development*. Apia: Government of Western Samoa.

Yen, D.E. 1974. Arboriculture in the subsistence of Santa Cruz, Solomon Islands. *Economic Botany*, 28, 247-284.

Zan, Y., and Hunter-Anderson, R.L. 1987. On the origins of the Micronesian 'savannahs': an anthropological perspective. Unpub paper, 3rd International Soil Management Workshop, Acid Soils of Oceania, Belau.

Index